THE BODY POLITIC

*Foundings, Citizenship, and Difference
in the American Political Imagination*

CATHERINE A. HOLLAND

ROUTLEDGE
New York London

Published in 2001 by
Routledge
29 West 35th Street
New York, NY 10001

Published in Great Britain by
Routledge
11 New Fetter Lane
London EC4P 4EE

Routledge is an imprint of the Taylor & Francis Group.

Copyright © 2001 by Routledge

Printed in the United States of America on acid-free paper.

All rights reserved. No part of this book may be printed or reproduced or utilized in any form or by any electronic, mechanical or other means, now known or hereafter invented, including photocopying and recording, or in any information storage or retrieval system, without permission in writing from the publisher.

Library of Congress Cataloging-in-Publication Data

Holland, Catherine A.
The body politic : foundings, citizenship, and difference in the American political imagination / by Catherine A. Holland.
  p. cm.
Includes bibliographical references and index.
ISBN 0-415-92858-3 — ISBN 0-415-92881-8 (pbk.)
1. Liberalism—United States—History.   2. Citizenship—United States—History.
    3. Political Culture—United States—History.   I. Title.
JC574.2.U6 H65 2001
320.51'0973—dc21   00-062813

Contents

Preface   vii

Acknowledgments   xi

1   Introduction: The Body Politic   xiii

I. FOUNDINGS AND THE PROBLEM OF THE PAST   1

   2   Notes on the State of America: Jeffersonian Democracy and the Production of a National Past   19

   3   Becoming Unnatural: The Federalist's Techniques of Government   57

II. RECONSTRUCTION AND ITS AFTERMATH: THE RELOCATION OF THE PAST   93

   4   Sexual Reconstruction: Gender, Political Friendship, and the New Techniques of Citizenship   109

   5   In the Beginning Was a Crime: Lynching, Rape, and the Reconstruction of the Political Imagination   139

POSTSCRIPT: RESTATING NEW POSSIBILITIES   169

Index   189

Preface

THERE ARE MANY WAYS, THESE DAYS, TO BE A CITIZEN. UNMODIFIED, citizenship connotes certain general protections and common responsibilities conveyed by membership in the modern national state. But this generic notion of citizenship has come, of late, to seem an insufficient guarantee; insufficiently attentive, that is, to the operation of power in late modern political culture. Thus, in recent decades we have witnessed the proliferation of forms of political identification that attempt to link the practices of citizenship with the particular identities of citizens. Not just citizenship unmodified, but African-American citizenship, feminist citizenship, queer citizenship (the list could go on). Along with this multiplication of political identities, we are also witness to a shift in the ground of politics itself, now recognizably a part of a much larger and more complex field of relationships. Where once the political sphere seemed well-defined and distinct, we now see politics in unlikely places, and, for example, speak of the politics of the household, the politics of the workplace, the politics of the schoolroom, the politics of higher education.

This eruption of difference onto the scene of politics, and of politics into everyday life, has occasioned much soul searching among political theorists and other publicly minded intellectuals. For some, it is an indication of a renewed democratic spirit in America. For others, these contending civic impulses suggest something considerably more ominous: the dissolution of a common public life altogether. Anxiety about the proliferation of the forms and venues of political action has been particularly acute in the academy, where debates over the place of race, gender, and sexuality in the curriculum have become particularly rancorous. To be sure, the turbulence brought about by the so-called culture wars of the 1980s and 1990s has calmed, but it has not gone away, at least not if the midwestern state university where I teach is at all representative. Certainly, today's college curriculum looks quite different from that of two decades ago, with much more attention paid to the contributions of non-Western cultures and to teaching about differences *within* the Euro-American tradition. The admission of difference into the curriculum, however, has come at a price.

Let me cite one, admittedly local and anecdotal, example. About a year ago, I received a telephone call at my office from a reporter for my university's student newspaper. In the midst of a campus debate over a remark another faculty member had made in the classroom (a remark that some students found deeply objectionable), the reporter was writing an article about the vulnerability of faculty who teach what he described as "controversial" courses. Intrigued, I asked him for clarification as to what he meant by the term. His response is telling: courses invite controversy, he suggested, when they present minority perspectives rather than generalize about what is true in the minds of most of the people, most of the time. As we spoke, it became increasingly clear to me that he had called because *my* courses were deemed controversial, not only my courses in feminist thought, but my courses in political thought more generally. Since the incident that generated that telephone call, a number of sympathetic colleagues have suggested that I include a disclaimer on my syllabi, warning students that the content of the course may make them uncomfortable, with some going so far as to recommend that I have students sign a waiver indicating that they have chosen to take the course in full knowledge of its "controversial" content.

I've resisted this suggestion, even though I am aware that doing so might offer at least some minimal protection against my becoming the focus of the next local commotion, because I worry about the broader implications. As much as I'm flattered by the fact that someone finds my courses challenging and controversial, it strikes me that there is little especially new or different or (presumably) unusual about them. What has happened to public discourse, or to the notion of critical inquiry itself, when (for example) a course that asks students to examine competing perspectives on the liberal doctrine of individual self-ownership as reflected in as diverse (dare I even say *balanced*?) a collection of texts as those by Robert Filmer and John Locke, by slaveholders and former slaves, by defenders as well as critics of nineteenth-century capitalism, and by late twentieth-century liberal feminists and their feminist critics, is deemed *controversial*? What, precisely, is controversial in this? The premise of liberal ownership of the self? Surely not. Rather, I suspect, it is the fact that the course resists offering students a single or unitary line of thought, and instead asks that they participate in a project that has long defined the discipline of political theory and the study of politics more generally: critical engagement with the contested and contestable intellectual traditions that shape us and the world around us. Put differently, a "controversial" course is one that neither seeks nor assumes consensus. Difference, it seems, can be admitted to the curriculum only as other, not as the irreducible ground of political thought itself.

In an era that encourages us to make snap judgments about important questions, to reduce and simplify complex political dynamics rather than exploit their richness, a course that asks students to take seriously a variety of competing perspectives, to engage others who think differently, to make reasoned judgments about fundamental political problems, and to revise those judgments if given good reasons for doing so, has become "controversial." I am not complaining, at least not entirely, for as much as I find myself deeply troubled by this state of affairs, I also harbor a certain fascination for it: what can it mean when the activity of political thinking, and the conventional disciplinary practices of political thought, come to be deemed "controversial" in a public place like the university? What, precisely, does this say about the state of American intellectual life, of American political life, and their convergence? What, moreover, can it mean when intellectual or political disagreement, *controversy*, comes to be treated as a breach of public etiquette, a form of impolite speech unsuited to public space, public institutions, and even public life?

The Body Politic can be read as an attempt to address these questions, if only obliquely. What if the culture wars are but one recent episode in a much longer debate over the meanings and practices of democratic citizenship in America? The culture wars and their consequences have served as a contemporary goad to my reading of past texts, prodding me to write an account of the development of citizenship in the United States that does not confirm familiar terms and categories of analysis, but seeks instead to render the familiar strange, to open the past to question and reinterpretation rather than closing it off as incontestable fact. Contemporary political life seems to demand that we return to the past not to establish the present as our inescapable heritage, but more pressingly to ask how the resources of the past might be turned to different purpose, enabling us to see politics with new eyes and to envision new ways of organizing and directing public power.

Politics is, of course, a messy (and sometimes downright mean and dirty) business, tantalizing us with the promise of neat ideological distinctions and clearcut lines of engagement and dispute, while at the same time violating every secure maxim and tidy formulation that it proffers. Theory is certainly no neater. If anything, it is an enterprise that invites trouble all the more, confounding received interpretations and confronting us with the surprise of the strange and the unfamiliar.

Acknowledgments

THERE IS SOMETHING HUMBLING IN THE ACT OF SENDING A MANUSCRIPT off to press, for in the very moment that an author most needs to proclaim her confidence in the originality of her project, she is also reminded of her extensive debts to mentors, critics, colleagues, friends, and family. This book began as a doctoral dissertation at the New School for Social Research. Beyond the first three words of the title, however, very little of the original dissertation has survived to publication. For that, I thank George Shulman, Ira Katznelson, and Don Scott, each of whom has read and commented upon many drafts of this project from its earliest stages. *The Body Politic,* and my own thinking more generally, has benefited immensely from their tutelage. Vicky Hattam joined the dissertation committee rather late in its existence, not only rescuing me as I was about to commit an unspeakable violation of university policy, but far more important, bringing to her reading of the work the political and intellectual vitality that one comes to understand as characteristic of all that she does.

Financial assistance, always welcome, came in the form of a dissertation fellowship from the American Association of University Women; and later, as a grant from the Research Board of the University of Missouri system and a summer salary stipend from the Research Council of the University of Missouri-Columbia. This book simply would not exist had it not been for a crucial one-semester release from teaching responsibilities in Fall 1998. For that, I thank the Department of Political Science, the Women Studies Program, and the office of the Vice Provost for Minority Affairs and Faculty Development at the University of Missouri.

Many others have sustained and enlivened this project. From its New York years (and in some cases beyond them as well), these include Elaine Abelson, Barbara Balliet, Paige Baty, Richard Bensel, Emma Bianchi, Greg Bongen, Jen Gaboury, Susan Gallagher, Andy Grossman, Sonia Kruks, Fred Langenegger, Melissa Matthes, Rayna Rapp, Lealle Ruhl, Nancy Shealy, Francesca Weisser, and Priscilla Yamin. In my other life, in Missouri, "the juniors" make going to work fun (don't tell the boss!) and they've offered the moral support that is vital to any sustained undertaking, so I thank Jay Dow (though junior no more), Corinna-Barbara Francis, Val Heitshusen, Joey Hewitt, Lael Keiser, Sharon Wright, and Garry Young. Linda Angst, Dave Kinsella, and (eventually) the marvelous Maddy-mo deserve special mention for making the American

Midwest hospitable, and for their continuing friendship after they left for other parts. Colleagues and friends in Women's Studies, Barb Bank, Jane Downing, Shelda Eggers, Sarah Gallagher, Magdalena García-Pinto, Kathy Lee, Geta LeSeur, Trudy Lewis, Mary Jo Neitz, Mary Neth, Tola Pearce, Linda Reeder, and LeeAnn Whites; in Political Science, Thad Brown and Greg Casey (both of whom read this manuscript in several incarnations); and the ultimately unclassifiable Karin Shutjer and Ben Alpers, all deserve particular mention and gratitude. John Petrocik arrived rather late in the life of the manuscript, but his arrival has made a world of difference for me. Dan Sabia, Jill Frank, and Angela Ledford rounded up a friendly audience at the University of South Carolina; and Karen O'Connor, Diane Singerman, Joe Soss, and others from the Department of Government at American University provided insightful comments.

At Routledge, Eric Nelson has been impeccably tolerant of my technological ineptitude, and what's more, he is the editor of whom authors can only dream. He saved my life, metaphorically at least, and possibly my career, several times over. Tom Dumm and Anne Norton combed through the penultimate draft for Routledge, offering constructive and engaged criticism, and supplying me with the courage I needed to face the manuscript one final time (actually, it was more like 426 final times, but who's counting?). An abbreviated version of Chapter 2 has been published in *Political Theory*, vol. 29, no. 2 (April 2001), benefitting enormously from the commentary of Michael Rogin, Stephen K. White, and an anonymous reviewer for that journal.

Whoever believes that work and family are unrelated is either dishonest or inexperienced with both. Lois and Lowell Hunter, and Jan and Joe Offredi, have been sources of unflagging encouragement. My parents, Alsie and J.T. Holland, and my brother, John, have endured years of attenuated holidays and foreshortened vacations to accommodate my work schedule, as well as regular Sunday telephone conversations that carefully (though perhaps not so gracefully) steered away from progress reports on the book—surely inequitable repayment for having raised me in an atmosphere that fostered critical inquiry and valued intellectual engagement. Finally, Geoff Swindells made countless sacrifices, giving up season tickets at the Brooklyn Academy of Music and pastrami at Katz's Deli to join me in Missouri, and he set aside his own research, frequently, to coax the important points out of my most tortured prose and my oddest formulations.

1

Introduction: The Body Politic

> In the beginning, all the world was *America*.
> John Locke[1]

> America is the country of the future . . . the land of desire for all those who are weary of the historical arsenal of old Europe.
> G.W.F. Hegel[2]

Rethinking the liberal tradition in America

NEARLY HALF A CENTURY HAS PASSED SINCE LOUIS HARTZ PUBLISHED HIS best-known work, *The Liberal Tradition in America*. While this work has been criticized, amended, and almost endlessly refined by subsequent scholarship, it nonetheless continues to stand as a highly influential interpretation of American political thought. Much of its power lies in its rare ability to define a field so that even Hartz's critics remain largely within the conceptual universe he established.[3] Briefly, Hartz's work brought theoretical sophistication to what he calls the "storybook truth about American history," namely, that America was settled as a place of escape from the restrictive religious, political, and social dogmas of the Old World by men whose public vision was "in the broadest sense liberal."[4] Writing in the midst of postwar American anti-Communist paranoia, Hartz understood the attenuation of intellectual freedom entailed by that crisis as traceable, paradoxically, to the peculiar development in the United States of the very doctrines such ideological narrowness most seemed to violate: the liberal freedoms America claims as its distinctive point of departure. Having escaped the feudal past, America, as Hartz characterizes it, was relieved of a whole variety of constraints that shaped the development of European liberal thought and politics, yet the legacy of this trajectory for modern Americans was not more freedom, but less. The "fixed, dogmatic liberalism of a liberal way of life"[5] produces in the United States a cult of liberal constitutionalism, he contends, a language of political rights that exerts an unshakable hold over the American political imagination, and thus effects a tyranny of unanimity by which American democracy (as Tocqueville had recognized over a century earlier) achieves the suppression of free thought and free speech with a dispatch and thoroughness that eluded centuries of European despots and Divine Right absolutists.[6] What most animates Hartz's book is its apprehension of a constitutive paradox at the heart of American politics: liberal freedom is most imperiled not by external adversaries but by liberalism's own internal logic.[7]

The Body Politic is an effort to understand this problematic feature of liberal democratic thought in America, particularly in light of the so-called culture wars of the late twentieth century. Like the McCarthyism of the 1950s, the culture wars originated in efforts by partisans on the political Right to discredit those on the Left, less by contesting their political vision than by vilifying it as un- or even anti-American. This time around, the perceived danger is not Communism, but a broad array of intellectual and political movements—feminism, multiculturalism, postcolonialism, queer studies—which, critics contend, strike at the very heart of what it means to be American by eroding the liberal universalist commitments said to undergird American democratic citizenship.[8] One thing that makes the culture wars especially interesting, however, is the way that convenient markers of Right and Left quickly became *in*convenient, muddied as a number of commentators who identified themselves with the political Left responded to the Right's invectives with their own defenses of liberal universalism—again figured as the conceptual tradition that defines and distinguishes America—in writings directed against many of the same targets, even if they did not promote the same political programs as their more conservative counterparts. What I find most striking (and most troubling) about this episode in American public life is the degree to which something called the liberal tradition in America is used to raise the question of citizenship, of what it means to be and to act as citizen, and is played like a trump card to authorize a particular vision of citizenship, stifling public debate by discrediting competing visions.

However, while this book takes the culture wars as its contemporary point of departure, I examine this debate, directly, only in the conclusion. Ultimately, I am less concerned with the culture wars themselves than I am with understanding the place of citizenship within the liberal tradition that occasions this dispute and serves as its more or less assumed ground. *The Body Politic* traces the development of competing languages of citizenship in two founding moments of American public life: the foundings of 1776–1787 and the era of post-Civil War Reconstruction. It argues that our notions of citizenship in America are not reducible to a coherent theoretical doctrine, but are instead the historical products of founding and refounding an American nation. Each attempt to articulate a vision of what it means to be American produces its own internal contradictions at the level of both theory and political practice, introducing new forms of subjection and inequality into American liberalism and endowing it with a complex lineage that underwrites rather than undermines its rhetorical power. Lest the reader mistake this account as a simple repetition of the Hartzian thesis, let me state at the outset that I am both indebted to Hartz's account of the liberal tradition in America and committed to rethinking and contesting it.

Hartz's "liberal consensus" thesis has been criticized by scholars who challenge it on a number of counts—most convincingly to my mind by those who find in American political development not a monolithic consensus over liberal ideals but a variety of competing and often *il*liberal traditions that shape civic activity, and by those who interpret American history not as a trajectory of uncontested liberal egalitarianism but instead see a "belated feudalism" marked by the "medieval hierarchy of personal relations, [and] a particularized network of law and morality . . . that the word 'feudalism' implies."[9] While I will address this latter challenge to Hartz's account momentarily, let me first focus on the former, which is most powerfully articulated in Rogers Smith's recent elaboration of the "multiple traditions" thesis in *Civic Ideals*.

For Smith, the defining feature of the American political tradition is not a Hartzian liberal consensus but rather a more variegated and historically contingent pattern of liberalism, republicanism, and what he calls "ascriptive Americanisms," inegalitarian and exclusionary doctrines of racial, ethnic, and gender supremacy. Over the course of American political development, Smith argues, "liberalizing and democratizing changes have often created the conditions for the resurgence of inegalitarian ideologies and institutions,"[10] and it is this complex and often internally contradictory mix that shapes recurring conflicts over the terms of American national identity. Smith's corrective to the Toquevillian-Hartzian thesis, then, turns on his effort to disentangle these three distinct traditions from one another and to comprehend their effects on American public life.

Smith's work brings to the study of American political thought a much needed sense of complexity and nuance, and it demonstrates the degree to which prior accounts have remained blind to the constitutive meshing of doctrines and traditions that, for all their mutual implication, nonetheless remain distinct. By understanding the American past in this way, Smith suggests, we are in a better position to recognize these discrete doctrines at work in the present moment and the way they inform contemporary political debates (foremost among these being the current impasse between what Smith calls "universalist integrationists" and "separatist pluralists").[11] Armed with this knowledge, he argues, we can identify and combat our own ascriptive Americanisms and achieve a more genuinely liberal, democratic, and inclusive common life. Only by recognizing how an uncritical embrace of the liberal tradition has blinded us to the illiberalisms at work in America, Smith contends, can we successfully defend and maintain liberal republican ideals.

What I miss in Smith's analysis, however, is the sense of paradox, even tragic irony, that shapes Hartz's account and makes it so compelling. In the end, Smith too fully exonerates American liberalism from its complicity in episodes of (sometimes extreme) brutality, and more problematically, he makes it difficult for us to recognize and come to terms with the ways in which these ascriptive languages of ethnic, racial, and gendered hierarchy may not be as fully external to American liberalism as he maintains. He misses, or miscasts as wholly and exclusively illiberal, the complex countertendencies and traces of archaic political and ideological commitments that inhabit both American liberalism and modern political thought more generally. Even as it contributes a valuable measure of complexity to our grasp of the American *political* tradition, in another sense *Civic Ideals* unnecessarily simplifies our understanding of the American *liberal* tradition by misrecognizing the variety of means by which, as Hartz put it, American liberalism can sometimes "pose a threat to liberty itself."[12]

The modern and its archaisms

Insofar as liberal democratic thought in America is articulated within the larger context of modern thought, it is both organized and inspired in the broadest possible sense by some of the central conceptual tenets of modernity. In a series of highly influential essays, political philosopher Claude Lefort sought to come to terms with the vicissitudes of democracy in a distinctly postmonarchical age, and his point of departure for that project was Alexis de Tocqueville's *Democracy in America*. Like Louis Hartz a century later, Tocqueville discerns the ambiguities of democratic power that accompanied the emergence of democracy in America. As Lefort puts it, Tocqueville's analysis "reveals the underside of both the positive—new signs of freedom—and the negative—new signs of servitude."[13] These ambiguities, Lefort argues, surface in consequence of an important mutation in the symbolic order by which power is represented, a mutation that marks the emergence of modernity. "Under monarchy," writes Lefort, "power was embodied in the person of the prince." Princely power was neither unlimited nor despotic, but rather functioned to mediate between mortals and gods, or in more secular terms, between mortals and the "transcendental agencies represented by a sovereign Justice and a sovereign Reason." Thus positioned at once as subject to the law and above it, the prince "condensed within his body . . . the principle that generated the order of the kingdom. His power pointed towards an unconditional, other-worldly pole, while at the same time he was, in his own person, the guarantor and representative of the unity of the kingdom." That kingdom "itself was represented as a body"—hence the early modern conception of a body politic—complete with a hierarchy of governing head, limbs that provided for the defense of the whole, and a common trunk to which each of the various parts was attached.[14]

Early modern "power was embodied in the prince, and it therefore gave society a body," Lefort suggests. With the overthrow of monarchy in western democracies, however, the prince is unseated, the place of power emptied of its occupant, and modern liberal democratic society "is instituted as a society without a body, as a society which undermines the representation of an organic totality." Consequently, modern democracy is both established and sustained by the dissolution of the palpable markers of certainty that undergirded the cosmic sense of place characteristic of early modern political society. "It inaugurates a history in which people experience a fundamental indeterminacy as to the basis of power, law, and knowledge, and as to the basis of relations between self and *other*, at every level of social life."[15] Lefort goes on to suggest that this fundamental indeterminacy has the effect of institutionalizing conflict, and hence fosters both a democratic social equality and a radically democratic intellectual culture: the first by ensuring that no distinct social class or group is granted special political privileges, and the second insofar as constitutive indeterminacy introduces ("without the actors being aware of it") "a process of questioning" into modern social practice itself.[16]

However, it is also the case that the "fundamental indeterminacy" produced by the unrepresentability of modern power can generate collective anxieties that give rise to totalitarian efforts to restore certainty by suppressing the spirit of intellectual contest born of modern social forms. Paradoxically, the modern democratic form that has vanquished the body inaugurates its return, for as Lefort points out, in moments of economic crisis, social fragmentation, class conflict, or the outbreak of war, "we see the development of the fantasy of the People-as-One, the beginnings of a quest for a substantial identity, for a social body which is welded to its head, for an embodying power, for a state free from division."[17] Just as Smith sees American political development as punctuated by the periodic surfacing of illiberal, ascriptive languages of gendered and racial supremacy, Lefort apprehends the sudden emergence of the body (or desire for a common body) in moments where there is a threat to the smooth maintenance of political order. However, for Lefort these disturbances are not so much the markers of external ideological commitments as the paradoxical consequences of modernity itself, internal forces working within modernity, formed of the very historic circumstances that also shape modern democratic society.

Perhaps it should be noted that Lefort does not end on so despairing a note, but proceeds to "examin[e] the underside of the underside,"[18] and here he finds a further value to modern democratic form. Its spirit of questioning exceeds ideological efforts to restore certainty, and democracy thus survives the totalitarian fantasies of absolute knowledge and absolute power. Lefort's turn to this more optimistic note, welcome though it may be, nonetheless leaves us with a number of questions about how we can understand the uncertain place of the symbolic body with respect to modern democracy. How can it be said that the body is deposed along with the prince when it remains available to moderns, conceptually and symbolically, to be put to political use in moments of political upheaval? How can we understand these sudden eruptions if we must assume that the elimination of the body from politics is a necessary precondition of the emergence of modern liberal democracy?

In separate meditations about the ways in which distinct forms of domination are preserved within a postwar welfare state that otherwise strives to institutionalize equality of well-being, both Sheldon Wolin and Wendy Brown confront a similar problem. Both ask if the late modern state is a reliable and appropriate resource to be embraced by the Left and both express skepticism about efforts to transform the state as a vehicle for economic redistribution (in Wolin's case) or as an arena for feminist political change (Brown). Most important, both are concerned with the apparently inexplicable reproduction within the late modern welfare state of the very forms of lordly prerogative that modern political thought prides itself in having overcome. For Wolin, the transformation of the early modern concept of Reason of State to a late modern Welfare-State Reason (*Wohlfahrtsstaaträson*) involves something of a paradox: while the emergence of the welfare state democratizes power and public resources, it also conveys a greater degree of state influence into the day-to-day lives of citizens, at times by virtue of intrusive and counterdemocratic means that disempower the very groups and classes it seeks to assist.[19] Brown makes a similar point when she reminds feminists that the concept of the state has never been a gender neutral one, but is marked by a variety of sometimes complementary and sometimes competing modalities of male power. One of these in particular—what Brown calls the "prerogative dimension"—institutionalizes the otherwise informal means by which men exercise control over women as an "expressly nonliberal" facet of the otherwise liberal state, establishing the state as a venue for "exchanging, violating, protecting, and regulating women."[20] In this respect, Brown emphasizes the gendered dimensions of a paradox similar to Wolin's: lordly prerogative is extended into the purportedly private lives of unmarried women and their children by the very programs and initiatives promoted by the late modern welfare state to benefit them.

In both cases, Wolin and Brown suggest that precisely those elements that are assumed to have been overcome by the emergence of the late modern state turn out to have been incorporated within it, and held in reserve by it, to be deployed in moments of crisis. Wolin formulates this by reference to the Hobbesian covenant that establishes a sovereign state: "Hobbes did not eliminate the state of nature by means of a covenant. The state of nature is repressed, not transcended. It exists as a permanent feature of international politics."[21] Brown's logic is similar: "There is another way of reading the origins of the liberal state, in which the arbitrary and concentrated powers of monarchy are not demolished. Rather, princely power is dissimulated and redeployed by liberalism as state prerogative that extends from war making to budget making. In this reading, the violence of the state of nature is not overcome but reorganized and resituated in, on the one hand, the state itself as the police and the military, and on the other, the zone marked 'private' where the state may not tread and where a good deal of women's subordination and violation is accomplished."[22]

To return, then, to the problem I have raised with regard to both Smith and Lefort—namely, that each recognizes, and recognizes as problematic, the sudden appearance of the body within a modern order—let me suggest that we address the matter by employing a logic similar to that formulated by Wolin and Brown. That the body erupts on the scene of politics in moments of public crisis suggests that it is never fully eliminated from a liberal democratic order, but is instead reconfigured by and incorporated within it. The body may be made invisible to or transparent within the modern public realm, but it is nonetheless held in reserve as a political force that becomes visible (or is made visible) in the very moments when order itself is at its most vulnerable. In this respect, we might begin to view the body as a somewhat more complicated symbol than Smith's account suggests, an unstable signifier of modernity's relation to the past—sometimes liberatory, sometimes limiting, but most often a complex of competing impulses.

To put this another way, it could be said that modern political thought does not fully overcome or abandon its premodern past, but instead recharacterizes elements of that past as archaisms that inhabit and work in new ways within the modern. One way of illuminating modernity's production of archaisms—and more specifically, modernity's production of the body as an archaic figure—is to retell with new emphases and a slightly shifted focus one of the foundational modern tales of the origins of political society, namely, that of man's passage from the prepolitical state of nature to an established political order. According to that tale, historical time and political order are preceded by an extended moment called the state of nature. Antecedent to politics, nature is all that exists: prior to the emergence of common culture, nature is the preface to progress, a time anterior to the development of language, institutions, politics. The nature that thrives in that period prior to the beginning of history is devoid of chronological time—days pass and conditions change, but there is as yet no logic to that time, no developmental motif by which "natural man" makes sense or sequence of events. This state of nature is at once a chaotic and incomprehensible predicament as well as a self-sustaining universe: immutable, timeless, and enduring.[23]

Politics erupts in the form of some uncontainable conflict and it sweeps man into a new order of progressive time, leaving nature in its wake. Or so we suppose. As the vehicle of progress, modern politics redirects time and transforms it into history, transforming nature into governable political society as well. Yet even as history steps in to carry political society up and away from the state of nature, nature is never entirely effaced from this narrative of modern politics. Rather, as natural man becomes citizen in the transition from nature to society, he brings with him into the social order a trace of the (dis)order he left behind: the body. Put another way, modern political thought does not so much dispense with the prediscursive state of nature as distill it and invest it in the body of the citizen. The sudden appearance of the body from time to time on the scene of politics is often understood and experienced as the abrupt materialization of "nature" that may take a variety of forms ranging from Lefort's antifantasy of an "embodying power" to what Todd Gitlin has recently called "tribalism rampant," the resurgence of ethnic identitarian movements not just in Bosnia, but also (albeit to a lesser degree) in Oakland, California.[24]

One premise of this book is that the figure of the human body operates within modern schemas of politics as one of modernity's archaisms, harbored within and on occasion deployed by the very order that gains its coherence through the claim of having vanquished, exiled, or displaced it. It is a figure of modern freedom, a sign of modern sovereignty, and at the same time a vehicle for establishing new means of subjection.[25] In the American context, the archaic body lives on most palpably within constitutional languages of citizenship, languages that take distinct forms and assign distinctive places to the body in different constitutional moments, but never fully eliminate it from our vernaculars of political membership. Identifying the place of the body and analyzing its operation on and within our languages of citizenship, then, constitute an important part of the project of rethinking the liberal tradition in America.

Why America? Why, in other words, is the American political imagination so distinctly (if *not* uniquely) shaped by the operation of archaic symbols of the past? The answer to this question, I would suggest, lies partially in the symbolic place that America holds in the modern European tradition, and partially in the consequent creative power of the very notion of pastlessness in American political thought.

America, the modern

Read together, the two epigraphs with which I opened this chapter tell us much about the place "America" occupies in the European political imagination: a (once) pristine and unsettled land (as Locke suggests), it becomes the settlement of the future for those seeking escape from the European past (Hegel). As Anne Norton has put it, America symbolizes an "Edenic innocence [where] men would be born to a perfect equality, and [in which] the nations of Europe would see in their relations the lineaments of a long-forgotten nature."[26] Indeed, from the moment the Mayflower sailed within sight of land, the American continent has been viewed as a natural ground on which Europeans might, in the words of the Mayflower Compact, "plant" a new society.[27] Myra Jehlen expresses it nicely: "Americans saw themselves as building their civilization out of nature itself, as neither the analogue nor the translation of Natural Law but its direct expression."[28]

"America" signifies the ancient ground on which the future will be forged, a fertile territory awaiting the cultivation and construction of a future purified of the contaminants of the European past. Yet even Locke complicates this familiar picture, for that oft-quoted passage ends not by *a*ssociating but by *dis*sociating America with an untouched nature: "In the beginning, all the world was *America*, and more so than that is now; for no such thing as *Money* was anywhere known." Put this way, the passage suggests a considerably more tangled and complex relation between and among past, present, and future; between America and the world; between America and itself; and even between money and modernity than any reading of Locke as the original American exceptionalist can acknowledge. For in this invocation, "America" recalls an original state even as it suggests an already-accomplished departure from it: America is no longer as it once was, the world is no longer what it (or what America) has been, even "the beginning" may signify something other than what it once did. Indeed, America is now (and was, for Locke, writing in the latter half of the seventeenth century) *less* American than the rest of the world was "in the beginning."

Perhaps it can be said, then, that America symbolizes the complex relation between past, present, and future where a past declared to be left behind is resurrected as phantasm and hence it survives in an all the more powerful, if vestigial, form into the present and is projected onto the future. In this light, it seems useful to take another look at the historic and conceptual bases of American exceptionalism, the "storybook truth about American history" that Louis Hartz analyzed so powerfully yet so problematically five decades ago. For if it was once clear that America lacks a feudal past, such a truth may, strictly speaking, be true no longer. In *Belated Feudalism*, Karen Orren contends that America's postfeudal political development cannot accurately be equated with the *absence* of a feudal past and she demonstrates the continued vitality of English Tudor, even Plantagenet, traditions of the law of master and servant in nineteenth-century American labor regulation up through the Gilded Age.[29] For Orren, Hartz's exceptionalist view of American liberalism succeeds only to the degree that Hartz was himself able to filter out the traces of feudal hierarchy and feudal tradition that otherwise survived and thrived in the canons of American law up until the early twentieth century. The feudal past, by this account, is not at all past, but lives on in American institutions.

Making a similar point (and one that I will develop further in Chapter 3), Sheldon Wolin has suggested that the supporters of the 1787 Constitution recognized in the Articles of Confederation and commensurate post-Revolutionary political practices a distinct set of feudal elements and localist tendencies that the advocates of the new Constitution set out consciously to suppress, but did so only incompletely.[30] Where Orren corrects the Hartzian record by identifying the historic traces of feudal social organization retained within American institutions, Wolin demonstrates the ways in which certain feudal commitments are retained and maintained *conceptually* at the heart of American liberal doctrine. Between Orren and Wolin lie a number of potential points of both theoretical and methodological disagreement, but together they help to establish an important corrective to a standard interpretation of the American political tradition, namely, that not one but several feudal traditions survive in the United States and shape important political and legal debates through (at least) the end of the nineteenth century.[31]

However, despite these correctives to the Hartzian account, it remains the case that Hartz's analysis taps into an American folk wisdom that is every bit as culturally powerful as it is historically misguided; it is a folk wisdom that enshrines the American citizen as a fully self-made man, and his nation a self-originating entity. Politics in the American political imagination suggests a field of infinite possibility unfettered by preexisting intellectual traditions or institutional structures where, as Hartz put it, "the words of Locke are used [but] a prior Filmer is absent."[32] That is, it is not so much the content of the American past that marks it as an "exception" to the rules of modern historical development, but America's purported *lack* of a foundational past on which Revolutionary statesmen constructed the new republic that, in Hartz's formulation, distinguishes American from European liberalism. Put another way, the claims of American exceptionalism may be historically wrong in the strict sense, but they nonetheless describe an important theme that runs throughout the history of American political thought, one that remains a creative force in shaping the American political imagination. Indeed, the strictly symbolic nature of America's purported pastlessness does not weaken but rather strengthens its purchase in American political culture. As Toni Morrison has written of America's, and Americans', persistent difficulty in coming to terms with the historic fact of slavery: "We live in a land where the past is always erased and America is the innocent future in which immigrants can come and start over, where the slate is clean. The past is absent, or it's romanticized."[33] Romanticized, I might add, as absence itself.

It is precisely this romanticization of America's (putative) pastlessness that calls into question the "exceptional" qualities the nation is said to embody. If America has come to symbolize the new by virtue of the romanticization of an absent past, then America is not exceptional but *exemplary* of an important aspect of modern thought, preoccupied as it is with the pursuit of novelty. Certainly, for political theorists, the mark of the modern is the effort to clear a space for the establishment of political society by reference to the fictive "past" of politics, the so-called state of nature. If it is the case that modern thought needs a state of nature, then "America" is not so much that fictive past as, perhaps, the pastless *setting* for the conceptual development of that body of work we call modern political thought.

Paradoxically enough, it is in America that the question of the past takes on particular significance precisely insofar as the American past is almost nowhere assumed (at least not in any coherent or consistent form), but must instead be produced, established, endowed with political meaning, and eventually abandoned in favor of new and different accounts. America's, and Americans', celebration of pastlessness, in other words, *is* a preoccupation with the past of a particular sort, a preoccupation made possible by the abandonment of one past (the European), and the commensurate effort to begin anew. Yet as I have argued above, even conceptual pasts and fictive foundations are rarely, if ever, abandoned simply or wholly. They live on to find new conceptual lives and take on new conceptual forms at the heart of the very innovations that are designed to lay past problems and past traditions to rest.[34] In America, and for Americans, it is (ironically) in the reiteration of the modern romance of American pastlessness that certain archaisms—which take the form of some distinctly novel feudalist sympathies and practices, and are repeatedly symbolized by the human body—are resurrected within, and at the heart of, the American political tradition.

The body politic: constitutional moments, constitutive tensions

This book proceeds by examining two critical moments in American political development, namely the years of the Revolution and early Republic, and the years of Reconstruction following the American Civil War. In each of these moments, distinct political languages of rights and citizenship are articulated, contested, reformulated, and finally formalized through incorporation into the Constitution. To emphasize the link between and among the diverse venues in which these languages of citizenship are promulgated—venues that range from conventional political and theoretical texts, to letters, popular pamphlets, and even the melodrama of a widely-followed, scandalous criminal trial—I use the phrase "constitutional moment" to describe an era during which a widely varied set of political discourses and practices coalesce, however precariously. I use that term not as a scholar of American constitutional law, but rather as a political theorist who considers constitutions, following the lead of Sheldon Wolin, as both political and hermeneutical events: political in the sense that they represent a settlement about the terms of power to which their signatories have agreed; hermeneutical insofar as, even if their content is agreed upon, their meanings are not. "The Founders," as Wolin writes (and I would include here the architects of Reconstruction as well), "did not produce *a* particular meaning that was subsequently ratified. Rather, they set in motion a form of politics, a good part of which would be absorbed by contests to settle the meaning of the Constitution by unsettling some competing meaning."[35] Constitutional moments, then, are periods of both construction and contest, in which political actors struggle to articulate, give meaning to, and inhabit a particular form of politics. It is my purpose in this book to take a close look at the constitutive tensions that inhere in these moments, to attend to both what holds them together and what threatens to pull them apart. Close attention to these generative moments reveals a recurring figure at the very heart of the American imagination: the human body. If, to recall Lefort, the symbolic vanquishing of the prince's body accomplished by modern liberal-democratic revolutions imparts a radical indeterminacy as to the locus of modern power, I argue that the figure of the human body remains as a powerful resource for visions of both political order and imminent collapse, an unstable signifier at the center of public life.

In a very real sense, then, America is a body politic, and the figure of the human body is fundamental to our understanding of the American nation. However, I am all too aware of the inadequacy of this phrase, "the human body," of the ways it is at once a maddeningly vague and overly specific marker of the complex of meanings that are accumulated within it. "The" overstates the consensus over meaning(s) attached to it; "human" misstates the universality of species that is almost nowhere assumed or asserted in discourses of citizenship and nation that repeatedly differentiate individuals by race and gender; and "body," with its suggestion of solidity and materiality, understates the ways in which the body functions as a *conceptual* principle of an ordered (or disordered) polity. However, it is precisely this ambiguity that this book seeks to engage and exploit, not in the service of offering definitive answers, but to prompt us to begin to look at "the liberal tradition in America" in new ways, ways that might help us reshape the American political imagination.

Part I focuses on the political thought of the Revolution and early national eras. It opens with the question of foundings. Foundings are rare moments in politics, when the laws and practices that once governed public life are renounced and new possibilities are envisioned. How, then, can we speak of the operation of the past within that most political of moments, when political order is established *anew*? This question has preoccupied scholars of the American founding over recent decades, a number of whom have demonstrated the degree to which American Founders relied upon preexisting models drawn from European liberal and republican thought to envision a new and different social order formed, in America, on distinctively American ground. While I appreciate the meticulousness with which this scholarship has established both the continuity of, and the innovations made in, particular strands of European thought in early America, I take a slightly different approach by looking to the production of new and different visions of the past—of what represents a distinctively American past—marshalled in this project of imagining a different future.

Thomas Jefferson's *Notes on the State of Virginia*, the focus of Chapter 2, identifies in American nature a past proper to the democratic project, one that might be refigured as a foundation for both a newly independent nation and a national citizenry. In keeping with the historic and historical significance with which Jefferson freights nature, his treatment of Virginia's landscape identifies in it a complex principle of time and change that he seeks to transport into the new nation's political institutions as a dynamic and democratizing force. Jefferson's natural history of the new nation is not concerned simply with the construction of new and innovative institutions, however, for it also mobilizes a retrospective logic which produces a new past that both generates and legitimates these new political traditions. For Jefferson, the link between America's natural past and its democratic future is to be found in an historicized conception of the citizen's body, a body that connects European creoles to the ancient American past through their physical and cultural similarities with Native Americans. Jefferson's genealogical nationalism also confirms the historic and political disconnectedness of African Americans from the American past and indicates their misplacement in the new nation. This genealogical nationalism establishes the body as the noumenal ground of citizenship in America, a point of origin upon which a philosophy of belonging—by birth or by naturalization—is fashioned.

Of course, Jefferson was by no means alone in the effort to legitimate the revolutionary break with the Old World and establish different foundations for the new one. Chapter 3 looks to a variety of other meditations, roughly contemporary with the *Notes*, on the relation among citizens, institutions, and America itself—meditations promoting localist orientations and an unruptured unity of citizenship that linked individuals to one another and to the distinct political cultures of the states in what I call, following Sheldon Wolin, a feudal-republicanism. This chapter examines the competing formulations of local bodies and general population to which (among other things) the 1787 Constitution responds, and out of which the most elaborate defense of that Constitution, *The Federalist Papers*, is developed. Bringing to these debates about citizenship and institutions the insights of Michel Foucault's late writings on governmental rationality, I identify in the 1787 Constitution the development of a distinctive language of governance that I call "aggregate universalist citizenship." Briefly, the technique of aggregation represents a central element of the federal state's efforts to develop democratic institutions that are responsible to the citizenry, a technique that works by producing a comprehensive knowledge about both citizens and institutions and by combining, integrating, and generalizing the diverse resources available to the state in its effort to guarantee the well-being of the whole. What the proposed Constitution, defended in the pages of *The Federalist Papers*, gives us is the principle of a citizenry that is sovereign of itself, made so by virtue of the aggregation of unlike things.

The 1787 Constitution thus pays little, if any, direct attention to citizens' bodies in any narrow or literal sense. However, its strategy of defining general rules did not simply eliminate the body, or the particularities of bodies, from American languages of citizenship, but first invoked the body and then rendered it archaic in the public realm. The citizen's local body was not left behind in the move from the Articles of Confederation to the federal Constitution; rather, it was integrated into American public life as the central figure around which a new form of national citizenship coalesced. My reading thus challenges those interpretations of citizenship in the early national era that stress its disembodiment, the explicit abstraction of the national citizen from the particulars of his or her local body. While I would agree that the techniques of citizenship promoted by the Founders certainly departicularize the citizen, I argue that these accounts cannot help us understand the ensuing politicization of the body in the decades leading up to the American Civil War. The antebellum movements for the abolition of slavery and for the guarantee of women's suffrage are emblematic of the place of the body under the principles of aggregate citizenship. While I do not treat these movements, or the Civil War itself, in any detail here, what they suggest is the ultimate failure of an aggregate universalism which locates citizens' bodies at the center of the American political imagination, but offers us no political means of addressing the inequalities of public power that come to define the place of the raced and gendered body in America.

Part II focuses on the effort to remake the federal Constitution, and with it the American body politic, in the aftermath of the Civil War and the concomitant collapse of the techniques of aggregate universalism. Reconstruction saw the development of two variants of this earlier vernacular, variants that did not supplant so much as overwrite their predecessor. Part II looks simultaneously at the new formulations promoted in the aftermath of the war and examines the shadows of the old order that not only survived the war but were actively reconfigured and produced anew during the period. It opens with the tangled politics of the post-Civil War suffrage movements, which required, in the end, that women defer their demands for suffrage so that freedmen might be guaranteed the franchise. If conventional accounts of the period tend to identify in the Reconstruction Amendments the formalization of women's exclusion from the right to vote, my analysis emphasizes something else at work: the development of a grid that counterposes race and gender, formalizing and fixing the requisite criteria for acting as a citizen in the attributes of individual bodies. This is to say that the forms and techniques of political identification were fundamentally altered by Reconstruction. The body that had long been present, if only dimly visible, within constitutional schemas of citizenship, came to occupy a far more prominent place.

The citizen's body takes on new meaning under the terms of Reconstruction: once a figure of a suppressed past, the raced and gendered body becomes an expression of that past, both a marker of political interest and a symbol of the citizen's future. Chapter 4 traces this complicated reconfiguration of the public sphere by looking to the events surrounding the 1875 adultery trial of Henry Ward Beecher. This very public scandal can be read as an elaboration, in the political realm, of what Eve Kosofsky Sedgwick has called "male homosocial desire," where the male citizen's body is afforded a new kind of public visibility, while women are redefined as visible, but silent, citizens. While this episode is indicative of Reconstruction's establishment of a gendered understanding of citizenship, the body's new visibility marked a loss for male citizens as well, a loss that I explore by reference to John Adams' earlier elaboration of a principle he called the "passion for distinction."

Chapter 5 draws on this analysis to examine the consequences of this new place of the body in the American political imagination and to trace the development during this period of two languages of citizenship that remain with us today. The first part of the chapter looks at the ways in which the aggregate universalism of the Founders was transformed in and through the categories of embodied citizenship articulated in the Reconstruction Amendments, establishing a new mode of genealogical nationalism and a new technique of citizenship that we have come to identify as abstract universalism. However, rather than focus my attention on the mainstream of political life, I develop my discussion of abstract universalism by looking to the margins, specifically to the white supremacist fraternities of the Reconstruction South. I do this not to suggest that abstract universalism is always and only a racist doctrine, but because this allows me to analyze the ways that liberalism itself, and not simply Smith's "ascriptive Americanisms," can be developed and deployed as an exclusionary ideology and practice. The chapter ends by looking to a late nineteenth-century meditation on the consequences of Reconstruction by suffragist Victoria Woodhull. Woodhull returns to a central myth of origins, the story of the Garden of Eden, to ponder the question of sexual difference and its distinctly political significance in America just prior to the turn of the century. Rereading Genesis as an allegorical tale of the origin of political society in the rape of Eve and extending this allegory to the place of women within the post-Reconstruction constitutional order, Woodhull advocates a new form of feminism: a feminism founded in injury, thus an early instance of the kind of politics that we associate with late modern identitarian movements.

The Body Politic concludes with a meditation on the persistence of the body in recent, late twentieth-century debates over the nature of citizenship in America and suggests ways of engaging this persistence differently. Despite the enormous (albeit incomplete) changes wrought by the feminist, Civil Rights, and gay rights movements, the American political imagination remains caught in the categories established during Reconstruction. I develop this point through an analysis of the contemporary culture wars, and end by returning to Victoria Woodhull to explore how we might productively rethink the place of the body in American politics.

Endnotes

1. John Locke, *Two Treatises of Government*, ed. Peter Laslett (Cambridge: Cambridge University Press, 1960), II §49.

2. G.W.F. Hegel, *Lectures on the Philosophy of World-History: Introduction—Reason in History*, trans. H.B. Nisbet (Cambridge: Cambridge University Press, 1975), 170–71.

3. As should become clear below, this claim is somewhat different from one made by Rogers Smith, who argues that within the Hartzian tradition even America's dissenters have tended to be portrayed as articulating radical versions of the dominant liberal-republican discourse. Smith, too, is concerned with the ways in which the Hartzian framework tends to swallow up and assimilate all American political discourse within the ambit of liberalism. Yet Smith is concerned with the nature of ideology; by contrast, I am speaking here of a specific *conceptual* move that is common to both Hartz and his critics—including (even especially) Smith—a means of defining a distinctly American liberalism by extracting impurities from it. In Hartz's case these impurities consist in a lingering feudalism; in Smith's, in illiberal discourses that exist (in his depiction) alongside but not within American liberalism. See Rogers M. Smith, "Beyond Tocqueville, Myrdal, and Hartz: The Multiple Traditions in America," *American Political Science Review* 87:3 (September 1993), esp. 550.

4. Louis Hartz, *The Liberal Tradition in America* (New York: Harcourt Brace & Company, 1952), 3.

5. Louis Hartz, *The Liberal Tradition in America*, 9.

6. For Tocqueville's formulation of the "tyranny of the majority" and its stultifying effects on freedom of thought, see Alexis de Tocqueville, *Democracy in America* (New York: Vintage, 1945), I:269–78.

7. Thomas Dumm puts it this way: "The *Liberal Tradition in America* highlights the conditions under which a polity might be able to grow without maturing, expand while protecting a studied ignorance concerning the ends of power. In this sense, even the deeply illiberal politics of the past decade [Dumm published this in 1994] have been a part of the liberal tradition." Thomas L. Dumm, *united states* (Ithaca: Cornell University Press, 1994), 15.

8. The first, classic, and in some ways most sophisticated of these attacks is Allen Bloom, *The Closing of the American Mind* (New York: Simon & Schuster, 1987). Building on the enthusiasm unleashed by Bloom's book are a number of texts that include William J. Bennett, *Our Children and Our Country: Improving America's Schools and Affirming the Common Culture* (New York: Simon & Schuster, 1988); Lynne V. Cheney, *Tyrannical Machines: A Report on Educational Practices Gone Wrong and Our Best Hopes for Setting Them Right* (Washington: National Endowment for the Humanities, 1990); Roger Kimball, *Tenured Radicals: How Politics Has Corrupted Our Higher Education* (New York: Harper & Row, 1990); Dinesh D'Souza, *Illiberal Education: The Politics of Race and Sex on Campus* (New York: Free Press, 1991); William J. Bennett, *The De-Valuing of America: The Fight for Our Culture and Our Children* (New York: Summit, 1992); Russell Jacoby, *Dogmatic Wisdom: How the Culture Wars Divert Education and Distract America* (New York: Doubleday, 1994).

9. Karen Orren, *Belated Feudalism: Labor, the Law, and Liberal Development in the United States* (New York: Cambridge University Press, 1991), 2. For a very different yet equally important interpretation of feudal development in the United States, see Sheldon S. Wolin, *The Presence of the Past: Essays on the State and the Constitution* (Baltimore: The Johns Hopkins University Press, 1989), esp. Chapters Four and Seven.

10. Rogers M. Smith, *Civic Ideals: Conflicting Visions of Citizenship in U.S. History* (New Haven: Yale University Press, 1997), 5.

11. In Smith's reading, each represents a different strategy for promoting greater inclusiveness in public life: the former by virtue of an improved universalism, the latter by calling for increased public recognition and preservation of group differences. Bibliographically, Smith associates the former strand with the work of John Rawls, the latter with that of Iris Marion Young. See Rogers Smith, *Civic Ideals: Conflicting Visions of Citizenship in U.S. History*, 473.

12. Louis Hartz, *The Liberal Tradition in America*, 11.

13. Claude Lefort, *Democracy and Political Theory*, trans. David Macey (Minneapolis: University of Minnesota Press, 1988), 14. Mark Reinhardt does an excellent job of getting at the ways Tocqueville both recognizes and (re)produces the ambiguities of

modern democratic society. See Mark Reinhardt, *The Art of Being Free: Taking Liberties with Tocqueville, Marx, and Arendt* (Ithaca: Cornell University Press, 1997).

14. Claude Lefort, *Democracy and Political Theory*, 17. For a similar formulation, see also Claude Lefort, "The Image of the Body and Totalitarianism," *The Political Forms of Modern Society: Bureaucracy, Democracy, Totalitarianism*, ed. John B. Thompson (Cambridge: Polity Press, 1986), 292–306.

15. Claude Lefort, *Democracy and Political Theory*, 17–19 *passim*. Emphasis in original.

16. Claude Lefort, *Democracy and Political Theory*, 19.

17. Claude Lefort, *Democracy and Political Theory*, 19–20.

18. Claude Lefort, *Democracy and Political Theory*, 15.

19. Sheldon S. Wolin, "Democracy and the Welfare State: The Political and Theoretical Connections between *Staatsräson* and *Wohlfahrtsstaaträson*," *The Presence of the Past: Essays on the State and the Constitution*.

20. Wendy Brown, "Finding the Man in the State," *States of Injury: Power and Freedom in Late Modernity* (Princeton: Princeton University Press, 1995), 186–91.

21. Sheldon S. Wolin, "Democracy and the Welfare State," 167.

22. Wendy Brown, "Finding the Man in the State," 187.

23. For this reason, the term "state of nature" is malleable enough to accommodate the many, competing and sometimes contradictory depictions of it throughout the history of modern political thought—as Lockean fact or Kantian fiction, as Hobbesian dystopia or Rousseauian utopia.

24. Claude Lefort, *Democracy and Political Theory*, 20; Todd Gitlin, *The Twilight of Common Dreams: Why America Is Wracked by Culture Wars* (New York: Metropolitan Books, 1995), 230.

25. "If men wish to be free," Arendt has written, "it is precisely sovereignty they must renounce." See Hannah Arendt, *Between Past and Future: Eight Exercises in Political Thought* (New York: Penguin, 1961), 165.

26. Anne Norton, *Alternative Americas: A Reading of Antebellum Political Culture* (Chicago: The University of Chicago Press, 1986), 1.

27. "The Mayflower Compact," *An American Primer*, ed. Daniel J. Boorstin (New York: Penguin, 1985), 21.

28. Myra Jehlen, *American Incarnation: The Individual, The Nation, and the Continent* (Cambridge: Harvard University Press, 1986), 3.

29. Karen Orren, *Belated Feudalism: Labor, the Law, and Liberal Development in the United States*.

30. Sheldon S. Wolin, *The Presence of the Past: Essays on the State and the Constitution*, esp. Chapters Four and Seven.

31. Acknowledging this does not in any way suggest that *other* traditions, most

prominently liberal and republican ones, exercise no influence in the United States.

32. Louis Hartz, *The Liberal Tradition in America*, 6.

33. "Living memory: a meeting with Toni Morrison," in Paul Gilroy, *Small Acts: Thoughts on the Politics of Black Cultures* (London: Serpent's Tale Press, 1993), 179. I am grateful to George Shulman for bringing this essay to my attention.

34. Joan DeJean makes a similar point, differently, in *Ancients Against Moderns: Culture Wars and the Making of a Fin de Siècle*. DeJean's examination of the literary culture wars of the 1690s in France suggests the ways in which the Moderns, by defining themselves against the Ancients (e.g., their seventeenth-century contemporaries who advocated the superiority of classical texts to "modern" ones), actually depicted themselves as the legatees of the "original ancients, the ancients in antiquity," and hence (ironically) as "quite literally older than their precursors in antiquity, coming as they do at the end of what . . . Moderns clearly present as a long development leading straight from antiquity to the late seventeenth century" (18). The distinctively modern picture of developmental progress that was essential to Moderns' self-definition required of them a certain pessimism not about the past, but about the present and the future. In holding that "Our century has reached the summit of progress," Moderns inadvertently admitted that "progress was literally always/already over" (17), and hence their own formulations gave rise to the seventeenth-century advocacy of classicism articulated by the so-called Ancients, who countered that pessimism with the embrace of classical notions of cyclical decline and regeneration. "The claim to Modern status," DeJean writes, "is at the same time a recognition of the burden of tradition and an admission of a sense of belatedness, of decadence. Inseparable from the rallying cry 'we are the Moderns' is 'we are the Ancients,' a clear sign of a fin de siècle mentality" (18). See Joan DeJean, *Ancients Against Moderns: Culture Wars and the Making of a Fin de Siècle* (Chicago: The University of Chicago Press, 1997).

35. Sheldon S. Wolin, *The Presence of the Past: Essays on the State and the Constitution*, 3. Emphasis in original.

I

FOUNDINGS AND THE PROBLEM OF THE PAST

———◆———

FOUNDINGS ARE UNIQUE AND POWERFUL MOMENTS, RARE OPPORTUNITIES not simply to begin, but to begin *again*, to remake the present in terms that are seemingly unconstrained by the past. Writing early in 1776, on the brink of the American Revolution, Thomas Paine enjoined the colonial residents of North America to commence "the birthday of the New World" by seizing the first opportunity "since the days of Noah" "to begin the world over again."[1] Nearly six decades later, Alexis de Tocqueville echoed Paine's analogy. For Tocqueville, the discovery of the New World represented a kind of providential redemption, a gift bestowed on the future at the very moment when the (European) present had become unliveable:

> When the earth was given to men by the Creator, the earth was inexhaustible; but men were weak and ignorant, and when they had learned to take advantage of the treasures which it contained, they already covered its surface and were soon obliged to earn by the sword an asylum for repose and freedom. Just then North America was discovered, as if it had been kept in reserve by the Deity and had just risen from beneath the waters of the Deluge.[2]

For both Paine and Tocqueville, the unprecedented character of the American founding requires the invocation of providential powers and mythic tales in order to rethink the present in wholly new terms. Their imagery also suggests a more complex relation between founding moments and the past(s) out of which they spring. Even the biblical story of the flood tells of a new beginning inaugurated not from a moment outside of time but from within it, a beginning accomplished by putting old elements to new use. The Old Testament deity, as Edward Said has put it, "does not begin completely from nothing, [for] Noah and the ark comprise a piece of the old world initiating the new world."[3]

In this sense, we might say that however much founding moments are oriented toward the construction of new futures, they also involve the (re)construction of the past. They imply a return to and a repetition of past languages, practices, and ideas as a means of marking a difference from them and making difference(s) of them. Foundings require a kind of vision that is at once prospective and retrospective. Their products are neither wholly new entities nor simply replications of the given. By anchoring new departures to some element of the past, we curb the radical indeterminacy of new beginnings and clear a space for innovation by opening a gap between what has been and what may be. In terms of the American founding, one of the primary mechanisms by which Founders imagined a past that also enabled a vision of the future was by reference to a concept of nature. Taking "nature as [their] guide"[4] (as Paine put it), Americans might confront the unprecedented prospect of developing a new nation fearlessly and creatively, meeting this challenge with unscripted formulations of public life and political power.

Yet the construction of an imaginary past may itself involve the elision of the terms of its own construction, and such a denial may turn out to be necessary to the success of the new order. The political thought of Thomas Jefferson is a case in point. If there is truth to Judith Shklar's observation that, for Jefferson, "a democratic people did not need a past of any kind [but] must live entirely in the present," I would argue that it resides in the degree to which he was able to obscure the "pastness" of the fiction of nature that his vision of democracy relied upon, and depict it as both contiguous to and continuous with the present. Indeed, this elision of the past in and by the present is precisely what gives appeal to Jefferson's radically democratic vision, to his insistence that democracy requires perpetual refounding, and hence to his oft-repeated remark that each generation would have to make its own revolution or else live under the tyranny of the laws of dead men. As Shklar puts it, Jefferson "wanted not merely *new* politics, but a politics of perpetual *newness*,"[5] but I would add, one that at once depended upon, incorporated, and yet obscured the presence of a past within it.

Not only democrats like Paine and Jefferson, but later advocates of the stronger and more centralized state promoted by Federalists touted the originality of the American revolutionary project. As John Adams put it, "the United States of America have exhibited, perhaps, the first example of government erected on the simple principles of nature . . . contrived merely by the use of reason and the senses."[6] To take them at their word, members of the revolutionary generation understood themselves to be radically unconstrained by the structuring character of history and freed from the tyranny of social hierarchies, political institutions, laws, and traditions that might limit the range of possibilities envisioned by their *novus ordo saeclorum*.

For Jefferson and for other American Founders, this meant not simply *identifying* a past that was distinctively American, but *supplying* one, one that could be divorced from the "ancestor worship" of European history,[7] and which by virtue of its very Americanness could be assimilated to the present, as the present. The past was not erased, nor was it abandoned. It was made a transparent component of the political present and (contra the conclusions of twentieth-century commentators as diverse as Louis Hartz and Judith Shklar) American democracy was established not through the forswearing of the past, but by virtue of incorporating that past within the present.[8] We might ask how that incorporation is possible, how a figurative past is sustained within the political present, how it operates, and by what mechanisms the past comes to be elided or erased even as it is (re)constructed within the American political imagination. This constellation of concerns raises important questions of reading. How might we retain a healthy skepticism of the self-understanding of Founders' invocations of pastlessness without losing sight of the creative force of those invocations themselves? How might we remain attentive to historical insights about the specificities of meaning and understanding without reifying past conceptual languages, enabling ourselves to bring new concerns and novel formulations to the study of past texts and past events—particularly to the study of texts and events that insist upon their own novelty and pastlessness?

Pastlessness and the bind of history

The fantasy of pastlessness, of political and historical unfetteredness, is as tempting for late-modern thinkers as it was for those of the revolutionary generation. As Paige duBois has noted, "the erasure of history reduces anxieties; we need no longer consider the past, or even the difficulties of the future."[9] This desire finds its expression in a variety of forms within post-World War II political thought in the United States and operates there to radically different effect: from Hannah Arendt's privileging of natality as the model of new beginnings and of political action to John Rawl's heuristic device of a "veil of ignorance" that obscures the particulars of each individual's embeddedness in a social hierarchy in the critical moments when codes of procedural justice are established.[10] As Sheldon Wolin has argued, even (indeed, especially) the enterprise of

American political science—with its commitments to objectivity, detachment, fidelity to facts, and elevation of method over virtually all other concerns—can be viewed as yet another instance of a "typically American" way of thinking that denies the implication of its own theoretical commitments in the conceptual, and even ideological, traditions that precede it.[11]

However much American political thinkers have been drawn to this myth of pastlessness, a wealth of scholarship suggests the depth with which men like Paine and Adams, Jefferson, Madison, and Hamilton drew upon a variety of legal- and political-theoretical traditions stretching from the ancient Roman republic through the English Revolution and into the French Enlightenment.[12] Indeed, if the claim of being radically freed from the weight of the past was conceptually central to the Founders' own self-understanding, the historical truth of that claim has long been discredited.[13] For ideas do have histories, thinkers do draw on traditions even if they do not acknowledge (or may not be conscious) that they do so, and our understanding of the political dimensions of the present is deepened and enriched by identifying and tracing the influence of traditions of thought even when they have been disavowed.

Still more important than tracing the sources of the Founders' thinking is another set of concerns about the historical character of ideas themselves, namely the recognition that just as historical conditions and circumstances shape us, they shape the ways in which we understand and engage particular concepts or political problems.[14] Perennially-cited concepts like "democracy," "equality," and "freedom" not only have their own lineages, but their meanings were radically different for Americans of the late eighteenth century than they were for Athenians of the fourth century B.C.E. Understanding the social and political mileau out of which particular concepts emerge and are transformed, and the conventions of meaning that prevailed in the moment at which a particular thinker formulated and composed a political argument is critical if we want to avoid the presumption that these texts constitute the expression of timeless truths and universally applicable formulations.[15] The Founders touted their liberation from the past, still, their sense of pastlessness may differ in important ways from our own.

But these historical approaches to the study of political thought are not without problems that may make them as burdensome as they are enlightening. First, there is the aim of recuperating authorial intent, which (if we take seriously the historical insight that readers in the present are shaped by historical forces utterly foreign to the authors of past texts) may be impossible in any "pure" sense. Not only that, the recovery of intention may be beside the point if we are concerned with the political *effects* of a given text, for meaning invariably exceeds intent and no author can fully or successfully confine and control the interpretations of readers. Perhaps more important, and more problematic, is the scholastic conservatism that tends to accompany these approaches. For even as they promote a recognition of the very otherness of past ways of thinking and hence help to displace our own fixity in the present, they may also promote what Margaret Leslie has called an "historical asceticism" that rules out all but the most narrowly academic uses of the past.[16] These attempts to fix our interpretations of past texts can have the effect of blinding us to the political value of historical *mis*interpretation. As Nietzsche reminds us, texts may not only be time-bound, but they may also be *untimely* insofar as they may provoke in us a response that has little to do with the historic moment or purpose for which they were intended, but which is nonetheless critically, politically, and even historically significant.[17]

As Gordon Wood has put it, "'historicism' is as restrictive as it is permissive, as conserving as it is liberating,"[18] and it does as much to confine the nature of questions we might ask of past texts, or of insights we might draw from them, as it does to expand them. My task here is different, to clear new directions for inquiry not by ignoring the past or leaving it behind, but by opening the past to the present, by making the present speak to the past and, in doing so, developing a new relationship to the texts and ideas of the past. For "it may actually be necessary to have certain sorts of preoccupations in the present in order to be able to understand certain things in the past. It may actually be an advantage at times not to approach the past with an open mind but to become interested in a particular historical problem because it has links with one's own train of thought."[19] I raise these issues here because they are critical to the means by which we interpret Founders' claims of having freed themselves from the binds of tradition and in preparation for introducing into my own analysis a critical representative figure of the past that structures Founders' thinking and informs their grasp of the importance of political institutions, but is nowhere explicitly theorized by them. In this sense, my own preoccupation with the place of the past as imagined by Founders is inextricable from my concern with more recent formulations of the place of racial and sexual difference in contemporary public life. Taking another look at past texts and past debates might not only revolutionize our understanding of the past, but also promises to revolutionize our understanding of the politics of the present.

That said, I believe there is much to recommend historical inquiry of a particular sort. Our ability to apprehend the richness of texts and events for our own purposes depends upon it, at least in some cases and to some extent. In the effort to liberate critical thought and political possibility from the rules of the past, political theorists too often turn their backs on history and historical insight, and by doing so ironically impoverish their own interpretive contributions. Hannah Arendt's celebrated discussion of the American founding is a case in point.

Declaring independence

For Arendt, the American Revolution initiates what Bonnie Honig has called a "non-foundational founding," one that does not close off political possibilities or privatize political spaces by hardening the terms of political action into a (nonnegotiable) language of identity.[20] The permeability and malleability that Arendt attaches to the American founding, what makes it nonfoundational and creatively open to the future, consists (at least in part) in what she sees as the Founders' "profoundly revolutionary acting and thinking [that] broke the shell of an inheritance which had degenerated into platitudes." One instance of that breakthrough is suggested by the Declaration of Independence, the greatness of which, Arendt argues, "owes nothing to its natural-law philosophy—in which case it would indeed be 'lacking in depth and subtlety'—but lies in the 'respect to the Opinion of mankind', in the 'appeal to the tribunal of the world . . . for our justification', that inspired the very writing of the document, and it unfolds when the list of very specific grievances against a very particular king gradually develops into a rejection on principle of monarchy and kingship in general."[21] For Arendt, the Revolution brought into being a whole series of new political forms and concepts.[22] While she acknowledges the degree to which the Founders did turn to the past in search of exemplars (in this case to antiquity as well as the more recent intellectual framework of the European tradition), she attributes that move primarily to failure of nerve and imagination: they turned to the past in search of reassurance that their own innovations were not radical but derivative.[23] That quest for reassurance was wrong-headed, Arendt suggests, for their actions were unprecedented and brought into being something altogether new. The "grandeur" of the Declaration, for Arendt, consists in its capacity to combine word and deed and by doing so to bring "something new into being that did not exist before."[24]

If Arendt takes the Founders' own claims about the originality of their enterprise at their word, there are important theoretical reasons for doing so. For Arendt, preserving the uniqueness of politics—its reliance upon the fact of human plurality and consequent openness to forces of contingency and unpredictability—requires that our capacity for acting not be limited by factors prior to or outside of the political moment; hence the particular antagonism she directs at what she calls the "realm of necessity" which draws us back to our "mere bodily existence" and the "ways of life chiefly devoted to keeping one's self alive."[25] At stake for Arendt is the possibility of democratic freedom, our capacity to act as "participator[s] in the government of [public] affairs,"[26] and to disclose our unique identities through political action, rather than seek our freedom in the private realm, as freedom from public life and thus enclose ourselves in and by private being. The sharp distinction she draws between the freedom of public life and the realm of necessity is also a distinction between politics and violence, and between politics and nature. The introduction to *On Revolution*, Arendt's extended meditation on foundings and on the American and French revolutions, concludes with a long consideration of the limiting capacities of nature:

> In so far as violence plays a predominant role in wars and revolutions, both occur outside the political realm, strictly speaking, in spite of their enormous role in recorded history. This fact led the seventeenth century, which had its share of experience in wars and revolutions, to the assumption of a prepolitical state, called "state of nature" which, of course, never was meant to be taken as historical fact. Its relevance, even today lies in the recognition that a political realm does not automatically come into being wherever men live together, and that there exist events which, though they may occur in a strictly historical context, are not really political and perhaps not even connected with politics. The notion of a state of nature alludes at least to a reality that cannot be comprehended by the nineteenth-century ideal of development, no matter how we may conceive of it—whether in the form of cause and effect, or of potentiality and actuality, or of a dialectical movement, or even of simple coherence and sequence in occurrences. For the hypothesis of a state of nature implies the existence of a beginning that is separated from everything following it as though by an unbridgeable chasm.[27]

It is the unbridgeability of that chasm that Arendt must maintain in order to keep her ideal of the political realm unsullied by the limiting necessity she associates with nature. In short, Arendt demands that politics be understood as accomplishing a sharp break from nature—a break that is in many ways the defining feature of modern political thinking[28]—and the success of the American Revolution (by her account) hinges on Revolutionaries' ability to achieve that break and, later, to institutionalize it in the Constitution.

As much as I appreciate the aims of Arendt's treatment of the American founding, I want to highlight the ways in which her enthusiasm for discovering in it the production of new political forms and concepts also involves the cultivation of a sort of blindness. Arendt's ability to discover something altogether new produced in and by the political writings of the Founders hinges on her ability to ignore their conceptual (re)production and mobilization of a whole variety of symbols of the old. To the extent that it could be said that Arendt herself wrings new meaning and new significance from founding texts like the Declaration of Independence, her own project (like that of the Founders she admires) also participates in the conceptual production of a past that is necessary to, yet is necessarily viewed as apart from, her understanding of the founding, and even more significantly, of politics itself.

The Declaration of Independence is a deceptively straightforward document: an indictment of King George III on a whole series of abuses and failures to govern a colonial people fairly and effectively, an announcement to the world of the dissolution of the political ties between the colonies and the Crown, and a mutual promise among its signatories to commit "our lives, our fortunes, and our sacred honor" to securing independence. Drawn up by Jefferson, who wrote on behalf of the Committee of Five appointed by the Continental Congress,[29] and revised by representatives to the Congress, the Declaration speaks through a complex relay of plural authors and multiple levels of representation. "Jefferson" writes for members of a Committee, a Committee that in turn represents a Congress of representatives convened in the name of (as the Declaration puts it) "one people"—who are not only not yet "one" but are also not yet "a" people. To the extent that the Declaration repeatedly cites a "We" ("We hold these truths to be self evident . . . ," "We have petitioned for redress in the most humble terms . . . ," "We therefore the representatives of the United states of America in General Congress assembled . . . ")[30] this is a "We" not only, and not simply, assumed by the Congress but produced by it, through what Jacques Derrida has called a "fabulous" chain of representative acts.[31]

To put the matter in slightly more historical terms, there was nothing inevitable about an American nation, certainly nothing contained within the terms of the founding that made that nation an ineluctable outcome of the events of 1776. Nor was the cohesiveness implied by a national "We" a foregone conclusion at the moment that Jefferson sat down to compose the Declaration. The challenge confronting its authors and signatories was both to engage and to elide that fact: to declare the independence of a people who did not yet exist as a people—let alone an independent people—until after the

Declaration's work had been performed. The activity of performing that work of declaring independence required a speaking subject, a "We" that can nonetheless be only illusory until after the fact of (the) Declaration.[32] Declaring independence installs at the origin of the act of declaring, as the origin of that act, a "We" that the act of declaring in fact produces.

That American "We" names a collective that is accomplished rather than simply described by the Declaration, a text that works retrospectively to transplant and transform that "We" from end-product to origin. What brings a sense of coherence and (deceptive) straightforwardness to the Declaration is the systematically retrospective frame through which "we" are able at once to interpolate it into our present, and to interpolate subsequent events into it. In other words, the degree to which the Declaration sets into motion a revolution and the entire constellation of forces that have shaped America as a nation is the degree to which we are able to naturalize both it and everything that develops historically as a consequence of it. By doing so, we sign onto that relay of representation, "we" join ourselves and our era into its "We" and thus (re)enact the "self-evident" truths given by "nature and nature's god," but pronounced in the name of America by "Jefferson." "What is at stake prior to any question of Jefferson's authorship as representative of the people," writes Bruce Burgett, "is the democratic coup that establishes the people as sovereign and capable of authorizing representations."[33] Indeed, what is at stake, what makes this "coup" a democratic one is the establishment of a sovereign people as prior to that which is authorized by the Declaration.

There is something very powerful and very important, both politically and intellectually, that comes of Arendt's willingness to take the Founders at their word and deliberately not question their claims of pastlessness and originality. Doing so enables her to resist the enclosure of the world through the unthinking repetition of "clichés, stock phrases, [and] adherence to conventional, standardized codes of expression and conduct" that "have the socially recognized function of protecting us against reality, that is, against the claim on our thinking attention that all events and facts make by virtue of their existence."[34] By attending to the novelty of Founders' thinking, Arendt discovers in their actions the rudiments of a different kind of public life and a different means of conceptualizing and organizing public power—a form of life and an organization of power that could emerge only once Founders were able to recognize that "the so-called old values" no longer served. By Arendt's account, the dissolution of old orders and the novelty of the Founders' historic situation present *for us* a unique opportunity that would be missed if we were to concern ourselves with tracing the intellectual traditions that shaped their thinking: "permit[ting] us to look on the past with new eyes, unburdened and unguided by any traditions, and thus to dispose of a tremendous wealth of raw experiences without being bound by any prescriptions as to how to deal with these treasures."[35]

But there is also something problematic that comes of Arendt's attribution of novelty to the Revolutionaries, and this too governs her interpretation of the Declaration. For, as Honig has pointed out, while Arendt recognizes the Declaration as producing "new relations and realities," she misses the ways in which that text also mobilizes a set of concepts that must precede the production of that new world in order to make it possible, and which must, therefore, temper if not extinguish our enthusiasm about its novelty: namely, the Declaration's reliance upon "self-evident" truths, and on the "nature and nature's god" that endows these truths with their self-evidentiary character. Such concepts mark the text not simply as a creative force, but one that is dependent upon elements it must assert as prior to it, elements that by virtue of their very priority come to operate as forces of absoluteness.[36] As Honig argues, "Arendt wants to celebrate the American Declaration of Independence as a purely performative speech act, but in order to do so she must disambiguate it. She dismisses its constative moments and holds up the Declaration as an example of a uniquely political act . . . an authoritative exemplification of human power and worldliness."[37] Arendt misses the important insight (developed by Derrida and others)[38] that these absolutes are a structural feature of language itself, therefore powerful forces of which politics is never free, and they pose challenges that political actors need to account for and engage.

Arendt's treatment of the Declaration of Independence dramatizes (even if it does not admit) that the act of making something new involves the simultaneous creation of what I will call here a *past*. This past may not be strictly historical but is necessary as a conceptual undergirding and foundation for what is being fabricated, and being fabricated as new, novel, or unprecedented. In this sense, foundings and the political thought that inspires them have something of a double life: in establishing a new and different present, founders also create new pasts. It is a truism that we cannot change or undo history, at least not in any literal sense. In acting to (re)shape the present, however, we inevitably configure alternative pasts. The present, as Sheldon Wolin has suggested, "is another name for the political organization of existence." Insofar as the present is "constituted by competing/cooperating structures of power that advance and secure the expectations and advantages of certain classes, individuals, groups, and organizations whose combination of authority and material resources enables them to concert power and thereby exert a major influence over which of the possible presents a society is going to have,"[39] then it is also the case that competitions over the shape and character of the political present involve the construction of competing pasts. In our competition over the present, we do not dissolve or discard those "so-called old values" but engage them, contest them, rethink them, and by doing so reconfigure and transform them.

Generally speaking, the terms of competition over the political present tend to draw the attention of political theorists, and the commensurate task of cultivating a past necessary and proper to the (proposed) present fades into the background, if not altogether into oblivion. This is particularly so in the case of theoretical studies of the American founding, where a number of Founders insisted on the necessary pastlessness of their enterprise. My task in the two chapters that follow is to shift the focus somewhat and by doing so illuminate the political operation of elements that need to be accounted for but which are too often obscured.

This suggests that we need to ask a somewhat different order of questions about the founding: not what set of intentions, shaped by what tradition of conceptual languages, governed the Founders' thinking, nor what wholly new resources for establishing the authority of the founding can we identify within the terms of the founding itself. I ask, instead, to what extent are Founders' assertions of the novelty and originality of their enterprise dependent upon their mobilization of preexisting concepts of a prepolitical, or even an eminently political, past? How do their appropriations of this past, in the project not of reproducing or reinstating it, but instead of producing a new and different present involve the misappropriation of tradition, of the past, and produce not only a novel present but also a novel figure of the past? Finally, what is the political career of that past, if pastlessness itself is understood to be the condition for the commencement of political life in America?

Endnotes

1. Thomas Paine, *Common Sense, The Rights of Man, and Other Essential Writings of Thomas Paine*, ed. Sidney Hook (New York: New American Library, 1969), 66.

2. Alexis de Tocqueville, *Democracy in America, Volume I*, ed. Phillips Bradley (New York: Vintage, 1945), 302.

3. Edward W. Said, *Beginnings: Intention & Method* (New York: Columbia University Press, 1985), 34.

4. Thomas Paine, *Common Sense*, 63.

5. Judith N. Shklar, "Democracy and the Past: Jefferson and His Heirs," *Redeeming American Political Thought*, ed. Stanley Hoffmann and Dennis F. Thompson (Chicago: The University of Chicago Press, 1998), 174.

6. John Adams, *The Political Writings of John Adams*, ed. George A. Peek (Indianapolis: 1954), 117.

7. The phrase is Shklar's, 175.

8. I do not mean to be understood as conflating Hartz's interpretation of American politics with Shklar's. As I understand her posthumously published work on American political thought, Shklar is not reiterating Hartz's insights so much as she is contesting them. Hence, as Shklar concludes, "Forswearing the past was not so much a matter of being an American," as Hartz had more or less argued, "as a democratic citizen" (178). While the elision of the past is a central component of American democratic thought for both Hartz and Shklar, each assigns that elision to a different element: Hartz to American distinctiveness, Shklar to democratic distinctiveness.

9. Paige duBois, *Sappho Is Burning* (Chicago: The University of Chicago Press, 1995), 2.

10. On the ways in which Americans seek to reinstate a prelapsarian innocence by obliterating the past, see Thomas L. Dumm, *united states* (Ithaca: Cornell University Press, 1994); also Myra Jehlen, *American Incarnation: The Individual, The Nation, and the Continent* (Cambridge: Harvard University Press, 1986). Although Arendt speaks often about natality, her most elaborate statement of it can be found in *The Human Condition* (Chicago: The University of Chicago Press, 1958). For an explanation of the "veil of ignorance," see John Rawls, *A Theory of Justice* (Cambridge: Harvard University Press, 1971).

11. Sheldon S. Wolin, "Political Theory as a Vocation," *American Political Science Review* 63:4 (December 1969), 1063.

12. To those familiar with this debate, it will be immediately clear that I have collapsed an extensive, and extended, discussion into very brief compass, siding in the end with those who see in the thought of the Founders a complex and sometimes inconsistent synthesis of (ancient) republican and (modern) liberal traditions (as Michael Lienesch has put it, a tradition that is "neither entirely republican nor exclusively liberal, neither classical nor modern, but a curious combination of both"). For excellent discussions of this synthesis, see Michael Lienesch, *New Order of the Ages: Time, the Constitution, and the Making of Modern American Thought* (Princeton: Princeton University Press, 1988); Isaac Kramnick, "Republican Revisionism Revisited," *American Historical Review* 87: 3 (June 1982) 629–64. For the classic argument about the origins of American thought in the liberal (mostly Lockean) tradition, see Louis Hartz, *The Liberal Tradition in America*; also: Joyce Appleby, " The Social Origins of American Revolutionary Ideology," *Journal of American History* 64:4 (March 1978), 935–58; and

more recently, Michael P. Zuckert, *Natural Rights and the New Republicanism* (Princeton: Princeton University Press, 1994); Joshua Foa Dienstag, "Between History and Nature: Social Contract Theory in Locke and the Founders," *Journal of Politics* 58:4 (November 1996), 985–1000. The interpretation of the Revolution as inspired by classical republican thought is promoted in Bernard Bailyn, *The Ideological Origins of the American Revolution* (Cambridge: Harvard University Press, 1967); Gordon S. Wood, *The Creation of the American Republic, 1776–1787* (Chapel Hill: University of North Carolina Press, 1969); and more recently, Carl J. Richard, *The Founders and the Classics: Greece, Rome, and the American Enlightenment* (Cambridge: Harvard University Press, 1994). For an extended discussion of what is missed by *both* sides of this dispute, but remains central to American political thought, see Rogers M. Smith, *Civic Ideals: Conflicting Visions of Citizenship in U.S. History* (New Haven: Yale University Press, 1997).

13. For an important elaboration of the political stakes in discrediting the originality of the Founders' (and also the Hartzian) view of the founding, see Karen Orren, *Belated Feudalism: Labor, the Law, and Liberal Development in the United States* (New York: Cambridge University Press, 1991).

14. Both the intellectual and institutional purchase of this contention is attested to by the development of the "Ideas in Context" series published by Cambridge University Press. The policy statement included in the first volume explains its purpose: "The books in this series will discuss the emergence of intellectual traditions. . . . The procedures, aims, and vocabularies that were generated will be set in the context of the alternatives available within the contemporary framework of ideas and institutions. . . . [and] it is hoped that a new picture will form of the development of ideas in their concrete contexts." See Richard Rorty, J.B. Schneewind, and Quentin Skinner, eds., *Philosophy in History: Essays on the Historiography of Philosophy* (Cambridge: Cambridge University Press, 1984).

15. For more programmatic statements about this approach to the study of political thought, see Quentin Skinner, "Meaning and Understanding in the History of Ideas," *History and Theory* 8:1 (1969), 3–53; Quentin Skinner, "Some Problems in the Analysis of Political Thought and Action," *Political Theory* 2 (1974), 277–303; J.G.A. Pocock, "The History of Political Thought: A Methodological Inquiry," *Philosophy, Politics, and Society*, eds. Peter Laslett and W.G. Runciman (Oxford: Basil Blackwell, 1962). For a different, and more recent, formulation of a similar approach, see Adolph L. Reed, Jr., *W. E. B. Du Bois and American Political Thought: Fabianism and the Color Line* (New York: Oxford University Press, 1997), esp. 177–86.

16. Margaret Leslie, "In Defence of Anachronism," *Political Studies* 18:4 (1970), 436.

17. Friedrich Nietzsche, "On the Uses and Disadvantages of History for Life,"

Untimely Meditations, trans. R.J. Hollingdale (Cambridge: Cambridge University Press, 1983). Peter Euben makes a similar case about the value of reading ancient political texts in an untimely fashion. See J. Peter Euben, "Introduction" to *Greek Tragedy and Political Theory* (Berkeley: University of California Press, 1986), esp. 3–6. This approach also inspires his more recent work: J. Peter Euben, *Corrupting Youth: Political Education, Democratic Culture, and Political Theory* (Princeton: Princeton University Press, 1997).

18. Gordon S. Wood, "The Fundamentalists and the Constitution," *New York Review of Books* (February 18, 1988), 40. Of course, Wood writes as a historian, and his argument about the "conservative" nature of historicism is directed not so much against historical methods (as I have put him to use here) as against Straussians who also aim to recuperate the author's original intent not by reference to context but by decoding the clues they believe to be contained within the text itself. For classic statements of Straussian "method" and aims, see Leo Strauss, *What Is Political Philosophy and Other Studies* (Chicago: The University of Chicago Press, 1989); also, Leo Strauss, "Introduction" to *The City and Man* (Chicago: The University of Chicago Press, 1964), esp. 6–12.

19. Margaret Leslie, "In Defence of Anachronism," 445.

20. For a more detailed account, see Bonnie Honig, *Political Theory and the Displacement of Politics* (Ithaca: Cornell University Press, 1993), Chapter Four.

21. Hannah Arendt, *On Revolution* (New York: Penguin, 1981), 129.

22. Including, for example, the eighteenth-century revolutionaries' break with a tradition of thought that stretched as far back as antiquity by which tyranny was conceptually opposed to the rule of law. For Arendt, one of the breakthroughs accomplished by American revolutionary thought is that "tyranny . . . was [reconceived as] a form of government in which the ruler, even though he ruled according to the laws of the realm, had monopolized for himself the right of action, banished the citizens from the public realm into the privacy of their households, and demanded of them that they mind their own, private business." For perhaps the first time, the revolutionaries came to oppose tyranny not to the rule of law but to republicanism, to a form of governance that recognized and "granted to every citizen the right to become 'a participator in the government of affairs', the right to be seen in action." See Hannah Arendt, *On Revolution*, 130.

23. See Arendt, *On Revolution*, 185–86, 199. See also Honig, *Political Theory and the Displacement of Politics*, 96–104.

24. Hannah Arendt, *On Revolution*, 129. Elsewhere she writes that "the men of the American Revolution, whose awareness of the absolute novelty in their enterprise amounted to an obsession, were inescapably caught in something for which neither the historical nor the legendary truth of their own tradition could offer any help or precedent." See Hannah Arendt, *On Revolution*, 212.

25. Hannah Arendt, *The Human Condition*, 176, 12.

26. The phrase is Thomas Jefferson's, quoted by Arendt. See Thomas Jefferson, "Letter to Joseph C. Cabell" (February 2, 1816) in *The Life and Selected Writings* (New York: Modern Library), 661; see also Hannah Arendt, *On Revolution*, 127.

27. Hannah Arendt, *On Revolution*, 19–20.

28. On this point, I am inclined to agree with Seyla Benhabib's suggestion that what Arendt gives us is neither a whole cloth rejection of the modern project nor an uncritical embrace of it but a "reluctant modernism," and that Arendt's "purported 'Graecocentrism' is as much a fiction created by us her readers as it is based upon her own texts." In this respect, see Seyla Benhabib, "The Pariah and Her Shadow: Hannah Arendt's Biography of Rahel Varnhagen," *Feminist Interpretations of Hannah Arendt*, ed. Bonnie Honig (University Park, PA: Penn State University Press, 1995), 95; also Seyla Benhabib, *The Reluctant Modernism of Hannah Arendt* (Newbury Park, CA: Sage Publications, 1996).

29. The other four members of the Committee of Five included John Adams, Benjamin Franklin, Roger Sherman, and Robert R. Livingston. What happened next is disputed. According to Adams, this Committee appointed a subcommittee of two—Jefferson and Adams—to draft their announcement, but Adams delegated the task to Jefferson. "Reason 1st:" Adams recalled the terms in which he put it to Jefferson, "You [Jefferson] are a Virginian and a Virginian ought to appear at the head of this business. Reason 2nd. I am obnoxious, suspected and unpopular; you are very much otherwise. Reason 3rd. You can write ten times better than I can." By 1823, Jefferson reconstructed the events differently. "The Committee of 5 met, no such thing as a subcommittee was proposed, but they unanimously pressed on myself alone to undertake the draught. I consented; I drew it; but before I reported it to the committee I communicated it separately to Dr. Franklin and Mr. Adams requesting their corrections. . . . Their alterations were two or three only, and merely verbal. I then wrote a fair copy, reported it to the committee, and from them, unaltered to the Congress." For a more detailed, historical account of the writing of the Declaration, see Carl Becker, *The Declaration of Independence: A Study in the History of Political Ideas* (New York: Alfred A. Knopf, 1964), esp. Chapter Four. These passages are quoted from Becker, 135–36. For a somewhat broader account of the practices and theories of rhetoric, and the culture of performance that informed the Declaration, see Jay Fliegelman, *Declaring Independence: Jefferson, Natural Language, and the Culture of Performance* (Stanford: Stanford University Press, 1993).

30. Quotations from the Declaration are taken from "The Declaration of Independence as originally reported to Congress," as appended in Jay Fliegelman, *Declaring Independence*, 203–08.

31. Here is Derrida: "Let us distinguish between the several instances within your

Declaration. Take, for example, Jefferson, the 'draftsman [*rédacteur*]' of the project or draft [*projet*] of the Declaration. . . . No one would take him for the true signer of the Declaration. *By right*, he writes but he does not sign. Jefferson represents the representatives who have delegated to him the task of drawing up [*rédiger*] what they knew *they* wanted to say. He was not responsible for *writing*, in the productive or initiating sense of the term, only for *drawing up*, as one says of a secretary that he or she draws up a *letter* of which the spirit has been breathed into him or her, or even the content dictated. Moreover, after having thus drawn up a project or a draft, a sketch, Jefferson had to submit it to those whom, for a time, he *represented* and who are themselves *representatives*, namely the 'representatives of the United States in General Congress assembled.". . . . As for the 'representatives' themselves, they don't sign either. In principle at least, because the right is divided here. In fact, they sign; by right, they sign for themselves but also 'for' others." See Jacques Derrida, "Declarations of Independence," trans. Tom Keenan and Tom Pepper, *New Political Science* 15 (1986), 8–9. Emphasis in original. For discussions of Derrida's reading, and similar accounts of the performative nature of the Declaration, and later, the Constitution, see Michael Warner, *The Letters of the Republic: Publication and the Public Sphere in Eighteenth-Century America* (Cambridge: Harvard University Press, 1990), esp. Chapter Four; and Bonnie Honig, *Political Theory and the Displacement of Politics,* esp. Chapter Four.

32. Jay Fliegelman's extraordinary book, *Declaring Independence*, develops the richest and most complex picture we have thus far of the political and intellectual culture that shaped the late eighteenth-century events in America known, all too simply, as the founding. Fliegelman's project begins from a deceptively simple premise: that the Declaration of Independence was not so much a text to be preserved and displayed and viewed (as it is, on occasion, in the Rotunda of the Capitol building, or more regularly at the National Archives) as a proclamation to be read aloud to assembled groups—an object of rhetorical performance that constituted its audience not simply as an audience but as an *American* audience. Hence, as Fliegelman suggests, "Jefferson's fascination with Homer, Ossian, Patrick Henry, and the violin"—all linked through the culture of performance—may be seen as of equal or "greater significance than his indebtedness to Locke or Hutcheson." See Jay Fliegelman, *Declaring Independence: Jefferson, Natural Language, and the Culture of Performance.*

33. Bruce Burgett, *Sentimental Bodies: Sex, Gender, and Citizenship in the Early Republic* (Princeton: Princeton University Press, 1998), 182, n. 54.

34. Hannah Arendt, *The Life of the Mind* (New York: Harcourt Brace & Company, 1978), 4. Similar formulations of the importance of thinking can be found throughout Arendt's work, especially in *Eichmann in Jerusalem: A Report on the Banality of Evil* (New York: Penguin, 1983). Dana Villa makes a similar point about Arendt in "The

Philosopher versus the Citizen: Arendt, Strauss, and Socrates," *Political Theory* 26:2 (April 1998), 147–72.

35. Hannah Arendt, *The Life of the Mind*, 12.

36. Honig refers to these concepts mobilized as prior terms within and by the Declaration as constative utterances, which stand in contrast to the performativity of the Declaration itself. The distinction between the performative utterance (which allows the speaker to act by means of speech itself) and the constative utterance (which asserts itself as a fact) is made by J. L. Austin, *How to Do Things with Words* (New York: Oxford University Press, 1962).

37. Bonnie Honig, *Political Theory and the Displacement of Politics*, 101.

38. See Jacques Derrida, "Declarations of Independence," 7–15; also "Signature, Event, Context," *The Margins of Philosophy*, trans. Alan Bass (Chicago: The University of Chicago Press, 1982), 307–30. Of course, Honig makes this point as well in *Political Theory and the Displacement of Politics*, Chapter Four.

39. Sheldon S. Wolin, *The Presence of the Past: Essays on the State and the Constitution* (Baltimore: The Johns Hopkins University Press, 1989), 1.

2

Notes on the State of America: Jeffersonian Democracy and the Production of a National Past

> To articulate the past historically does not mean to recognize it "the way it really was" (Ranke). It means to seize hold of a memory as it flashes up at a moment of danger.
>
> Walter Benjamin[1]

IF THE DECLARATION OF INDEPENDENCE PERFORMS THE WORK OF transforming the colonial inhabitants of a territory ("America") into a geopolitically distinct people that precedes and authorizes the very acts that bring them into being, Jefferson's *Notes on the State of Virginia* accomplishes the similar transformation of an as yet nationally-unstructured territory into a (potentially) sovereign nation. Like the Declaration, Jefferson's *Notes* depends on the operation of a largely undefined yet elaborately worked out concept of nature, one that he directs to distinctly national purposes. As Charles A. Miller puts it, "insofar as nature symbolized America in its entirety, nature *was* America for Jefferson. His interest in nature and his use of the word are therefore a form of nationalism. In Europe national sentiment was expressed through a common history, a royal family, a culture, or a literature. In America and for Jefferson it was expressed through, and as, nature."[2] Nature is central to Jefferson's writings. It pervades his private and official correspondence as well as his more public and collectively authored works like the Declaration. It is in *Notes on the State of Virginia*, however, that he most clearly articulates his philosophy of nature as a political philosophy of American nationalism. Jefferson does not simply marshall nature as a preexisting setting upon which an American nation is to be constructed, but rather produces nature anew by representing it as a necessary precursor to national history, a naturalized past that makes an American nation appear to be its logical, chronological, and inevitable outcome. For Jefferson, nature is more than the given properties of a landscape; more than the state of indigenous plant, animal, and human life in the New World; and more than an immanent order of being. Nature is a means by which America may be made intelligible as a nation, and natural history a technique by which Jefferson recasts people(s), places, and topographic features into a single entity, continuous in both time and space. Nature is the retrospective logic by which he integrates diverse objects and peoples into a coherent and wholly new national form.

Historically, the establishment of permanent colonies in America is not only coincident with modernity,[3] but as Benedict Anderson has pointed out, the New World was also the location where new forms of national consciousness first emerged. Our ability "to 'think' the nation,"[4] as Anderson puts it, hinges at least in part on a distinctively modern reorganization of temporal modes of understanding. Where premodern thought is characterized by a strange simultaneity of archaic and contemporary elements that fuse "past and future in an instantaneous present," what Walter Benjamin refers to as messianic time,[5] Anderson suggests that modernity brings with it a new understanding of time as organized serially in an "endless chain of cause and effect or of radical separations between past and present."[6] *Notes on the State of Virginia* can be read in this light, as Jefferson's attempt to think the nation, to transform a pre-modern messianic landscape into an ordered and orderly, progressive national state.

What is significant about Jefferson's mobilization of nature in *Notes* and elsewhere is not only his ability to present us with a nature that is historical, but one that operates to establish territorial antiquity in the name of a modern, national America. In doing so, Jefferson forges a fiction of kinship between the aboriginal inhabitants of the continent and its more recent settlers, a fiction that undergirds Americans' ability to imagine themselves bound together, as John Jay would later put it, as "one connected country . . . one united people."[7] Natural history, then, is the technique by which Jefferson establishes territorial antiquity in the name of a modern national state, but it is also a means by which he establishes genealogical antiquity in the service of what Shklar calls "the living citizenry of a democracy."[8]

This genealogical nationalism is, perhaps, Jefferson's most troubling legacy. In *Notes*, the essential link between America's natural past and its democratic future is forged through an historicized conception of the citizen's body, where the raced body becomes the foundation of citizenship itself. For Jefferson, the correspondence between creole (persons of European descent born in the

Americas) and Native American bodies provides continuity between an ancient American past and the national future, while also ensuring the eventual transubstantiation of Indian into citizen. At the same time, this genealogical nationalism confirms the inadmissiblilty of African Americans to national citizenship, for the black body cannot be assimilated to the American past and therefore, for Jefferson, has no place in the national future.

Jefferson's national natures

Written during the war years of 1780–81, *Notes* responds to a survey drawn up by François Marbois, the secretary of the French legation at Philadelphia, and circulated among selected members of the Continental Congress. Transmitted to Jefferson by Joseph Jones, a member of the Virginia delegation, this simple questionnaire was turned by him into an elaborate treatise on the state of Virginia and, more generally, on the state of the new American nation. Indeed, his exacting treatment of Marbois' queries, as Frank Shuffelton puts it, "transformed *Notes* from the local report that the Frenchman had hoped for into a scientific inquiry of a larger, American significance."[9] *Notes* sought both to provide a detailed catalogue of colonial resources and to enliven wavering French support for the Revolutionary cause by promoting America as the embodiment of Enlightenment rationalism. This tension between objective description and teleological purpose runs throughout the work and it shapes Jefferson's treatment of the Virginia landscape as well as his organization of the book itself.

In a variety of ways, *Notes* makes for difficult and, at times, mind-numbing reading. Jefferson's first and only full-length book, it can be a "notably rebarbative text . . . difficult and unrewarding to read, if one is looking to it from any point of view other than that of extracting the 'information' it so densely and insistently accumulates."[10] Lengthy descriptive passages relentlessly catalogue both the natural bounty of America and the productivity of her industrious inhabitants. Its pages are interspersed with long lists of vegetable species and taxonomies of native fauna. There is a census of America's human, as well as its bird and mammal, populations; an extensive table showing the variations in Virginia's weather from month to month, and another measuring distances along the Ohio River; and a seventeen-page list of state-papers, which Jefferson himself characterizes as a "tedious detail."[11]

There is more to *Notes* than mere description, however. The work is also interspersed with impassioned argument. Curiously, for a text written in the midst of war, Jefferson's passions are not stirred by the republican cause so much as by the natural history he reads in the American landscape, in its quadrupeds and bipeds, and in its native peoples. The primary target of such intellectual ardor is the Comte de Buffon's *Histoire Naturelle*, which had argued that American animal and aboriginal life was degenerate by contrast with that of Europe. Countering Buffon, Jefferson goes to elaborate lengths to establish the equivalence of both continents, if not, indeed, the superiority of American nature over its European counterpart.[12]

In her reading of *Notes*, Myra Jehlen attributes Jefferson's movement from an "almost aggressive objectivity" of exact technical description to an impassioned discussion of American fauna, not to his having "risen from fact gathering to political pleading," but instead to his having "sunk below facts, to the contemplation of a deeper level [of meaning] . . . the level at which America is precisely *not* in the process of becoming viable or valuable because it has been what it is, as a natural given, all along."[13] For Jehlen, the political project suggested by *Notes* consists of simply implementing an order already immanent within American nature.[14] While Jehlen is right to recognize the intimate connection between nature and politics in *Notes*, her reading tends to miss the fragility of that connection, a connection marked by its suffusion with time. *Notes* is Jefferson's effort to place America in time, and while the notion of serial time is what enables him to secure a place for the new American nation on the ancient American continent, chronology is in many ways the central political problem of the text.

Jefferson's project of imparting chronological and narrative order to the American nation is evident in the structure he brings to Marbois' queries. The text of *Notes* is divided into twenty-three chapters, each a response to a given query, though importantly, Jefferson took the liberty of rearranging the order of Marbois' questionnaire in organizing his response.[15] This is not a standard chronology in the conventional historical sense. But Jefferson's reordering of the questions tells a story immediately recognizable to political theorists, for it recalls a foundational (European) fiction of modern politics: the tale of man's passage from the state of nature into political society.[16] *Notes* moves from the given to the made, from the prior to the present, and from the natural to the artistic and institutional—in short, from nature to politics. The chapters travel from space to time (from the "Boundaries of Virginia" to "Histories, Memorials, and State-Papers"), from natural givens to political institutions (from "Rivers," "Sea-Ports," and "Mountains," to "Public Revenues and Expences"), and from a prehistoric American nature to a democratic modernism that flowed from its natural origin as fluidly and continuously as the Ohio River flowed from its source to Fort Pitt.

Jefferson's retelling is not a simple one, however. In *Notes*, he at once repeats and revises prevailing (modern) understandings of the relationship between nature and politics, infusing nature with the capacity for change in order to (re)claim America for itself. For Jefferson, nature is not the absolute (and absolut*ist*) other of politics;[17] it is neither fully oppositional to politics, nor its abandoned conceptual origin; rather, he figures nature as necessary to politics, both prior and internal to it. Refusing to depict it as a space or a moment outside of or prior to history, he installs nature within the realm of the historical. Jefferson's *Notes* thus assigns purpose to nature, attaching it to the cause of democratic governance as *arche* to *telos*. The work provides a mapping in both space and time of how democracy might work in America, of how democracy is in some ways already at work in America, of how democracy constitutes a form of governance autochthonous to America because visibly at work in its natural productions. He mines nature for what he finds valuable in it, extracts its most precious resources, and sets them to work as politics within history. From the shifting of the sandbars of the Mississippi River, to the regular but unpredictable overflowing of the Missouri,[18] to his "more philosophical view of mountains" that suggests the complicated ways in which "this earth has been created in time,"[19] nature for Jefferson is saturated with time and the capacity for change. In this light, we might understand Jefferson's much-noted offense at the Comte de Buffon's assertion of the inferiority of American nature as taken less from the claim itself (a claim that for Jefferson was empirically false) as from his insinuation that, as Jefferson paraphrases, "nature is less active, less energetic on one side of the globe than she is on the other."[20]

To return for a moment to Jefferson's Declaration then, that text (like Paine's *Common Sense*) could promote political insurrection against the Crown as a restoration of nature because monarchy had deformed and disappointed a *natural* order insofar as it hindered *political* development. Indeed, over half of the "repeated injuries and usurpations" with which the Declaration charges the King are complaints against monarchy's obstructionism. Monarchy violated nature, the Declaration suggests, by suppressing historical change. Jefferson's nature then, is nature with a difference, not so much a foundation for a fixed order that ties us to origins, but a past produced as a necessary part of the larger project of forming a new and different national present.

Much later in his life, Jefferson returned to the project of mapping America in time. In an 1824 letter to William Ludlow, he imagines America as containing within its borders the entire history of anthropological development, a history that could be read by a "philosophic observer" on an imagined walk across the continent from west to east. Such a journey would traverse not only a physical terrain, Jefferson mused, but would also lay bare the stages of human social and political development, the "progress of society from its rudest state to that it has now attained":

> The savages of the Rocky Mountains . . . he would observe in the earliest stage of association living under no law but that of nature, subsisting and covering themselves with the flesh and skins of wild beasts. He would next find those on our frontiers in the pastoral state, raising domestic animals to supply the defects of hunting. Then succeed our own semi-barbarous citizens, the pioneers of the advance of civilization, and so in his progress he would meet the gradual shades of improving man until he would reach his, as yet, most improved state in our seaport towns.

Jefferson imagines anthropology historically, even as he maps geography through history, as history. Human history lends intelligibility, here, to an otherwise conceptually unstructured space. What makes the journey interesting (and what is most problematic about it) is that it is less a *tour de monde* than an *histoire de l'homme*.

> I am eighty-one years of age, born where I now live, in the first range of mountains in the interior of our country. And I have observed this march of civilization advancing from the seacoast, passing over us like a cloud of light, increasing our knowledge and improving our condition, insomuch as that we are at this time more advanced in civilization here than the seaports were when I was a boy. And where this progress will stop no one can say. Barbarism has, in the meantime, been receding before the steady step of amelioration; and will in time, I trust, disappear from the earth.[21]

The frontier provides Jefferson with not only a spatial but also a temporal dimension by which to articulate a language of American nationalism. Unexplored or barely explored territories to the west represent not only an opportunity for westward expansion (though, to be sure, Jefferson did understand the west in these terms),[22] but also a virtually unprecedented opportunity to observe human history, to view an otherwise lost and inaccessible past without leaving the present (one might argue in the case of his letter to Ludlow, without even leaving *home*). The letter paints a complex, polychronic portrait of America as the setting where distant and distinct eras of human civilization coexist in the same calendrical moment. Yet Jefferson gives structure to this picture and sets it into motion by endowing it with an Enlightenment notion of progress. What was long past in Atlantic seaports may be present in the Mississippi Valley yet a still-distant future for the Rockies. In this sense Jefferson's account has the effect of fusing, or to use Lauren Berlant's more apt term, of "suturing" together plural, diverse, complex, and competing presents into something that extends well beyond the boundaries of Virginia to give shape to a national whole, a state of America.[23]

Stressing the developmental nature of the relation between inhabitants of the west and the east, Jefferson establishes a veneer of continuity among them. The difference between the "savages of the Rocky Mountains" and the "most improved state [of man observable] in our seaport towns" is not only temporal but temporary, soon to be elided by the inevasible "march of civilization." In the end, the success of Jefferson's national vision rests on "the steady step of amelioration," the progressive integration of disparate peoples into the American nation; but the portrait Jefferson paints in his letter suggests other possibilities as well, for these stages of anthropological development do not simply represent extant traces of the American past, but in fact illuminate the complex social history of the American present.

Bridging the chasm?

For Jefferson, the nature represented by the Virginia landscape suggests ordered contingency and the capacity for change. Hence, he could promote nature as a special kind of foundation for a new and revolutionary political order, a past that does not bind us to origins but which nonetheless supplies some degree of guidance, and offers something of a metaphorical corrective to a politically corrupt European order. But even his best efforts at supplying the fledgling nation with a past are complicated by the fact that his experience of the force of nature exceeds his attempt to render it a purely abstract entity. Jefferson is not only inspired but at times overwhelmed and even frustrated by the American landscape, and the exhaustion fostered by precisely what exhilarates him most is particularly evident in two instances: his discussion in *Notes* of Virginia's Natural Bridge, and considerably later, his correspondence with a prospective publisher concerning a revised edition of the book.

In a short passage of *Notes* describing the Natural Bridge, that "most sublime of Nature's works," Jefferson begins with a dispassionate and detailed survey of the Bridge's topographic features ("The fissure, just at the bridge, is by some admeasurements, 270 feet deep, by others only 205. It is about 45 feet wide at the bottom, and 90 feet at the top. . . . Its breadth in the middle, is about 60 feet, but more at the ends, and the thickness of the mass at the summit of the arch, about 40 feet . . ."). The tone of the passage then shifts abruptly:

> Though the sides of this bridge are provided in some parts with a parapet of fixed rocks, yet few men have resolution to walk to them and look over into the abyss. You involuntarily fall on your hands and feet, creep to the parapet and peep over it. Looking down from this height about a minute, gave me a violent head ach [sic]. (This painful sensation is relieved by a short, but pleasing view of the Blue ridge along the fissure downwards, and upwards by that of the short hills . . . and, descending then to the valley below, the sensation becomes delightful in the extreme. It is impossible for the emotions, arising from the sublime, to be felt beyond what they are here: so beautiful an arch, so elevated, so light, and springing, as it were, up to heaven, the rapture of the Spectator is really indiscribable [sic]!)[24]

There is something about the Bridge that Jefferson finds both inspiring and overwhelming, something that disrupts his efforts at pure description, something that is uncontainable within the terms of description alone. That something drives Jefferson to his knees, it provokes headache, it presses him to back away from the precipice and to seek anaesthetic relief in the "pleasing view" of the nearby mountains. His retreat from the abyss, his search for respite, is accomplished only by virtue of an abrupt shift into the persona of the Spectator. It is in this mode that the passage continues to its conclusion, for Jefferson cannot leave us with this sense of the uncontainable power of nature, of contingent forces, of violent headache and "indiscribable" rapture. Nature, it seems, must be contained if it is to be conceived as a foundation for national life. Contained, first, in and by the mundane details of geography:

> The fissure continues deep and narrow and, following the margin of the stream upwards about three eights [sic] of a mile you arrive at a limestone cavern, less remarkable, however, for height and extent than those before described.

Contained, second, in and by political boundaries:

> This bridge is in the county of Rockbridge, to which it has given name, and affords a public and commodious passage over a valley, which cannot be crossed elsewhere for a considerable distance.

Contained, finally, in and by the requirements of industry and technological progress that it is made to serve:

> The stream passing under it is called Cedar creek. It is a water of the James river, and sufficient in the driest seasons to turn a grist-mill, though its fountain is not more than two miles above.[25]

Despite Jefferson's attempt to reassert narrative control, the pastoral vision that ends the passage remains at odds with what Richard Slotkin calls the "sublime terror" at its heart.[26]

Decades later, in 1814, this anxiety reappears in a slightly different register. Declining an invitation from a publisher to revise and update *Notes* for a new edition, Jefferson wrote:

> I consider . . . the idea of preparing a new copy . . . as no more to be entertained. The work itself is nothing more than the measure of a shadow, never stationary, but lengthening as the sun advances, and to be taken anew from hour to hour. It must remain, therefore, for some other hand to sketch its appearance at another epoch, to furnish another element for calculating the course and motion of this member of our federal system.[27]

Jay Fliegelman reads this letter as an admission of exhaustion: "Tired from correcting the manuscript of *Notes*, Jefferson articulated the core futility of his descriptive project."[28] I would suggest that there is something more significant at work here. Jefferson was famously cognizant of the structural tensions between generations. "We seem not to have perceived that, by the law of nature, one generation is as one independant [sic] nation to another," he wrote to Madison in 1789, referring to the inadvisability of incurring national debt, "the earth belongs always to the living generation." Constitutions and laws expire every nineteen years, he continues, and "if [they] be enforced longer, it is an act of force, and not of right."[29] In this light, we might view Jefferson's reluctance to revise the work yet again as, in the words of Susan Manning, "one of Jefferson's acknowledgments of the limitations of the human condition that he believed us to have only fragmentary access to partial information."[30] Jefferson's effort in *Notes* to "think the nation" in and through time is in this sense a necessarily incomplete and provisional one, at best only a preliminary account of the national past insofar as the past is itself perpetually augmented by events of the present.

Juxtaposed with his account of feeling overwhelmed by the force of nature at the Natural Bridge, we might also discern in Jefferson's admission of futility something of an intuition of the complexity, even the political undesirability, of his own project in *Notes*, a recognition that the plural and contingent forces of nature make it unrepresentable in any simple or final terms; that the plural and contingent forces that he so admires in the natural world are also forces that shape the political world; and for this reason that the effort to think and write a nation cannot be simply accomplished—not by one man, not by one text, and certainly not in one revised edition.

This is to say that Jefferson's effort to capture and distill the temporality of American nature and put it to work as a force of American nationalism is frustrated by the very properties of nature that he most admires. However much Jefferson attempts to bring purpose to nature, there is something in and of nature, something in and of the world, that complicates and confounds his ability to do so, at least his ability to do so completely. What he expresses in early chapters of *Notes* as anxiety about the force of contingency outside of political life might be linked to his later expressions of anxiety about differences in political life, about the place of difference in political life, and about the relationship between and among the inhabitants of the multiple pasts (or competing presents) he described in his letter to Ludlow. The chapter immediately following his discussion of the Natural Bridge offers Jefferson his first opportunity in the book to discuss the peoples who inhabited the American landscape.

American ancients

Jefferson's most impassioned treatment of American nature turns on his discussion of Native Americans in the chapter entitled "Productions Mineral, Vegetable, and Animal." It is here that he expands the scope of his conception of nature to take in another of its significant "productions," namely the human body. Placing Indians in a landscape rich with mineral deposits and rock formations, a diverse collection of native plants, and animal life ranging from the tiniest mouse to the great mammoth ("or big buffalo, as [it is] called by the Indians"),[31] Jefferson reserves the "man of America" as ammunition for his strongest case yet against Buffon. What he takes particular exception to are Buffon's charges that

> The savage is feeble, and has small organs of generation; . . . and no ardor whatever for his female; swifter than the European [but] less strong in body; . . . less sensitive, and yet more timid and cowardly; he has no vivacity, no activity of mind.[32]

Jefferson takes pains to counter each of these claims, arguing that the American Native was in fact every bit as virile as his European counterpart, profoundly affectionate and loyal to both family and friends, and (not least) as accomplished in the arts of rhetoric and oratory as were Demosthenes and Cicero.[33] In fact, Jefferson insists that Native Americans differ from the European inhabitants of America only developmentally, taking pains to establish the racial likenesses that link them: "we shall probably find," he speculated, "that [Indians] are formed in mind as well as in body, on the same module with the 'Homo sapiens Europaeus.'"[34]

Jehlen suggests that Jefferson's defense of the vitality of Indians' physical and intellectual powers seems to sit uncomfortably with his larger project: "Indeed, Buffon's denigration of the Indians, and of the wilderness, might seem a more useful premise for arguing the rectitude and likely success of the Revolutionary cause." How then, she asks, are we to understand the political significance of the position Jefferson articulates with such passion? Buffon, after all, "had not impugned Jefferson's manhood, but only that of a native population whom Jefferson and his fellow colonizers, when they were not killing them outright, were energetically displacing."[35] For Jehlen, Jefferson's refusal to espouse the superiority of European civilization is consonant with what she reads as his nondevelopmental view of American nature. "An American land transformed by European civilization," she reasons, "would be Europe's permanently dependent derivative."[36] Independence from the European past could be secured most effectively by imagining an America whose landscape, natural resources, and peoples were self-founding, self-sustaining, and eternal. It is here that Jehlen's emphasis upon the messianic aspects of time in Jefferson's *Notes* meets its own limits. Jehlen's reading doesn't quite enable us to get at the degree to which Jefferson *does* take Buffon's denigration of Indians personally and that this sense of identification is comprehensible only if we understand Jefferson's placement of Native Americans in time, at (and as) the origin of a temporal continuum that leads directly to Jefferson himself. If Jefferson's focus on the Native's body—the size and vitality of the Indian's "organs of generation," his strength, body hair, motility, and so on—takes its cue at least initially from Buffon, then, it turns out to hold further significance in *Notes*. The Native's body suggests to Jefferson another kind of natural bridge between American nature and the American nation.

This becomes clear when we turn to his next discussion of Indians in *Notes*, in the chapter entitled (fittingly enough) "Aborigines." This chapter appears in an intermediate section of the work, immediately following his treatment of queries regarding "Population," "Military Force," and "Marine Force." On the face of it, the chapters in this middle section appear to be situated oddly with respect to those that precede and follow them, interrupting the nature-culture teleology that otherwise seems to structure his project. But in fact, they constitute an integral part of that larger narrative, a necessary bridge between the natural features described in Jefferson's answers to the first seven queries, and the discussion of colonial institutions that occupies the remainder of the book. In brief scope, these four chapters tell the story of European settlement and the armed break with the European past. They end by supplying European creoles with new ties to a different past, in this case, figurative ties of kinship to the ancient inhabitants of the New World.

The aboriginal peoples of America were perhaps most interesting, and most significant, to Jefferson insofar as they represented the living relics of an ancient past, an ancient *American* past. Natives were a living museum, an archaism within modern America from whom important knowledge about human civilization (in epochs that were otherwise no longer available for study) could be gleaned. *Notes* includes a lengthy table that lists, enumerates, and indicates territorial habitations of tribal populations known to Jefferson, comparing these records to those compiled by earlier explorers.[37] "Great question has arisen," he notes, "from whence came these aboriginal inhabitants of America?"[38] For Jefferson, the answer is to be discovered through the study of native languages, for "a knowledge of their several languages would be the most certain evidence of their derivation which could be produced. In fact, it is the best proof of the affinity of nations which ever can be referred to."[39] Jefferson's attempt to identify ancient filiations and (once-) common cultures through a comparison of Natives' vocabularies was frustrated, however, by the paucity of historical documentation: "It is to be lamented then, very much to be lamented, that we have suffered so many of the Indian tribes already to extinguish, without our having previously collected and deposited in the records of literature, the general rudiments at least of the languages they spoke."[40] What little evidence was available, he concludes, revealed that tribal tongues had, quite significantly, "lost all resemblance to one another."[41] Unlike the languages of Northern Europe which, though distinct, nonetheless retain traces of their common origin, the loss of all commonality among Indian vocabularies indicates to Jefferson the measure of a tremendous passage of time, and he speculates that the "red men of America" are likely "of greater antiquity than those of Asia," and, indeed, may be among the earliest human inhabitants of the earth itself.[42] "A separation into dialects may be the work of a few ages only," he notes, "but for two dialects to recede from one another till they have lost all vestiges of their common origin must require an immense course of time; perhaps not less than many people give to the age of the earth."[43]

From the vantage point of the present condition of Indian civilization(s), Jefferson integrates "aborigines," retrospectively, into the American past that he calls nature. The very pastness of American nature enables him to imagine, in turn, a form of kinship between Native Americans and native creoles of European extraction, one that would help to naturalize, as citizens, the American-born descendents of British colonials. Imagining aborigines as American ancients, Jefferson laid the groundwork for American creoles to imagine themselves as descendants of Native Americans, their ancient ancestors who were also, strangely enough, their contemporaries.

An 1812 letter from Jefferson to John Adams can help to illustrate this fabulous kinship at work in his recollections of his own childhood. Following a detailed discussion of works that might shed light onto what Adams had referred, in earlier correspondence, as the "confused traditions of Indian Antiquities,"[44] Jefferson turns to a memorable event from his own life. He recalls being present, in his youth, for the farewell oration made to his people by "the great Outassete, the warrior and orator of the Cherokees" just before he left for England to be received by the King. Outassete's "sounding voice, distinct articulation, animated action, and the solemn silence of his people at their several fires filled me with awe and veneration, altho' I did not understand a word he uttered."[45] Outassete, a frequent guest of Jefferson's father, Peter Jefferson, when Thomas was a boy, spoke so movingly that the memory of the farewell address, as Jay Fliegelman reads it, calls to the younger Jefferson's mind the death of the elder, and it constitutes what Fliegelman characterizes as "one of the extremely rare references [Jefferson made] to his father." The recollection, he writes, "seems to have served Jefferson as a way of addressing, mourning, and ennobling the death of his father, a deeply traumatic event that left him 'at 14 years of age' head of the family with 'the whole care and direction of myself . . . thrown on my self entirely, without a relative or friend qualified to advise or guide me.'"[46] To expand upon Fliegelman's analysis, it might be said that the account of Outassete's oratory sparks in Jefferson a nostalgic and mournful chain of memories that positions the Native as a figurative equivalent of the father, and by extension positions Native Americans as the figurative progenitors of creoles.

This is a fabulous kinship indeed. Consider, for example, the complicated kinship terms and tangled historical relations contained in a short passage from Jefferson's address to a delegation of the Osage, delivered in 1804, the year following the completion of the Louisiana Purchase:

> My children. By late arrangements with France & Spain, we now take their place as your neighbors, friends and fathers: and we hope you will have no cause to regret the change. It is so long since our forefathers came from beyond the great water, that we have lost the memory of it, and seem to have grown out of this land, as you have done. Never more will you have occasion to change your fathers. We are all now of one family, born in the same land, & bound to live as brothers; & the strangers from beyond the great water are gone from among us.[47]

This passage illustrates the complex place of the Native in Jeffersonian nationalism. Eliding the memory of creoles' European ancestry, and recasting the French and Spanish as strangers to Indians and creoles alike, Jefferson writes creoles into the natural history of the continent, so that they now "seem to have grown out of this land, as [Indians] have done." The new relations between Native and creole formed of this fiction are far from straightforward, however, for Jefferson positions Natives here as both the siblings ("we are . . . bound to live as brothers") and the offspring ("My children") of British creoles, "born in the same land," and living in the same calendrical moment, but developmentally distinct from one another. These complicated kinship terms might be read, in fact, as foreshadowing stages in the development of national citizenship. Insofar as Indians preceded Europeans on the continent, they could be seen as creoles' forebears. Yet in time, as creole civilization became more established in America, creoles became more like sibling equals; eventually, as creoles consolidated their hold on the continent and became a dominant power, Indians were transformed in the creole imagination into their less developed children.

If Natives had somehow remained unchanged by the "march of civilization [that] pass[ed] over us like a cloud of light," Jefferson was confident that, with the proper guidance, they too could reap the benefits of industrious modernism. As he advised the Cherokee chiefs in 1806:

> When a man has enclosed and improved his farm, builds a good house on it and raised plentiful stocks of animals, he will wish when he dies that these things shall go to his wife and children, whom he loves more than he does his other relations, and for whom he will work with pleasure during his life. You will, therefore, find it necessary to establish laws for this. When a man has property, earned by his own labor, he will not like to see another come and take it from him because he happens to be stronger, or else to defend it by spilling blood. You will find it necessary

then to appoint good men, as judges, to decide contests between man and man according to reason and to the rules you shall establish.[48]

In the case of Indians, becoming citizens required that they become moderns by reproducing the general contours of European history. However, even as he sought to tutor Natives into the modern political era, Jefferson came to regard those tribes that (as he saw it) refused the gift of government as dangers to America and American creoles. In the same letter to Adams where he praises the rhetorical powers of "the great Outassete," Jefferson acknowledges the possibility not only of Natives' "cultural obstinacy," but of cultural regression. Writing on the eve of the War of 1812, Jefferson addresses the possibility of Native collaboration with the British: "On those [Natives] who have made any progress, English seductions will have no effect. But the backward will yeild [sic], and be thrown further back. These will relapse into barbarism and misery, lose numbers by war and want, and we shall be obligated to drive them, with the beasts of the forest into the Stony mountains."[49]

Bernard Sheehan has argued that this ultimate "elimination of the tribal order" is an unintended (if not unimaginable) consequence of "Jeffersonian philanthropy"[50]; however, this explanation downplays the extent to which creole self-identity was bound up with the figure of the Indian. Jefferson's comments point to the short distance that separates paternalism from violence, a violence that would find its most tragic expression in Indian policy executed by the Jackson administration. Following Michael Rogin's analysis of Jackson in *Fathers and Children*, I would argue that this is not a case of unintended consequences so much as an indication of the dual character of paternal authority itself.[51]

Native Americans figure in Jefferson's creole nationalism as a bridge linking an American nation that was still very much in the process of becoming (and was by no means historically or politically assured) to the precolonial American past, and it is precisely their status as American ancients that defines the terms of Indians' incorporation in the political future of the new nation. Native society was an archaic remnant of the past, a proper antecedent for the American nation, but no more. Benedict Anderson has traced a similar process at work in colonial Peru: "San Martín decreed in 1821 that 'in the future the aborigines shall not be called Indians or natives; they are children *and citizens* of Peru and they shall be known as Peruvians.'"[52] Natives can be "'invited into' the imagined community"[53] of the nation, Anderson suggests, but not as Natives. However much Anderson grasps the terms of Indian integration into a new nation, his insight that "from the start, the nation was conceived in language, not in blood"⁵⁴ does not quite get at the place of the past in the nationalist project, not, at least, in Jefferson's articulation of that project. Somewhat closer to my reading is that of Werner Sollors, who recognizes the significance of the Native past for American culture. As Sollors puts it, creoles saw the aboriginal inhabitants of the continent as "legitimating ancestors who support the[ir] adoptive descendents,"⁵⁵ ancestors of choice, not (like Europeans) of strict lineal descent. Unlike Sollors, I do not read this embrace of new and different ancestors as the triumph of consensual heterogeneity. I would argue that particularly in the case of Jefferson the embrace of American ancients as forebears represents the complex reincorporation of the old within the new, of Indians within a creole nation. Descent is not so much overthrown by, but contained within, Jefferson's effort to think the nation, and the figure of the Native (if not Natives themselves) gains new purchase in the American political imagination. As Joseph Lowndes has written, "one must become an Indian to become independent, and replace the Indian to become an American,"⁵⁶ but, I would add, that replacement is not a simple one.

Even as Jefferson promotes the integration of Indians as citizens into the creole nation, he secures for these American ancients a new role. In the third and last section of *Notes*, Jefferson shifts his vision from the land and its native peoples to the laws and institutions of the new nation. However, Natives do not disappear from the narrative. In the chapter entitled "Colleges, Buildings, and Roads," for example, Jefferson criticizes the terms of the Brafferton endowment at the College of William and Mary, which had provided for the establishment of an institution dedicated to "the instruction of the Indians, and their conversion to Christianity." This endowment, he suggests, would be better employed by "maintaining a perpetual mission among the Indian tribes, the object of which, besides instructing them in the principles of Christianity, as the [endowment] requires, should be to collect their traditions, laws, customs, languages, and other circumstances which might lead to a discovery of their relation with one another or descent from other nations."⁵⁷ Significantly, Jefferson is not arguing against Indian conversion in this passage, but rather suggesting that conversion is not enough. Even as he advocates the integration of Indians into creole culture, Jefferson seeks to preserve and maintain some form of *Indianness* at the heart of the American imaginary. American ancients are not simply incorporated within the nation, they are made the animating force within nationhood itself: Indian history becomes creole history so that Indians may become citizens and creoles may become Americans. While Anderson is right, then, to argue that "from the start, the nation was conceived in language, not in blood," this is performative strategy framed as a generative logic, a genealogical nationalism formed through recourse to a fabulous kinship, imagined retrospectively, that secures the prospect of citizenship in a creole nation.

African moderns

If Jefferson imagines creoles and Native Americans as developmentally distinct generations linked to one another both retrospectively and prospectively, his treatment of African Americans in *Notes* and elsewhere is strikingly different. Jefferson's position with regard to slavery is, of course, well known.[58] Confronting the political question of slavery in his initial draft of the Declaration of Independence, he condemned the King for having "waged cruel war against human nature itself, violating it's [sic] most sacred rights of life and liberty in the persons of a distant people who never offended him, captivating & carrying them into slavery in another hemisphere or to incur miserable death in their transportation thither."[59] In *Notes*, an entire chapter is devoted to the deleterious effects of slavery on the "manners of our people."[60] Yet in turning to the question of the slaves themselves, Jefferson was far less decisive. Briefly put, slaves pose a different kind of problem for Jefferson's creole nationalism than Indians, for they cannot be incorporated into the American natural past. It is precisely slaves' lack of ties to American nature that calls to mind what it is that they hold in common with whites: they, too, are creoles.

In a very important sense, slaves cannot be fully or comfortably integrated as American citizens within the terms of Jeffersonian nationalism because they are, paradoxically enough, not products of American nature but creations of the law itself, or more precisely, of what is most injudicious in American law. In fact, Jefferson's only substantive discussion of slaves in *Notes* takes place in the chapter entitled "Laws." Responding to Marbois' query about "the administration of justice and the description of the laws," Jefferson takes pains to point out that the emancipation of slaves constitutes an important aspect of republican efforts to remove monarchical elements from the colonial statutes. In a passage that seems, on the face of it, not so very different from his occasional writings on Indian removal (and which, it turns out, may have little basis in fact),[61] he outlines the particulars of an "amendment to be offered to the legislature whenever the bill [to revise Virginia's code] should be taken up":

> To emancipate all slaves born after passing the act . . . and further directing, that they should continue with their parents to a certain age,

then be brought up, at the public expence, to tillage, arts or science, according to their geniusses [sic], till the females should be eighteen, and the males twenty-one years of age, when they should be colonized to such place as the circumstances of the time should render most proper.[62]

Jefferson's proposal for African colonization partakes of much of the same tutelary impulse, much the same desire to lead what he views as a developmentally backward people into the full flower of industrious modernism, as we saw with Natives. All is not entirely as it seems, however. As he soon makes clear, unlike Natives who inhabited an ancient moment in political and anthropological development, and who might therefore have a (different) future in the new nation, for Jefferson, Africans were moderns, creole contemporaries whose very presence on the continent threatened the foundations of Jefferson's national vision.

Immediately following his discussion of the proposed amendment, Jefferson makes clear his reasons for promoting colonization. "It will probably be asked, why not retain and incorporate blacks into the state . . . ?":

Deep rooted prejudices entertained by the whites; ten thousand recollections, by the blacks, of the injuries they have sustained; new provocations; the real distinctions which nature has made; and many other circumstances, will divide us into parties, and produce convulsions which will probably never end but in the extermination of the one or the other race.—To these objections, which are political, may be added others, which are physical and moral.[63]

For Jefferson, the political problem facing the new nation was not simply the institution of slavery, but the presence of black Americans themselves. To retain African Americans in the same territory with European creoles, he suggests, is to risk genocide. The apocalyptic tone of this passage, Jefferson's firm belief that blacks and whites possessed incommensurable natures, histories, and interests, is mirrored in his later writings on St. Domingo. Commenting, in a much-cited 1797 letter to St. George Tucker, on the aftermath of slave rebellion on that island, he notes:

Perhaps the first chapter of this history [of the emancipation of slaves], which has begun in St. Domingo, & the next succeeding ones, which will recount how all the whites were driven from all the other islands, may prepare our minds for a peaceable accommodation between justice, policy & necessity; and furnish an answer to the difficult question, whither shall the colored emigrants go? and the sooner we put some plan underway, the greater hope there is that it may be permitted to proceed peaceably to it's [sic] ultimate effect. But if something is not done, & soon done, we shall be the murderers of our own children. The 'murmura venturos nautis prodentia ventos' has already reached us; the revolutionary storm, now sweeping the globe, will be upon us, and happy if we make timely provision to give it an easy passage over our land. From the present state of things in Europe & America, the day which begins our combustion must be near at hand; and only a single spark is wanting to make that day to-morrow.[64]

For Jefferson, the lesson of St. Domingo was that the presence of blacks on American soil was not simply a threat to the present peace, but to future generations "of our own children."

What I find especially interesting in *Notes* is not so much Jefferson's frequently commented upon bias against the intellectual capacities of African Americans, that is, his deployment of natural history as racial science, but something more: his attempt to join that taxonomy of racial development with a chronoscopic vision of American nationalism. For Jefferson, race is both a measure of and a proxy for a people's genealogical connection with the American past—that is, with a past produced as natural history—and therefore also an indication of their place in the nation's future. In the end, Jefferson's speculation in *Notes* that Africans and European creoles may belong to "different species of the same genus," or to distinct "varieties of the same species," works not only to naturalize, as racial, the apparent differences between blacks and whites, but also to obscure precisely what blacks and whites most hold in common. African Americans are not foreigners who, as Jefferson had famously worried in an earlier section, "infuse into [the nation] their spirit, warp and bias its direction, and render it a heterogeneous, incoherent, distracted mass."[65] Quite the contrary. The "many millions of [slaves who] have been brought to and born in America"[66] are of the same stock as whites, native-born descendants of the "persons [white and black] imported for the establishment of our colony in its infant state."[67] Occupying the "same stage with the whites,"[68] slaves were creoles of a different color.

In this regard, we might view the passages of *Notes* that are frequently interpreted as evidence of Jefferson's racial prejudice in a slightly different light. Immediately following his rationale for colonizing slaves (quoted above), Jefferson catalogues a variety of observed "physical and moral" markers of the inferiority of black creoles when compared to their white creole contemporaries. He ends the passage with a call for further study, a caution lest our "conclusion would degrade a whole race of men," and yet a "suspicion" that "blacks are inferior to the whites in the endowment of both body and mind."

> To our reproach it must be said, that though for a century and a half we have had under our eyes the races of black and of red men, they have never yet been viewed by us as subjects of natural history. I advance it therefore as a suspicion only, that the blacks, whether originally a distinct race, or made distinct by time and circumstances, are inferior to the whites in the endowments both of body and mind. It is not against experience to suppose, that different species of the same genus, or varieties of the same species, may possess different qualifications. Will not a lover of natural history then, one who views the gradations in all the races of animals with the eye of philosophy, excuse an effort to keep those in the department of man as distinct as nature has formed them?[69]

I do not mean to minimize the racism at work here.[70] Like American Natives, African Americans were, for Jefferson, a developmentally arrested people whose cultural productions fell far short of the modern standards set by their white European and American creole contemporaries. But quite unlike the not-yet-civilized Natives who were simply unschooled in modern ways (as, at least, Jefferson's more optimistic portrayals would have it), African Americans were full inhabitants of the modern era trained in the fine arts, the "handicraft arts," and mathematics and the sciences, yet nonetheless lacking the "restraint of reason and taste" that made them capable of producing work that demonstrated generous "endowments of the head."[71]

There is prejudice at work here to be sure. It is a form of prejudice that Jefferson justifies by recourse to racial science. To leave it at that, however, is to miss the important ways that race comes to be established as central to the symbolic order through which citizenship is imagined and imaginable in America. For Jefferson does not simply deploy languages of racial science and biological determinism as justification for colonization and exclusion. He also identifies a form of racial difference constituted explicitly by *historical* antagonisms, and he freights it with permanent political meaning. Jefferson perceives racial tensions in terms of incompatible histories that produce *cultural* differences in such a way that, as Renata Salecl has written, "culture itself functions as a 'natural' determinative force" by locking individuals and groups "a priori into their cultural genealogy."[72] This is racial difference established not (only) in and by nature but, significantly, in and through time insofar as, for Jefferson, American nature is permeated by American time. Jefferson's project in *Notes* of placing America—and its various human inhabitants—in time works to naturalize white creoles as citizens, and to denaturalize black creoles by making them appear culturally and politically (as well as biologically) incompatible with both whites and Indians.

In this light we can make sense of the sudden appearance of Native Americans in Jefferson's comparison of whites and blacks:

> Some [slaves] have been liberally educated, and all have lived in countries where the arts and sciences are cultivated to a considerable degree, and have had before their eyes samples of the best works from abroad. The Indians, with no advantages of this kind, will often carve figures on their pipes not destitute of design and merit. They will crayon out an animal, a plant, or a country, so as to prove the existence of a germ in their minds which only wants cultivation. They astonish you with strokes of the most sublime oratory; such as prove their reason and sentiment strong, their imagination glowing and elevated. But never yet could I find that a black had uttered a thought above the level of plain narration; never see even an elementary trait of painting or sculpture.[73]

Although they have had far greater exposure to Euro-American civilization than Indians, Jefferson contends, blacks show considerably less propensity for it and no benefit from it. They are developmentally and biologically disconnected from both Native and naturalized Americans, as anthropologically advanced as they are ever likely to become. For Jefferson, Indians and white creoles occupy different developmental moments along the same cultural and historical trajectory. Black slaves, by contrast, inhabit not a different developmental moment, but a different national trajectory altogether.

Unlike Indians, slaves are not historical anomalies of the present, they are not contemporary ancients, but moderns whose presence in America was decidedly unnatural, a product of corrupt monarchical laws. Viewing slaves as creatures exclusively of that aspect of American law that most demanded repeal, Jefferson could not imagine a place for free blacks in the national future precisely because they could not be retrospectively integrated into the precolonial, preslavery American past. They were a danger to the integrity of the nation itself, perpetual reminders of what was destructive in the past.

Here, Jefferson's genealogical nationalism shifts from the figurative to the literal as he equates the slave's body with an eternally unchanging nature that stands in sharp contrast to the timeliness he sees in American nature: what was most threatened by the coexistence of European and African creoles in the same national space was the creole bloodline itself, and thus the future of the American people. Unlike emancipated Roman slaves, Jefferson mused, Africans would not be able to "mix with, without staining the blood of his master. . . . When freed, he is to be removed beyond the reach of mixture."[74] This is to say that Jefferson's efforts to supply a past for the late eighteenth-century national project encounters a genealogical double bind: he cannot or will not imagine an ancestral link that integrates African slaves into the American national past, but he is all too aware of the means by which free blacks might make their way into national life as creole competitors pitted against their former owners for control of the American nation. Indeed, Jefferson went so far as to recommend the exile of white women who consorted with black or mulatto men, and proposed to the Virginia legislature a bill requiring that any white woman who had given birth to a mulatto child must leave the state or be placed "out of the protection of the laws" and into a virtual state of nature.[73] Where fostering a sense of kinship—even if only a figurative one—between European creoles and Native Americans gave shape and purpose to Jefferson's Indian policy, his policy toward slaves was notably different, oriented instead to the prevention of those ties. What Jefferson fears with respect to slaves is not a cleavage between past and future that could be bridged historically, but the ultimate incompatibility of two groups, both of whom are fully a part of the present. This incompatibility is founded in the law and fixed by both history and nature, and evidence of that fixity is written on the slave's body itself, "that immoveable veil of black which covers all. . . ."[76]

Mapping a new American past

Late bound and distributed copies of the privately printed 1785 edition of *Notes,* and subsequent English-language editions published both in the United States and abroad, include a map of Virginia and surrounding areas of Maryland, Delaware, and Pennsylvania.[77] The map is Jefferson's own correction and updating of an earlier work, "A Map of the Inhabited Part of Virginia," drawn in 1751 by Jefferson's father, a self-taught surveyor and cartographer, and his partner Joshua Fry.[78] Jefferson's 1786 map accomplishes more than just cartographic description, and a comparison of the two versions is instructive, for Jefferson's map can also be read as a kind of coda to the book itself, a spatial summation of his genealogical nationalism as well as a projection onto the land of a new national future. In fact, Jefferson's map does not simply reflect and record, but it "anticipate[s] spatial reality," providing (as Thongchai Winichakul has characterized a very different national mapping project) "a model for, rather than a model of, what [it] purports to represent."[79] Even as Jefferson's map marks off and describes a given space, it views that territory from a distinct perspective and orients its users to a particular future, promoting national expansion and contributing to the construction of a new national vision.[80]

As Benedict Anderson has noted, the development of national consciousness is dependent on changing apprehensions of both time and space.[81] The increasing scientific accuracy of new cartographic techniques, coupled with the new knowledge of the world gained, in America, through westward expansion, made possible the development of novel strategies of imagining and representing state power in spatial terms. On Jefferson's map, these two innovations come together in his depiction of a spatial and temporal foundation for a new American nation. The 1751 Fry and Jefferson map contained considerable gaps in its depiction of territory west of the Appalachians and admitted of imprecise placement of important landmarks.[82] Thomas Jefferson's revision corrects these deficiencies, and it is drawn with a considerably greater degree of longitudinal precision.[83] The later map is not simply more complete or technically precise, however. Jefferson's 1786 revision does not just describe a landscape that is overlaid with political boundaries, it also projects national ambition onto the land. Most notably, Jefferson's map points to territorial potential beyond the established contiguous states, designating each of three demarcated territories to the west as "A New State." In doing so, the map reconfigures territory in terms of the national plan proposed by the Ordinance of 1784, a plan drafted by a committee Jefferson chaired, which had "[r]esolved, that the territory ceded or to be ceded by Individual states to the United states shall be formed into distinct states. . . ,"[84] drawing political boundaries that reshape a colonial past into a national future.[85]

Yet Jefferson's revision is interesting not only in terms of what it adds to the earlier map, but also in terms of its omissions and elisions. The cartouche of the Fry and Jefferson map—which contains its title, names its authors, its commissioner, and its printer—is dominated by a detailed engraving of a wharf in a Virginia port. Amid the barrels collecting on the dock is an assortment of Virginia's inhabitants. A gentleman checks a ship's lading order, others sit in conversation with a serving woman, and slaves dressed in loincloths labor over the freight and serve drinks to the assembled party. Jefferson's revised map eliminates the explicit depiction of slavery, and with it all traces of African Americans are erased from the land, save for the occasional creek named "Negro Run." Of course, as Jefferson was all too aware, slavery persisted in the land about which he composed his *Notes*, but like the three "New State[s]" that he draws onto the northwestern territory, the effacement of slavery and slaves from his map projects an imagined future onto the landscape itself.

The two maps differ in another sense as well. The 1751 version records a number of active Indian roads and trading paths as well as tribal settlements both occupied and deserted. With the exception of a handful of scattered Indian cabins, these indications of Indian presence are missing from Jefferson's 1786 revision. Unlike slaves, who disappear from the map altogether, in the place of these paths and settlements something new appears: markers pointing to the location of Indian Grave(s). These graves evoke traces of precolonial, and certainly of prenational, pasts that are not only retained within but have also been transformed by the colonial and national present. In this sense, Jefferson's map registers changes in the land born of expanded creole settlement while also retaining the shadows of a more recent and distant past. Replacing paths and habitations with gravesites suggests not only the passage of time and a commensurate shift in population, but also the transformation of the past itself. The Indian Graves and the bodies they contain have become relics of the past, present to the scene of national imagination, but they are also indications of a new kind of past, tailored for a new national future.

The body is a central but unstable figure in Jefferson's effort to construct a national past. If the aboriginal body serves as an integrative principle that helps him link white creoles retrospectively to the American land, the black body figures as a principle of dissonance and disharmony in the national present. Signifying both past and future in Jefferson's treatment, the body works within *Notes* as a complicated proxy—a piece of the old world initiating the new, or what Benjamin has called "a past charged with the time of the now."[86] At once an *aide-mémoire* and a portent, the body holds both the promise of redemption from a corrupt European past, and the possibility of national conflagration in the future. Jefferson's genealogical nationalism is an example of what Bruce Burgett calls the "*disestablishment* of the body" accomplished by the early national literature of late eighteenth-century America. Significantly, this alteration in the symbolic order does not signify the exile of the body from public life, but instead marks its transformation from an older status as "one of many phenomena ordered through pre-existing political, ethical, and theological systems" to "the noumenal grounding of existence itself—a point of origin upon which political, ethical, and theological systems are then erected."[87] Even as Jefferson's *Notes* and the appended map evoke a particular future, the past is not fully elided but is contained within it in a new form that melds a history into a nation: the citizen's racialized body. In this respect, Judith Shklar's suggestion that under Jeffersonian democracy a democratic people have no need for a past but "must live entirely in the present" turns out to be at once insightful and misguided.[88] Shklar rightly perceives that Jefferson promotes a politics of perpetual newness; however, his ability to imagine a democratic public life also depends on the absorption into the present of a past transformed. Jefferson's *Notes on the State of Virginia* might be said to supply a new past for a new nation, refiguring the citizen's body as the essential, though ultimately problematic, foundation for the national project.

The museum of America

American democracy, in Jefferson's hands, was framed as a legacy of American nature, and national citizenship became imaginable by reference to the human body. Yet as Lauren Berlant has put it, "Whenever citizenship comes to look like a question of the *body*, a number of processes are being hidden. The body's seeming obviousness distracts attention from the way it organizes meaning, and diverts the critical gaze from publicity's role in the formation of the taxonomies that construct bodies publicly."[89] I might add, the body's seeming prediscursiveness and its installation as the origin of politics continued, beyond Jefferson's meditation in *Notes*, to organize the terms and languages through which national citizenship would be articulated, particularly in the era during which the American Constitution was debated and ratified. As is well known, Jefferson himself initially opposed the Federal Constitution, for in a number of ways it departed from the institutional forms that he envisioned as most potentially democratic. Yet, the major models for citizenship proposed as part of the discussions surrounding the formulation of the Constitution retained Jefferson's figuration of the body as the (potentially dangerous) foundation of American national citizenship.

Jefferson's natural history of the American nation had a career beyond Jefferson himself, and as a way of concluding this chapter I'd like to turn briefly to a self-consciously Jeffersonian reformer whose own attention to race, though leading in a different direction than Jefferson's, may help to highlight the place of the body in republican thought. Frances Wright, who is perhaps best known as the first woman to conduct a public speaking tour in the United States, was a Scot raised by her uncle, the philosopher James Mylne. Between 1818 and 1820, Wright and her sister Camilla traveled unescorted through America, an experience she translated upon her return to Europe into a book-length account, extolling the institutions of the new republic as "*rues democrates*" where "the little inequalities of the ground are being removed with much trouble and expense."[90] Wright's chronicle opened to her the homes and conversations of numerous prominent political thinkers, including Jeremy Bentham, Albert Gallatin, and Jefferson himself. In her book, Wright marveled at the enduring pride the residents of Philadelphia professed for their Independence Hall decades after independence:

> Every friend or acquaintance that ever passed [the building] with me paused before it to make some observation. "Those are the windows of the room in which our first Congress sat." "There was signed the declaration of our independence." "From those steps the Declaration of Independence was read in the ears of the people."

Wright's pilgrimage to what she viewed as the fount of freedom brought only disappointment, however, for once inside she found herself in something of a museum—a monument to Jeffersonianism, but one she had not expected:

> The Statehouse, statehouse no longer in anything but name, is an interesting object to a stranger and, doubtless, a sacred shrine in the eyes of Americans. I know not but that I was a little offended to find stuffed birds, and beasts, and mammoth skeletons filling the place of senators and sages. It had been in better taste, perhaps to turn the upper rooms of this empty sanctuary into a library, instead of a museum of natural curiosities or a mausoleum of dead monsters.[91]

It seems that Wright, the European, recognized what native Philadelphians no longer could. In converting the meeting place of the 1776 Continental Congress to a natural history museum curated by Jefferson's friend Charles Willson Peale, a whole series of substitutions and transformations had been made. Nature had been emptied of any notion of diachronic time. The nature represented in Peale's museum was quite literally dead, frozen in time and thus made timeless by the art of taxidermy. Motionless, nature's "productions" (the term is Jefferson's) could then be extracted from the larger, systematic (we might say today ecological) web of relations that Jefferson described, and isolated as empty signs they were dislocated both geographically and temporally from the nature for which they had been substituted.[92]

Perhaps this is the substitution that Arendt fears, the normalization of a fixed and constraining nature that overcomes history and suffocates politics. In a sense, Arendt is more profoundly right about the nonfoundational character of the American founding that she associates with Jefferson than she recognizes, even if she misses the ways in which it is Jefferson's employment of a concept of nature—not his whole cloth refusal of it—that is central to a founding refusal of absolutes, setting into motion a particular form of democratic politics that is open to a different future rather than tethered to the originary terms of the past. For nature is not only a central feature of Jefferson's thought, it is a resource from which he derives the element of change that lends distinctness to his democratic vision, the means by which he supplies a (largely) nonconstraining past for his "politics of perpetual newness." For Jefferson (for the most part), nature is not opposed to politics or history, even if it is both a logical and a chronological precursor to democracy. Rather, nature provides Jefferson with the very model of historical change that he mobilizes in the name of democracy, in the project of a political founding that his Declaration of Independence can be said to initiate. It is through recourse to nature that Jefferson supplies the Revolutionaries' political project with a past that is more conceptual than it is strictly historical, a past that represents not so much a prior historic moment but an eternal dimension of the present—a kind of architecture that lies within the present, a structure around which the present is (to be) built.

Nonetheless, it is also the case that Jefferson reserved within his concept of nature a countervailing principle of fixity, of permanence and timelessness, that he represented by reference to the black body, and that he perceived this fixity as equally threatening as the contingencies he attached to the power of nature he experienced in the landscape of the Natural Bridge. If, in that case, Jefferson sought to contain the powers of nature in geographic, bureaucratic, and technological description, he takes a different course when he perceives contingent forces at work in politics. What he cannot assimilate, through nature, to the American past, he exiles from the nation altogether.

It is the notion of nature as change that Wright brought to bear on the very questions that most troubled Jefferson. She returned to America, accompanying the Marquis de Lafayette on his final visit in 1824, and stayed, settling eventually at Robert Owen's utopian socialist community in New-Harmony, Indiana. In 1828, Wright assumed the editorial responsibilities for the *New-Harmony Gazette*, the major publication of Owenite thought in America, and in that capacity she engaged in a sustained debate with Robert Dale Owen, son of New-Harmony's founder. In a letter to Owen, Wright challenged his representation of nature as an external standard against which political formulations could be measured for their truth value. What could be found that lay outside of nature? she asked. If, as Owen had insisted, nature was "every thing in its first brute state—untrained, uncleaned, unimproved,—then in proportion as every thing is rude and uncultivated and imperfect, should it be nearer to nature," she reasoned. What, then, of science, and of scientific progress? Were the scientific speculations of Benjamin Franklin to be considered unnatural, suspect for their very sophistication? What of common modifications of nature? Was a bent tree less natural than a straight one for having been twisted by a child at play? Answering these questions, Wright argued, would lead us to the conclusion that "nature therefore (if we are to apply a definite meaning to the word) can only mean *what is*." The term, she insisted, carried no inherent valence of the positive or the negative. Rather, everything in existence was a part of nature, as was change itself. "The straight tree is not more in nature than the crooked tree, nor the crooked tree than the straight, nor the wise man than the foolish, nor the foolish than the wise. Each is what circumstance operating upon its original, or, if we will, we may here use the word *natural* organization makes it to be."[93]

What Wright sought to accomplish was the breakup of a monolithic understanding of "nature" that, by 1828, had become both an intellectual and political weapon wielded against political action itself. "Nature" had become the watchword of social and political conservatism:

> Let us now translate the phrase above quoted from the work of the physiologist: "Nothing but ignorance would endeavor to govern Nature." That is—*Nothing but ignorance would endeavor to change things from what they are*. An assertion certainly never intended by an enlightened advocate of human improvement. Again: "Why will man alone disdain the laws of Nature, which takes so much care for the preservation of the species?" Translated, we shall read: *Why will man alone doubt the perfection of things as they are, which always exist in the best possible way for the preservation of the human race?*[94]

The task Wright undertook for herself was to do just that, to "doubt the perfection of things as they are" and demonstrate not only that change was an intrinsic part of nature, but that nature *could be* changed, and changed with an eye toward fundamentally altering what Jefferson had depicted as the greatest natural obstacle to universal democracy in America: the seemingly inalterable "stamp" of race.[95]

Leaving New-Harmony, Wright purchased congress lands on the Wolf River in Tennessee and established there a utopian community of a different sort, dedicated to the task of racial amalgamation. Populated with slaves she purchased along with the land, as well as with a few white volunteers, Wright set about a task that, she argued, had already been well-proven by slave owners who fathered children by their slaves: to demonstrate that racial amalgamation was not made impossible by "nature."

> Idle indeed is the assertion that the mixture of the races is not in nature. If not in nature, it could not happen; and, being in nature, since it does happen, the only question is whether it shall take place in good taste and good feeling and be made at once the means of sealing the tranquility, and perfecting the liberty of the country, and of peopling it with a race more suited to its southern climate than the pure European,—or whether it shall proceed, as it now does, viciously and degradingly, mingling hatred and fear with the ties of blood—denied indeed, but stamped by nature herself upon the skin. The education of the race of color would doubtless make the amalgamation more rapid as well as more creditable; and so far from considering the physical amalgamation of the two colors, when accompanied by a moral approximation, as an evil, it must surely be viewed as a good equally desirable for both.[96]

In the end, however, Wright's effort to (re)infuse nature—indeed, to reinfuse the citizen's body—with a capacity for change remained trapped in the same double-bind as Jefferson's racial science, for both treated racial difference as a threat to the national order. If Jefferson had sought to eliminate racial difference from the American nation by colonizing emancipated slaves to a distant territory, Wright sought to eliminate difference itself through the creation of a single, and singularly new, American race.

Endnotes

1. Walter Benjamin, *Illuminations*, ed. Hannah Arendt (New York: Schocken Books, 1969), 255.
2. Charles A. Miller, *Jefferson and Nature: An Interpretation* (Baltimore: The Johns Hopkins University Press, 1988), 3.
3. Gordon Wood has explained the particular purchase the American founding has attained in the Straussian interpretive project as linked, through the coincidence of that founding with modernity, to Leo Strauss's conviction that the emergence of modernity within political thought brings with it a realism that stressed the historic rather than the natural and eternal character of political life. For Strauss, this "historicism" promotes the erosion of (classical) beliefs in natural (or positive) right, and for his followers, "America"

thus symbolizes (at least the potential for) the permanent lowering of expectations for political life. By contrast, what I am suggesting here is that the coincidence of "America" as a national entity, and "modernity" as a shift in consciousness, does not so much abjure "classical" values as produce a new and different model of "ancientness," that is, the novelty of the American project necessitates the production of new antiquities which are, nonetheless, important to the nationalist project insofar as they provide an ancient foundation for a new world. See Gordon S. Wood, "The Fundamentalists and the Constitution," *New York Review of Books*, (February 18), 1988, 33–40.

4. Benedict Anderson, *Imagined Communities: Reflections on the Origin and Spread of Nationalism* (New York: Verso, 1991), 22.

5. For Benjamin, messianic time "comprises the entire history of mankind in an enormous abridgement." Anderson gives the example of the stained glass windows of medieval cathedrals that depict a nativity scene where the Christ child is attended by his parents, who may look like the offspring of Tuscan merchants; by shepherds, who bear the features of Burgundian peasants; and even by the patron responsible for commissioning the window itself, who appears in full burgher or noble costume. See Benedict Anderson, *Imagined Communities*, 22–24. Also, Walter Benjamin, "Theses on the Philosophy of History," *Illuminations*, ed. Hannah Arendt, 263.

6. Benedict Anderson, *Imagined Communities*, 23, 26.

7. "Number II: Concerning Dangers from Foreign Force and Influence," *The Federalist Papers*, ed. Isaac Kramnick (New York: Viking Penguin, 1987), 91.

8. Judith N. Shklar, "Democracy and the Past: Jefferson and His Heirs," *Redeeming American Political Thought*, ed. Stanley Hoffmann and Dennis F. Thompson (Chicago: The University of Chicago Press, 1998), 174.

9. "Introduction," *Notes on the State of Virginia*, ed. Frank Shuffelton (New York: Penguin, 1999), xix. The classic reading of *Notes* as "a vehicle of American nationality" is that of Merrill D. Peterson in "Thomas Jefferson's *Notes on the State of Virginia*," *Studies in Eighteenth-Century Culture* 7 (1978), 49–62.

10. Susan Manning, "Naming of Parts; or, The Comforts of Classification: Thomas Jefferson's Construction of America as Fact and Myth," *Journal of American Studies* 30:3 (1996), 347.

11. Thomas Jefferson, *Notes on the State of Virginia*, ed. William Peden (New York: W.W. Norton, 1972), 179. Citations to Jefferson's *Notes* refer to this edition unless otherwise noted.

12. Thomas Jefferson, *Notes on the State of Virginia*, esp. Query VI.

13. Myra Jehlen, *American Incarnation: The Individual, the Nation, and the Continent* (Cambridge: Harvard University Press, 1986), 44. Emphasis in original.

14. Myra Jehlen, *American Incarnation: The Individual, the Nation, and the Continent*, 57–59. Jehlen is by no means alone in viewing Jefferson's portrayal of American

nature as shaped by messianic notions of time. For similar, though less complexly formulated analyses, see: Christopher Looby, "The Constitution of Nature: Taxonomy as Politics in Jefferson, Peale, and Bartram," *Early American Literature* 22 (1987), 252–73; Harold Hellenbrand, "Roads to Happiness: Rhetorical and Philosophical Design in Jefferson's *Notes On the State of Virginia*," *Early American Literature* 20 (1985), 3–23. For a sharply contrasting interpretation, see Merrill D. Peterson, "Thomas Jefferson's *Notes on the State of Virginia*," *Studies in Eighteenth-Century Culture* 7 (1978), 49–62.

15. For the original order of Marbois' questionnaire, see "Marbois' Queries Concerning Virginia," *The Papers of Thomas Jefferson*, eds. Julian P. Boyd et al. (Princeton: Princeton University Press, 1951), 4:166.

16. For a different interpretation of Jefferson's arrangement of the queries, see Robert A. Ferguson, "Mysterious Obligation: Jefferson's *Notes on the State of Virginia*," *American Literature* 52:3 (November 1980), 381–406.

17. For a discussion of the place of nature in modern and liberal thought, see Shane Phelan, "Intimate Distance: The Dislocation of Nature in Modernity," *In the Nature of Things: Language, Politics, and the Environment*, eds. Jane Bennett and William Chaloupka (Minneapolis: University of Minnesota Press, 1993), 44–62. One of the clearest characterizations of the relation between nature and politics in modern thought can be found in Hannah Arendt, *On Revolution* (New York: Penguin, 1981), 19–20.

18. Thomas Jefferson, *Notes on the State of Virginia*, 7–9.

19. Thomas Jefferson, *Notes on the State of Virginia*, 18–19.

20. Thomas Jefferson, *Notes on the State of Virginia*, 47. For commentary on Jefferson's response to Buffon, see Paul Semonin, "'Nature's Nation': Natural History as Nationalism in the New Republic," *Northwest Review* 30:2 (1992), 6–41; Myra Jehlen, *American Incarnation: The Individual, The Nation, and the Continent*, Chapter Two; Daniel J. Boorstin, *The Lost World of Thomas Jefferson* (Chicago: The University of Chicago Press, 1993), esp. 98–108; Brooke Hindle, *The Pursuit of Science in Revolutionary America* (New York: W.W. Norton, 1974), esp. 320–23.

21. Thomas Jefferson to William Ludlow, September 6, 1824; in Thomas Jefferson, *Writings*, ed. Merrill D. Peterson (New York: Library of America, 1984), 1496–97.

22. Dumas Malone characterizes Jefferson's own movement in *Notes* beyond the formal territorial boundaries of Virginia (at the time by far the largest state in the Confederation) as an "irresistible impulse into the vastness of the West." See Dumas Malone, *Jefferson the Virginian* (New York: Little, Brown, 1948), 378.

23. Berlant is speaking of the nationalizing effects of the tablet held by the Statue of Liberty, on which is inscribed, simply, *JULY IV MDCCLXXVI*. That date names "the space of time that sutures 'the people' and the territory to the 'nation.' I use the term 'suture' deliberately here [Berlant writes], to signify the way in which the national totality does not demand the dissolution of the micro-boundaries of individuals or property

within its border; rather, as is the case with the statue's iconic construction, internal boundaries are conferred on citizens of a geographical and political territory and are legitimated as traces of the nation's sovereignty...." See Lauren Berlant, *The Anatomy of National Fantasy: Hawthorne, Utopia, and Everyday Life* (Chicago: The University of Chicago Press, 1991), 25.

24. Thomas Jefferson, *Notes on the State of Virginia*, 24–25. Throughout his life, Jefferson returned to his personal copy of *Notes* to add handwritten comments. The passage included in parentheses, above, represents one of these later insertions.

25. Thomas Jefferson, *Notes on the State of Virginia*, 25.

26. Richard Slotkin, *Regeneration Through Violence: The Mythology of the American Frontier, 1600–1860* (Middletown, CT: Wesleyan University Press, 1973), 245. For other interpretations of this passage, see Bernard W. Sheehan, *Seeds of Extinction: Jeffersonian Philanthropy and the American Indian* (Chapel Hill: The University of North Carolina Press, 1973), 91–92; Charles A. Miller, *Jefferson and Nature: An Interpretation*, 105–6.

27. Thomas Jefferson to John Melish, December 10, 1814, *Catalogue of the Library of Thomas Jefferson*, ed. E. Millicent Sowerby (Charlottesville: University Press of Virginia, 1983), 4:328.

28. Jay Fliegelman, *Declaring Independence: Jefferson, Natural Language, and the Culture of Performance* (Stanford: Stanford University Press, 1993), 152.

29. Thomas Jefferson to James Madison, September 6, 1789, *Papers*, ed. Julian P. Boyd, 15:392–98 *passim*.

30. Susan Manning, "Naming of Parts; or, The Comforts of Classification: Thomas Jefferson's Construction of America as Fact and Myth," 364.

31. Thomas Jefferson, *Notes on the State of Virginia*, 43.

32. Quoted in Thomas Jefferson, *Notes on the State of Virginia*, 58 *passim*.

33. Thomas Jefferson, *Notes on the State of Virginia*, 59–63.

34. Thomas Jefferson, *Notes on the State of Virginia*, 62.

35. Myra Jehlen, *American Incarnation: The Individual, the Nation, and the Continent*, 48.

36. Myra Jehlen, *American Incarnation: The Individual, the Nation, and the Continent*, 56.

37. Thomas Jefferson, *Notes on the State of Virginia*, 103–7. For a detailed treatment of Jefferson's anthropological investigations of native peoples, see Anthony F.C. Wallace, *Jefferson and the Indians: The Tragic Fate of the First Americans* (Cambridge, MA: Belknap, 1999).

38. Thomas Jefferson, *Notes on the State of Virginia*, 100.

39. Thomas Jefferson, *Notes on the State of Virginia*, 101.

40. Thomas Jefferson, *Notes on the State of Virginia*, 101.

41. Thomas Jefferson, *Notes on the State of Virginia*, 102.

42. Thomas Jefferson, *Notes on the State of Virginia*, 102.

43. Thomas Jefferson, *Notes on the State of Virginia*, 102. Jefferson's notion of Native autochthony stands in sharp contrast to popular, scholarly, and scientific discussions of Indians' origins that date to the Jeffersonian era and the years immediately preceding it. Indeed, these discussions tended to posit as the distant ancestors of American Indians a wide variety of peoples including lost tribes of Jews, Greeks, and Welshmen. Most prominent, however, was the theory that Indians' progenitors had migrated across an (as yet undiscovered) land bridge from Asia. Quite against the grain of many of his contemporaries who posited the Asian origins of American Natives, Jefferson argues in *Notes* for a reversal of the migratory direction, suggesting that American Natives were of far more ancient provenance than their Asian counterparts and hence were more likely to be their ancestors than their descendents. See *Notes on the State of Virginia*, 100–2; see also Bernard W. Sheehan, *Seeds of Extinction: Jeffersonian Philanthropy and the American Indian*, esp. Chapter Two.

44. John Adams to Thomas Jefferson, May 21, 1812, in *The Adams-Jefferson Letters*, ed. Lester J. Cappon (New York: Simon and Schuster, 1971), II:305.

45. Thomas Jefferson to John Adams, June 11, 1812, in *The Adams-Jefferson Letters*, II:307.

46. Jay Fliegelman, *Declaring Independence*, 98–99.

47. "Jefferson to the Osages," *Letters of the Lewis and Clark Expedition, with Related Documents, 1783–1854*, ed. Donald Jackson (Urbana, IL: University of Illinois Press, 1978), I:200; see also, I:280–83, I:284–89.

48. Thomas Jefferson, *The Writings of Thomas Jefferson*, ed. Merrill Peterson (New York: Library of America, 1984), 561. There is good reason to believe that Jefferson considered the Cherokees, and several other tribes, to have taken his advice. Six years later, in a letter to John Adams, Jefferson observed that the Cherokees and the Creeks were "far advanced in civilisation. They have good Cabins, inclosed fields, large herds of cattle and hogs, spin and weave their own clothes of cotton, have smiths and other of the most necessary tradesmen, write and read, are on the increase in numbers, and a branch of the Cherokees is now instituting a regular representative government." See Thomas Jefferson to John Adams, June 11, 1812, *The Adams-Jefferson Letters*, II:307.

49. The term "cultural obstinacy" is from Joyce Appleby, "Introduction: Jefferson and His Complex Legacy," *Jeffersonian Legacies*, ed. Peter S. Onuf (Charlottesville: University Press of Virginia, 1993), 1–16. See also Thomas Jefferson to John Adams, June 11, 1812, *The Adams-Jefferson Letters*, II:307–8.

50. Bernard W. Sheehan, *Seeds of Extinction*, 12.

51. Michael Paul Rogin, *Fathers and Children: Andrew Jackson and the Subjugation of the American Indian* (New Bruswick: Transaction, 1995). See also Susan Scheckel,

The Insistence of the Indian: Race and Nationalism in Nineteenth-Century American Culture (Princeton: Princeton University Press, 1998); Michael Rogin, *Ronald Reagan, The Movie, and Other Episodes in Political Demonology* (Berkeley: University of California Press, 1987), Chapters Two and Five; Richard Slotkin, *Regeneration Through Violence.*

52. Benedict Anderson, *Imagined Communities: Reflections on the Origin and Spread of Nationalism*, 49–50. Emphasis added by Anderson.

53. Benedict Anderson, *Imagined Communities: Reflections on the Origin and Spread of Nationalism*, 145.

54. Benedict Anderson, *Imagined Communities: Reflections on the Origin and Spread of Nationalism*, 145.

55. Werner Sollors, *Beyond Ethnicity: Consent and Descent in American Culture* (New York: Oxford University Press, 1986), 124.

56. Joseph E. Lowndes, "The Discourse of Antistatism in the Post-Civil Rights Era: Forrest Carter and *The Outlaw Josey Wales*," paper presented at the annual meeting of the American Political Science Association, September 2–5, 1999, 12.

57. Thomas Jefferson, *Notes on the State of Virginia*, 151.

58. The literature here is extensive. For the classic discussion, see Winthrop D. Jordan, *White Over Black: American Attitudes Toward the Negro, 1550–1812* (Chapel Hill: The University of North Carolina Press, 1968), Chapter Twelve. See also: Paul Finkelman, *Slavery and the Founders: Race and Liberty in the Age of Jefferson* (Armonk, NY: M.E. Sharpe, 1995); Frank Shuffelton, "Thomas Jefferson: Race, Culture, and the Failure of Anthropological Method," *A Mixed Race: Ethnicity in Early America*, ed. Frank Shuffelton (New York: Oxford University Press, 1993); *Jeffersonian Legacies*, ed. Peter S. Onuf (Charlottesville: University Press of Virginia, 1993); William D. Richardson, "Thomas Jefferson & Race: The Declaration & *Notes on the State of Virginia*," *Polity* 16:3 (Spring 1984), 447–66; Chester E. Miller, *The Wolf by the Ears: Thomas Jefferson and Slavery* (New York: Free Press, 1977); Fawn M. Brodie, *Thomas Jefferson: An Intimate History* (New York: W.W. Norton, 1973).

59. Jefferson's condemnation of slavery, included in his original draft of the Declaration, was struck out by Congress well before the document was approved and signed. See "The Declaration of Independence as originally reported to Congress" in Jay Fliegelman, *Declaring Independence*, 206.

60. Jefferson meant, of course, "our" *white* people. See Thomas Jefferson, *Notes on the State of Virginia*, Query XVIII, 162–63.

61. See Paul Finkelman, "Jefferson and Slavery: 'Treason Against the Hopes of the World'," *Jeffersonian Legacies*, esp. 196–97.

62. Thomas Jefferson, *Notes on the State of Virginia*, 137–38.

63. Thomas Jefferson, *Notes on the State of Virginia*, 138.

64. Thomas Jefferson to St. George Tucker, August 28, 1797, *The Writings of Thomas Jefferson*, ed. Paul Leicester Ford (New York: G.P. Putnam's Sons, 1896), VII: 168.

65. Thomas Jefferson, *Notes on the State of Virginia*, 85.

66. Thomas Jefferson, *Notes on the State of Virginia*, 139.

67. Thomas Jefferson, *Notes on the State of Virginia*, 82.

68. Thomas Jefferson, *Notes on the State of Virginia*, 139.

69. Thomas Jefferson, *Notes on the State of Virginia*, 143.

70. As Winthrop Jordan has argued, in the end even Jefferson's own efforts to recognize blacks' achievements seem to convince him only of their shortcomings. "No body wishes more than I do to see such proofs as you exhibit," he wrote to Benjamin Banneker in 1791, "that nature has given to our black brethren, talents equal to those of the other colors of men, and that the appearance of a want of them is owing merely to the degraded condition of their existence, both in Africa and America." Echoing this letter in 1809, he wrote to thank the Abbé Henri Gregoire for having passed along a book celebrating blacks' achievements: "[N]o person living wishes more sincerely than I do, to see a complete refutation of the doubts I have myself entertained and expressed on the grade of understanding allotted to [Negroes] by nature, and to find that in this respect they are on a par with ourselves." But some months later, he indicated to Joel Barlow that he had proffered a "very soft answer" in response to Gregoire's offering, insisting upon the counter-evidence of "what we know ourselves of Banneker." "We know he had spherical trigonometry enough to make almanacs, but not without the suspicion of aid from Ellicot, who was his neighbor and friend, and never missed an opportunity of puffing him. I have a very long letter from Banneker, which shows him to have had a mind of very common stature indeed." Similarly in *Notes*, Jefferson dismissed the poetry of Phyllis Wheatley and Ignacio Sancho as exhibitions not of the art of intellect but that of sentiment: Wheatley's work, he writes, is "beneath the dignity of criticism," and Sancho's "subjects should often have led him to a process of sober reasoning; yet we find him always substituting sentiment for demonstration." For a more detailed discussion, see Winthrop D. Jordan, *White Over Black: American Attitudes Toward the Negro, 1550–1812*, Chapter Twelve. Passages quoted above can be found in Thomas Jefferson to Benjamin Banneker, August 30, 1791 in *Papers*, eds. Julian P. Boyd et al., 22:97–98; Thomas Jefferson to Henri Gregoire, February 25, 1809, *Writings*, ed. Merrill D. Peterson, 1202; Thomas Jefferson to Joel Barlow, October 8, 1809, reprinted in *Notes on the State of Virginia*, ed. Frank Shuffelton, 279–80; Thomas Jefferson, *Notes on the State of Virginia*, 140–41.

71. Thomas Jefferson, *Notes on the State of Virginia*, 140, 142.

72. Renata Salecl, *The Spoils of Freedom: Psychoanalysis and Feminism After the Fall*

of Socialism (New York: Routledge, 1994), 12. See also Etienne Balibar, "Is There a 'Neo-Racism?'" *Race, Nation, Class: Ambiguous Identities*, eds. Etienne Balibar and Immanuel Wallerstein (London: Verso, 1991), 17–28.

73. Thomas Jefferson, *Notes on the State of Virginia*, 140.

74. Thomas Jefferson, *Notes on the State of Virginia*, 143.

75. Paul Finkelman, "Jefferson and Slavery: 'Treason Against the Hopes of the World'," *Jeffersonian Legacies*, ed. Peter S. Onuf (Charlottesville: University of Virginia Press, 1993), 195. See also John Chester Miller, *The Wolf by the Ears: Thomas Jefferson and Slavery*, 64.

76. Thomas Jefferson, *Notes on the State of Virginia*, 138.

77. For a brief account of the somewhat tangled publication history of *Notes*, and of the Jefferson-Fry map as well as its later revision, see Coolie Verner, *A Further Checklist of the Separate Editions of Jefferson's Notes on the State of Virginia* (Charlottesville: Bibliographical Society of the University of Virginia, 1950). See also the "Introduction" by William Peden in Thomas Jefferson, *Notes on the State of Virginia* (New York: Norton, 1972), esp. xv–xxi; Dumas Malone, *Jefferson the Virginian* (New York: Little, Brown, 1948), esp. 22–26.

78. See *The Fry & Jefferson Map of Virginia and Maryland* (Princeton: Princeton University Press, 1950). For details about Thomas Jefferson's revisions of the Fry and Jefferson map, see Coolie Verner, "Mr. Jefferson Makes a Map," *Imago Mundi* 14 (1959), 96–108. The clearest reproduction of Jefferson's 1786 map is the one enclosed in Thomas Jefferson, *Writings*, ed. Merrill D. Peterson (New York: Library of America, 1984).

79. Thongchai Winichakul, *Siam Mapped: A History of the Geo-Body of a Nation* (Honolulu: University of Hawaii Press, 1994), 130.

80. My language draws on Mark Reinhardt, *The Art of Being Free: Taking Liberties with Tocqueville, Marx, and Arendt* (Ithaca: Cornell University Press, 1997), 23.

81. Benedict Anderson, *Imagined Communities* (2nd edition), Chapter 10. For further discussion about the increasing reliance on maps by states in early modern Europe, see *Monarchy, Ministers, and Maps: The Emergence of Cartography as a Tool of Government in Early Modern Europe*, ed. David Buisseret (Chicago: The University of Chicago Press, 1992).

82. With respect to the problem of attempting to chart the western territory, for example, the Fry and Jefferson map depicts the continuation of mountain ranges beyond Virginia's western boundaries, then shows a virtually empty territory beyond, empty space broken now and then by rivers and the occasional mountain. Along the far western edge of the map is the indication of "Branches of the Mississippi River" running on a north-south axis between Lake Erie to the north and the westernmost boundary of

North Carolina to the south. Just below the area marked off as Lake Erie, the map offers the following disclaimer: "Maps differ much in the Longitude and Latitude of the Lakes, and wether [sic] Lake Erie in this Map is in its proper Situation or not must be left to further Discoveries."

83. At the time of the publication of *Notes*, cartography had only recently ascended to the status of science. For some time previously, the efforts of cartographers had been vexed by two critical gaps in knowledge: first, by the existence of vast territories not yet discovered by Europeans; these significant topographic discontinuities could be included only speculatively, if at all, on maps and charts, and were often indicated by drawings of sea-monsters or strangely-shaped human forms; and second, by the inability to calculate longitude in precise terms. If the age of exploration helped to fill the gaps in European geographic knowledge of the world, it took the invention of the chronometer by John Harrison in 1761 to establish the precise locations of topographic landmarks. For further discussion of the technological aspects of measuring longitude, see David S. Landes, *Revolution in Time: Clocks and the Making of the Modern World* (Cambridge: Harvard University Press, 1983), Chapter 9. For more on surveying in the American colonies, see Brooke Hindle, *The Pursuit of Science in Revolutionary America, 1735–1789* (New York: W.W. Norton, 1974), esp. Chapter 9.

84. Jefferson's committee recommended the establishment of 14 new states, though this number appeared only in private communications and was never formally specified in the Ordinance itself. The Ordinance was never implemented, however, for it was officially repealed by the Northwest Ordinance (approved in July 1787), which nonetheless borrowed extensively from its predecessor. See "Report of the Committee, 1 Mch. 1784," *The Papers of Thomas Jefferson*, ed. Julian P. Boyd (Princeton: Princeton University Press, 1952), vol. 6, 603–617, as well as the extended "Editorial Note" that precedes it on 571–600. See also Robert F. Berkhofer, Jr., "Jefferson, the Ordinance of 1784, and the Origins of the American Territorial System," *William & Mary Quarterly*, 3rd series, vol. XXIX, no. 2 (April 1972), 231–62; Peter S. Onuf, *Statehood and Union: A History of the Northwest Ordinance* (Bloomington: Indiana University Press, 1987).

85. The boundaries drawn between new and established states and indicated on Jefferson's map were a matter of considerable controversy at the time, for they required that Virginia cede its territorial claims to the trans-Appalachian west. Virginia's cession of claims on this land was accomplished in February 1784. For further detail, see Robert J. Berkhofer, Jr., "Jefferson, the Ordinance of 1784, and the Origins of the American Territorial System," 231–262.

86. Walter Benjamin, *Illuminations*, 261.

87. Bruce Burgett, *Sentimental Bodies: Sex, Gender, and Citizenship in the Early Republic* (Princeton: Princeton University Press, 1998), 15. Emphasis in original.

88. Judith N. Shklar, "Democracy and the Past: Jefferson and His Heirs," *Redeeming American Political Thought*, ed. Stanley Hoffman and Dennis F. Thompsaon (Chicago: The University of Chicago Press, 1998), 174.

89. Lauren Berlant, *The Queen of America Goes to Washington City: Essays on Sex and Citizenship* (Durham, NC: Duke University Press, 1997), 36.

90. Frances Wright, *Views of Society and Manners in America*, ed. Paul R. Baker (Cambridge: Harvard University Press, 1963), 13.

91. Frances Wright, *Views of Society and Manners in America*, 48–49.

92. This is similar, I think, to the process Benedict Anderson calls the "logoization" of national territories through the practice of producing "maps" of those territories that detach them from all geographic context. If this process began in the innocent practice of imperial states' marking their colonies on world maps with the same color, it created a "jigsaw effect" by which "each colony appeared like a detachable piece of a jigsaw puzzle"; once normalized, colonies "could be wholly detached from . . . geographic context," Anderson writes. "In its final form, all explanatory glosses could be summarily removed: lines of longitude and latitude, place names, signs for rivers, seas, and mountains, *neighbours*." This accomplished, the shape of a territory had been transformed into a pure sign, "an infinitely reproducible series, available for transfer to posters, official seals, letterheads, magazine and textbook covers, tablecloths, and hotel walls." Benedict Anderson, *Imagined Communities*, 175.

93. *New-Harmony Gazette*, 3:34 (June 18, 1828), 271. Emphasis in original.

94. *New-Harmony Gazette*, 3:34 (June 18, 1828), 271. Emphasis in original.

95. Frances Wright, *Views of Society and Manners in America*, 42.

96. *New-Harmony Gazette*, 3:17 (February 6, 1828), 133. Emphasis in original.

3

Becoming Unnatural:
The Federalist's Techniques of Government

> There is wildness in the world that exceeds the wish of humanity either to moralize or master it.
>
> William E. Connolly[1]

FOR THE MODERN IMAGINATION, GOVERNMENT IS A DECIDEDLY UNNATURAL enterprise. It is an effort to organize what is given to us in and by the past, to assert the power of human will over unthinking, perhaps unthinkable, forces. Insofar as it is one aim of modern political thought to imagine and produce structures, procedures, and institutions of government, modern political thinking relies on a distinction between what is fabricated (and fabricated by design) and what is not: shall we call this latter *nature*? If I hesitate before this term, it is because by the start of the twenty-first century our relationship to nature is already too complex to invoke or understand it simply, for nature has become so overinvested with meaning as to be suspicious (at best) and meaningless (at worst). In recent decades, the concept of nature has been mobilized by both the Right and the Left to justify inescapably political visions. The invocation of a language of nature serves to obscure the political forces at work in these visions and to give them a sense of inevitability and even divine sanction. This mobilization of nature as politics, however, is not new, and as we saw in the last chapter, neither is the ambivalence that accompanies it. This is part of the complex legacy of Jeffersonian politics. Joyce Appleby puts it this way: "Jefferson's framing of an American political creed is largely invisible because he offered his opinions as propositions about nature, and we, his cultural heirs, have so received them."[2] For Jefferson, in *Notes on the State of Virginia*, nature in the form of the American landscape and the bodies of citizens represents an ordered and orderly contingency, the cornerstone of his progressive democratic vision. Yet, as we saw, there are moments in *Notes* when Jefferson's best efforts to marshall nature as a foundation for the new nation encounters a nature (both landscape and bodies) that defies consolidation.

It is just this sense of the uncontainable power of nature that prompts Arendt to insist upon a foundational and inviolable distinction between the natural world and the political one. Such a distinction can be enabling, of course, for it helps us to make the world manageable, to relinquish delusions of infinite human mastery, and to focus on those places and those moments where human action can be directed, productively and creatively. Indeed, the distinction between nature and politics, culture, or history (whichever one prefers) makes a certain kind of sovereign governance possible by cutting into, and cutting off, the potential for chaos, those wild and unmanageable forces that threaten both to undercut and to overrun political life. It is also this division of the world that fosters what Jane Bennett, modifying Foucault's term for emphasis, calls "govern-mentality," the political mobilization of rationalized knowledge about what lies within, and what outside, the competence of the state, and the disciplinary power that accompanies this mobilization.[3] Developed with the most benign of objectives, that of ensuring the well-being of citizen-subjects and of generating and optimizing forces that Foucault calls "life" or "bio-power,"[4] the techniques of governmental rationality carry within them a policing function that disciplines citizen-subjects even as it enables and empowers their actions.[5]

This chapter examines the political operation of governmentality in the political thought of the early Republic, specifically, the conceptual place of the body within the languages of citizenship developed during the revolution and after, in the debates circulating around the adoption of the Constitution of 1787. The question of the citizen's body forms a persistent theme that cuts across a broad range of identifiable political positions. I explore this place of the body in the political imagination of the early Republic by reference to three metaphors—the closet, the boudoir, and the veil—all drawn from the political literature of the era. Each of these metaphors expresses a particular relation between politics and the body. Moreover, each, in its own way, treats the body as an archaism, a remnant of the prepolitical past in some cases and of the pre-Constitutional past in others, though always one with important political consequences. In the context of the 1787 Constitution, the project of governmental rationality involved a deliberate turn away from other, roughly contemporary efforts to develop forms of self-governance that would express or cultivate a natural American order. Accordingly, the governmentalist project in the United States effected an important shift in the meanings attributed to the citizen's body: while the body continued to represent the past in some sense, this past came to be seen as an explicitly historical and political—not a natural—one, a past associated by advocates of the federal Constitution with the localist republicanism of the immediate postrevolutionary years that they sought to overcome, and whose competing political enthusiasms they sought to contain within American institutions. By doing so, supporters of the new constitution developed a technique of national government that produced an important, though often misrecognized, language of American citizenship that I call aggregate universalism.

A distinctly American feudalism

In his account of the adoption of the American Constitution, Sheldon Wolin poses a direct challenge to the Tocquevillian-Hartzian orthodoxy that America's distinctive political and constitutional development follows from the absence of a feudal past. Wolin argues that America does have a feudal tradition, and that unlike the French Revolution, the American Revolution "was in its political theories importantly a revolution for, not against, feudalism."[6] If the feudal tendencies of the Revolution have been lost to students of American political thought, Wolin argues, this is due largely to two factors: first, American feudalism (like feudalism more generally) was never fully or coherently articulated by those who promoted it; and second, American feudalism was almost immediately overthrown by a second American revolution, that of the federal Constitution of 1787.

Wolin's case for the feudalist impulses of the first American Revolution rests not on the existence in America of conventional markers of feudal social organization (a system of land tenure, relations of protection and obligation between landowner and vassal, or a regime of inherited privilege and social status), but instead on a conception of political power that was polycentric and local, which placed a premium on the distinct political cultures present in each of the thirteen discrete colonial administrations. As Wolin points out, the opposition to British rule expressed by the generation of 1776 was characterized by repeated challenges to the centralization of power, rule from a distance, and the uniformizing tendencies of administrative governance. The support for "the dispersion of power among several centers," institutionalized later in the Articles of Confederation, "forms a striking contrast with the [Crown's] imperial emphasis upon unity and centered administration."[7] American Revolutionaries thus promoted a set of principles that, in contesting the legitimacy of the British Crown, reiterated and transformed a loose assemblage of feudalist and democratic political commitments, emphasizing the valuable diversity of local institutions and advocating a political form that vested political power in the periphery rather than a strong central state, "a unique compound of democratic and feudal elements which later reappeared in the antifederalist opposition to the Philadelphia constitution."[8]

If Wolin is right, then American political development is to be explained not by the absence of a feudal experience, but by its comparatively expeditious suppression. He identifies this suppression in a complex of historical forces and related epistemological shifts. The feudal-republican enterprise of the Revolution produced an internally unstable amalgam of competing political tendencies. It could not "jell into a coherent theory, primarily because there was no available theoretical language to give adequate expression to a distinctive blend of ideas that seemed at once progressive in the Enlightenment sense of emphasizing individual rights, responsible government, rule of law, and a certain formal equality, and, at the same time, regressive in the sense of emphasizing the values of place, local interests, and local arrangements while defending the status of local notables."[9] The events that brought to light the institutional inadequacies of the Articles of Confederation, together with a commensurate reaffirmation of centralized power and the need for political unification by proponents of the 1787 Constitution, brought about a second revolution in both political thinking and institutional form. Simply put, the feudal-republican advocates of localism and decentralized government had no alternative that cohered as powerfully, cogently, and rationally as did the argument outlined in *The Federalist Papers.*

Wolin argues that *The Federalist*'s case for the Constitution of 1787 effectively overthrew the premises of this distinctly American feudalism by instituting a new political grammar that conflated theory with generalization. In his terms, *pluris*—the ability to speak of and for the many—is overthrown by the principle of *unum*—a unifying Reason that conceives of the people as one, "a unified people whose oneness would for the immediate future be represented by the state."[10] In consequence, he writes, subsequent thinkers and political actors "who would theorize [difference and diversity] are put in the paradoxical position of seeking to generalize about difference, of trying to make a theory about exceptions, local idiosyncracies, regional differences."[11] Yet if the epistemological conflation of theory with generalization effectively suppressed the political justification for decentralization and the diversity of local institutions, it did not—indeed, could not—entirely remove difference from the American political landscape. However complicated the effort, and however seemingly incoherent the formulation may be, the case for *pluris* nonetheless continues to be articulated and refashioned, repeatedly and insistently, for as Wolin puts it, "American history, especially the history of the present, is a story of differences. It is a history that suggests that the true archaism is . . . [the] myth of a single people and a single narrative."[12]

Wolin's analysis, almost heretical in its departure from conventional conclusions about the liberal-republican character of the 1776 Revolution, can help us make sense of a whole variety of Revolutionary-era social and cultural tendencies that otherwise seem to sit uncomfortably in an interpretive framework that sees the 1787 Constitution as effecting a significant institutional transformation of American government, but only extending and expanding the ideals of the Revolution itself.

The citizen of the closet

In his work on the construction of a public sphere in eighteenth-century America, Michael Warner suggests that the complex reference point that we call "the public" is brought into being, at least in part, through a transformed and transformational understanding of print media. In print—newspapers, pamphlets, novels—authors surrendered their thoughts and ideas to an audience that was unknown to them, a readership that "was by definition indefinite." This anonymity of audience also fostered an increased appreciation on the part of essayists and pamphleteers of the ways that print media enabled them to engage their readers pseudonymously. Speaking as (personally) disinterested parties to public life, writers from Poor Richard to Publius flourished in an atmosphere that Warner calls a "utopia of self-abstraction" that would "allow people to transcend the given realities of their bodies and their status."[13] Yet as Warner notes, American public life in that period—as in our own—was also shaped by a complex set of countertendencies suspicious of this capacity of publicity "to alter or refract the individual's character and status," and viewed with concern its potentially distorting and corrupting influence on individual citizens. "The republican notion of virtue, for example, was designed exactly to avoid any rupture of self-difference between ordinary life and publicity," Warner writes. "The republican," therefore, "was to be the same as citizen and as man. He was to maintain continuity of value, judgment, and reputation from domestic economy to affairs of public nature. And lesser subjects—noncitizens such as women, children, and the poor—were equally to maintain continuity across both realms."[14] What Warner's analysis captures is the sense in which the early years of the republic witnessed a heightened tension between two competing models of the relation between the person and the citizen, between private and public life, between local and national life, and between household and commercial life. Indeed, this tension came to structure public conversations about the nature of national citizenship, and the question of how to preclude the development of ruptures between private and public, between nature and culture, and *within* individual subject-citizens formed an important preoccupation of Revolutionary-era republicans.

The republican emphasis on the continuity of self also placed a premium on the local institutions and forms of self-governance that fostered continuity and self-identity. This ontology of citizenship took a variety of forms. In 1774, Charity Clarke, a young woman from New York, explained in a letter to her British cousin that she was striving to *feel* "Nationly." After several generations of living as British colonials in America, she suggested, it was time for colonists to cultivate self-rule in order that they might "retire beyond the reach of arbitrary power, cloathed with the work of our own hands, & feeding on what the country affords." Clarke's vision of independence is achieved by virtue of an imagined organic link between the land and the people who work it, who cultivate and consume American resources and who are not, therefore, simply residents of a territory, but Americans formed *of America* so deeply and profoundly that they experience the nation as sentiment, as an integral component of their emotional lives.[15] Products of their own cultivation—not simply pastoral agrarians, but physically- and psychically-autochthonous embodiments of the land itself—Clarke imagines that Americans might thus remain innocent of British influence by conceptualizing monarchy as an unnecessary garment that can simply be removed from the American body: "the arms that supports [sic] my family shall defend it, though this body is not clad with silken garments, these limbs are armed with strength."[16]

Where Clarke imagined national sentiment as a current running in and through those formed of the American land, her anxiety about the excess of monarchical trappings that threatened to obscure this homespun Americanness, and distract Americans from their national project, found broader expression in a series of laws that cultivated authenticity by prohibiting public spectacles. Laws banning theatre, gaming, masquerade, and Tea Assemblies proliferated,[17] and editorialists pronounced their disapproval of the ruptures of self-difference produced by elaborate dress: "Country girls in their market carts, and upon their panniered horses [who parade] through our streets with their heads deformed with the plumes of the ostrich and the feathers of other exotick [sic] birds" dangerously blur distinctions between colony and Court, one commentator complained.[18] These efforts to legislate authenticity sought to fasten together in ever tighter bonds of association the private American self, experienced as national sentiment, and the public surfaces of the self visible in the streets, the marketplaces, and other venues of public life. The aim, in short, was to fashion the outer self, the public body, as a direct and unadorned expression of the sentimental individual self, eliminating any activity or form of ornamentation that might refract, obscure, or disguise the intrinsically, even elementally, American nature of republican citizens.[19]

Throughout the Revolution, suspected Tory spies and others believed to be masquerading as Americans while quietly harboring sympathies for the monarchy were subjected to public rituals designed to expose their dissimulations, at least symbolically. In the summer of 1776, Lorenda Holmes of New York smuggled messages to and from members of the King's invading army. Denounced by patriots as "the Damned Tory the penny Post," Holmes was publicly stripped of her clothing by an angry mob.[20] Similarly, the daughters of loyalist Major Allen MacDonald and Flora MacDonald of North Carolina were captured in November 1777 by patriot forces who put "swords into their bosoms, split down their silk dresses, and, taking them out into the yard, stripped them of all their outer clothing."[21] In Connecticut, Walter Bates, the sixteen-year-old son of a loyalist family was questioned by members of the Revolutionary army in regard to his older brothers' political activities. As he described it later, at "ten o'clock at night . . . I was taken out by an armed mob, conveyed through the field gate one mile for the two to back Creek, then having been stripped my body was exposed to the mosquitoes, my hands and feet being confined to a tree near the Salt Marsh, in which situation for two hours time every drop of blood would be drawn from my body. . . ."[22] While examples of the practice abound, the details of the various incidents are less important than the significance of the actions themselves. These exposures serve not only to punish and humiliate, but also to establish an identity between an individual's self and his or her acts, an identity installed in, and disclosed by, one's body once it has been shorn of adornment and artifice. If such acts appear disorderly, their aim is nonetheless to establish order and to do so publicly, through the identification of traitors and the ritual stripping away of the forms of artifice that disguised their political loyalties. If, following Clarke's nationly vision, bodies themselves were the autochthonous products of the cultivation of American soil, then loyalty to the Crown was not only treachery, but an abomination of (American) nature itself.

We might pause here momentarily to ask how Americans cultivated from the land might be anything but authentically American. How could patriots who viewed the body as a sign of American authenticity explain loyalist sympathies in native-born Americans? For some, like the anonymous author of a popular Christian tract of the Revolutionary and early republican eras, the problem was a function of publicity itself. Lives lived too much in public, caught up too much in political matters, became vulnerable to the distance that distinguished the land that gave Americans both life and livelihood from the world in which they lived that life. *The Closet Companion* was "intended to be fixed up in the Christian's usual Place of Retirement, in order to *remind* him of, as well as to *assist* him in the Work" of Christian self-scrutiny.[23] The pamphlet consisted of a litany of leading questions ("Do I really believe that I am a fallen Creature—that I derived from Adam a Nature wholly corrupt, depraved, and sinful—and that I am a Child of Wrath, by Nature, even as others?" "Do I hunger and thirst after Righteousness? Do I pant, and long, and pray to be holy?"),[24] as well as instructions ("Make *Conscience of performing this Duty.*" "*Be impartial,* or you lose your Labour." "Take Care, that you do not *trust* on your Self Examination, rather than on Christ." "Examine yourself *frequently.*"),[25] and warnings about the importance of constant vigilance in the practice of the self ("There is great Danger of being deceived; for every Grace in the Christian has its Counterfeit in the Hypocrite").[26] If the purpose of the instructions, reminders, and rejoinders contained in the pamphlet is to enable readers to come to "know . . . your real State" so as to "*be very serious in the Performance of it,*"[27] the process by which this might be accomplished suggests a series of techniques of intensive self-fashioning that carefully cultivate a self imagined as local, self-contained, self-generating, and perpetually self-identical. For the republican citizen of the closet, American authenticity, like American nature, needed to be carefully cultivated if it was to be marshalled as a political force that would consolidate an independent nation.

What I mean to illustrate by these vignettes is a fairly broad-ranging set of conversations and practices of the Revolutionary and early republican eras that placed a premium on self-unity as a distinctly public good, a means of establishing an unruptured continuity of sentiments, bodies, the household, and local institutions with the land itself. Place and person were to coincide to the degree that no rupture between them could be opened in and through the phenomenon of publicity; to the contrary, publicity became a means of confirming and reaffirming the unity of self and public. From within this ethic of self-continuity, the project of achieving national independence was twinned with, to the point of being indistinguishable from, that of governing the individual self; thus the phrase "self-governance" might be understood, as Joyce Appleby puts it, as a "*double entendre* . . . for which the Revolution was fought."[28] There was both depth and breadth to the republican project of producing self-continuous citizens: it reached vertically from the most superficial decisions about millinery apparel into an individual's most deeply experienced sentiments and sense of self; and it spanned a broad lateral range from the most private recesses of the household to the most public political and commercial spaces.

While the distinctively American feudal-republicanism that Wolin identifies posited sharp discontinuities between and among the thirteen colonies, it also drew upon and fostered a sense of internal coherence, promoting citizenship as an organic unity that connected individuals to themselves, to local institutions, and to the larger web of local political culture. The political problem for the new nation, however, was not simply the self-government of individuals or states, but also the government of the whole; and for the authors of *The Federalist*, the lesson of ten years under the Articles of Confederation was that the organic unity of citizen and locale was, in fact, a serious impediment to national unity. The constitutional solution advocated in the pages of *The Federalist* was to disrupt this continuity between self and place by supplying a new conception of national citizenship, as Wolin puts it, "abstracting the citizen from his local culture and reconstituting him as a new kind of being, one who would be the object of national administration rather than an active subject in local self-government."[29]

This process of abstraction had the effect of separating the public person from the private one, dislocating the citizen from the organic unity of person and place that had been an essential element of republican virtue. In doing so, it established a particular grammar of citizenship as constitutional principle, one that we are wont to refer to in a kind of contemporary shorthand as abstract universalism. In opening a chasm between the citizen and the person, this technique established a relationship of indeterminacy between the two, a relationship that operates at once to consolidate a certain disembodied quality of citizenship and, paradoxically, to produce the body as a complex site of local countermemory.

Abstraction and disembodiment?

Some two centuries after its ratification, a fairly standard interpretation of the 1787 Constitution's techniques of citizenship has emerged. One of the more comprehensive and nuanced of these formulations has been articulated by Lauren Berlant:

> The Constitution's framers constructed the "person" as the unit of political membership in the American nation; in so doing, they did not simply set up the public standard of white male embodiment—technically, in the beginning, property ownership was as much a factor in citizenship as any corporeal schema. Nonetheless, we can see a real attraction of abstract citizenship in the way the citizen conventionally acquires a new body by participation in the political public sphere. The American subject is privileged to suppress the fact of his historical situation in the abstract "person": but then, in return, the nation provides a kind of prophylaxis for the person, as it promises to protect his privileges and his local body in return for loyalty to the state.[30]

The form of liberal democratic equality enshrined by the Constitution, Berlant suggests, operates by suppressing in public life all historical markers of particularity and individuality that in private life distinguish one member of the nation from another. Placing a positive valence on a kind of generic individualism, the American Constitution offers citizens the means to participate equally in the public order on a common ground where, as Michael Warner puts it, "what you say will carry force not because of who you are but despite who you are."[31] There is a certain allure to this unique capacity of citizenship to disincorporate us, to enable us to step aside from our "local bodies," from the sociological facts that structure our lives, and inhabit—if only momentarily—the radically unstructured position of the citizen-subject. When we do so, we do not abandon our bodies altogether so much as we step into a new and different *citizen* body, a new and different subject position supplied by the terms of American constitutional discourse.

This "kind of prophylaxis for the person," or what Warner calls in a similar vein the "prosthetic person" of the citizen,[32] is neither reducible to the private and embodied individual, nor is it a fully disembodied condition. As Berlant points out, a long and creditable tradition of feminist criticism has demonstrated the ways in which the Framers encoded certain implicit (and sometimes even explicit) characteristics into their model of the abstract citizen. These characteristics reflected the sociological markers of the Framers themselves and thus presumed whiteness, maleness, and the qualities imparted by a classical education, among other things.

As Pateman, Landes, MacKinnon, and others have argued, the implicit whiteness and maleness of the original American citizen is thus itself protected by national identity: this is a paradox, because if in practice the liberal public sphere protects and privileges the "person's" racial and gendered embodiment, one effect of these privileges is to appear to be disembodied or abstract while retaining cultural authority. It is under these conditions that what might be an erotics of public life passes for a meritocracy or an order defined by objective mutual interests. The white, male body is the relay to legitimation, but even more than that, the power to suppress the body, to cover its tracks and traces, is the sign of real authority, according to constitutional fashion.

Needless to say, American women and African-Americans have never had the privilege to suppress the body: and thus the "subject-who-wants-to-pass" is the fiercest of juridical self-parodies as yet authored by the American system.[33]

Both the tendency to privilege certain bodies, specifically masculine ones, as "the relay to legitimation," and the power to suppress the body, "to cover its tracks and traces" are indicative of the complicated place of the body in this first constitutional moment. The so-called abstract citizen, in other words, is not disembodied so much as he is reembodied differently, as he moves from the particularized and particularizing private sphere into the more generalized public arena. We see this process at work in a 1776 letter from John Adams to James Sullivan, where Adams pondered the question of how best to specify the broad range of individuals eligible for the suffrage. "Society can be governed only by general rules," he argued. "Government cannot accommodate itself to every particular case as it happens, nor to the circumstances of particular persons. It must establish general comprehensive regulations for cases and persons. The only question is, which general rule will accommodate most cases and most persons." The question of specificity, he warned, "is dangerous to open," for

> there will be no end of it. New claims will arise; women will demand a vote; lads from twelve to twenty-one will think their rights not enough

attended to; and every man who has not a farthing, will demand an equal voice with any other, in all acts of state.[34]

For Adams, the question of specification raised the specter of endless debate about the terms of citizenship, of a politics uncontained, uncontainable, and out of control. In terms of citizenship, the mantle of the general endowed individuals with the authority not only to speak, but to speak comprehensively and independently, to speak and act as citizens rather than as private individuals shaped by private interests and concerns particular to the circumstances of their relatively restricted lives. The important point, however, is that in the end, these general rules reflect the privileges of propertied men, as Adams himself acknowledges at some level. Certainly, the terms most frequently deployed to characterize this move from the specific to the general, and from the individual to the universal—terms like *abstract* and *disembodied*, as in Berlant's analysis above—communicate a sense of the direction and sweep of this mental kinetics of citizenship. I am nonetheless uncertain that such terms quite comprehend the complexity and fleeting materiality of the place of the body, both literal and figurative, in the shift from the local and specific to the universal and general. As it happens, Adams also offers us a detailed and imaginative meditation on this very process, in the movement from, as he put it, the gentleman's boudoir into public life.

The citizen of the boudoir

Some years after the initial publication of his *Defense of the Constitutions of Government of the United States,* John Adams reassessed in a letter to a friend what that work had accomplished. Were he given the opportunity to retitle what his British editor called a "History of Republicks," Adams suggested that he call it "The American Boudoir." The boudoir, or the "pouting room," was a special chamber often found in the homes of the French gentry. As he described it, the boudoir

> is of an octagonal form, twelve or fifteen feet across, or thirty six or forty-five feet round, and all the eight sides, as well as the ceiling over head, are all of the most polished glass mirrors; so that, when a man stands in the centre of the room he sees himself in every direction, multiplied into a row of selfs, as far as the eye can reach. . . . So that persons can see themselves naked in every posture.

To Adams' mind, his book functioned as a sort of boudoir in that it offered an occasion not just for individuals but for the various states, as institutional bodies, to examine themselves "naked in every posture," in their most unadorned stances and circumstances. "Such a Boudoir," he concluded, "is the *Defence*. Our States may see themselves in it, in every possible light, attitude, and movement. They may see all their beauties and all their deformities. Happy they who are made cautious by others' dangers!"[35]

Let me pause here for a moment to consider two possible interpretations of Adams' metaphor of the boudoir, both of which begin by noting the centrality—not the absence—of the gentleman's local body to this meditation and, by extension, the position of the local body with respect to national citizenship more generally. One interpretation might proceed by exploiting the properties and the location of the mirrored room itself.

The boudoir enables individuals to subject themselves to meticulous examination from every possible angle of vision, in order that they might know themselves as fully and complexly as possible. The venue of this self-examination is all important here. The embodied individual that Adams describes undertakes this exhaustive inventory of his own particularities deep within the recesses of the private sphere of the household, in a room devoted primarily to that very purpose. In this light, the boudoir can be viewed as a means for shaping the self-understanding of individuals, for creating the conditions under which it becomes possible for private individuals to act as citizens. This shift—from private individual to public citizen—implies a shift of venue, and indeed, we might understand Adams to be suggesting that having first studied and then integrated their many aspects, individuals are to abandon the boudoir for the larger world.

To the degree that this process of leaving the boudoir enables political action, Adams both lays bare the terms within which action becomes possible and places on display those properties of individuals that he considers to have no place in public life, properties that are excessive, even dangerous, to citizenship and which must be eliminated or overcome as a condition for leaving the boudoir. It is in this sense that Adams' explanation of the more colloquial name for the quarters, the "pouting room," is especially suggestive. He continues the letter:

> When the lady of the house is out of temper, when she is angry, or when she weeps without a cause, she may be locked up in this chamber to pout, and to see in every direction how beautiful she is. There are settees and chairs round the sides and commonly a bath in the centre, which may be made hot or cold.[36]

If there is richness and complexity to be found in the very generality of a liberal-democratic state, for Adams there is also danger lurking within it, taking the form of imbalance, fragmentation, and instability. Adams imagines this danger by feminizing it. Insofar as the activities of individual self-scrutiny and self-fashioning that take place in Adams' boudoir are also metaphors for institutional development on the part of the states, the dangers that Adams perceives in the guise of the lady of the house, and the remedies he suggests for her, have institutional relevance as well. The dangers posed to the household by the lady's indispositions—hazards that justified locking her away in the mirrored chamber—find expression in the state in the form of political fragmentation. In this sense, it might be said that Adams' meditation on the boudoir justifies the conclusion that sexual difference (in his view) has no place in the state except as a source of danger and fragmentation; entering the public realm specifically as citizen means leaving the body and its particularities behind, for insofar as they may be meaningful within the household, they bode ill for the state.

This first interpretation, then, treats the boudoir as a complex metaphor that accomplishes a variety of tasks, one of which is to help Adams envision the resources from private life upon which individual citizens might draw, and to imagine the dangers to the state that are best left behind in the household. This reading helps get at the gender dynamics of the boudoir, but perhaps it is a bit too hasty in its consideration of the properties of the boudoir itself, and in its conclusions about the fate of the citizen's local body. A second interpretation, which I would formulate more as a supplement than an alternative to the first, begins by reconsidering Adams' meditation on the boudoir as a metaphor for the means by which knowledge about both citizens and institutions is acquired and accumulated by the state. In this sense, the imagery Adams calls to mind with his description of the chamber is that of a complex environment for imagining as general both citizens and institutions, an environment where the plural and heterogeneous properties of individual citizens (in their local bodies) could be reflected, refracted, multiplied, and incorporated into the institutions of the state. The medium by which this is to be accomplished is central to the metaphor, for the mirrored room does not simply reflect the qualities of its occupant, but reflects them from eight different lateral directions and from above. Each mirror, moreover, not only reflects but also refracts, bending each reflection and repeating it in an almost endless chain of reflections. Replicating within the state this complex, scopic property of the mirrors, provides Adams' general rules with a panoptic and comprehensive accounting of the object of the law. Doing so is critical, he seems to suggest, if the state is to work as an expansively democratic force in shaping the political public sphere. Ensuring that the law maintain its general sweep requires that political institutions address themselves not to each instance of each reflection, but aggregate them together into a singular and unified, if also complex and multifaceted, whole.

What is critical, and what distinguishes this interpretation from the previous one, is the placement of the citizen's local body with respect to the household as well as to the state: here, the body is by no means left behind in the private sphere, but is a central element of the state's effort to develop democratic institutions that are responsible to a politically and sociologically complex citizenry. The boudoir, then, is more than a device of institutional self-scrutiny and more than an implement of an individual's private circumspection and self-integration (though it is most assuredly both of those things). It is also Adams' proxy for a comprehensive knowledge about citizens and institutions that would be aggregated and generalized in and by the state, as well as an instrument of disciplinary power that orders and empowers citizens, to quote Foucault, through its "concerted distribution of bodies, surfaces, lights, gazes; . . . [it is] an arrangement whose internal mechanisms produce the relation in which individuals are caught up."[37] In the case of the "lady of the house" locked away in the pouting room, the boudoir works equally well as an instrument of disempowerment. Either way, the boudoir represents a disciplinary precursor to the panopticon insofar as "it does not link forces together in order to reduce them; it seeks to bind them together in such a way as to multiply and use them."[38]

My broader point is that even as the Constitution's framers sought to generate a language of citizenship by reference to general principles, the citizen's "local body" was not simply left behind in the move from the household to the public, but instead recharacterized as a central means by which national citizenship itself was imagined and imaginable. This entails a complexity and a degree of materiality that terms like abstraction and disembodiment do not quite capture, even if they do accurately characterize a certain ineffability with which the body comes to occupy the public space of appearance during the era.

Techniques of the general

The effort to comprehend the place and significance of the body in the Framers' strategies of citizenship is facilitated by reference to the array of practices described by Michel Foucault's neologism, *governmentality*. In his later lectures and writings, Foucault turned to the identification and analysis of a new form of political reason that, he maintained, emerged in Europe between the middle of the sixteenth and the end of the eighteenth century, a strategy of governance marked by the development of governmental rationality.[39] Briefly, governmentality entails the elaboration of new ways of thinking about power and population, the relation between states and their citizens. Whereas the central object of a genre of political literature prevalent in classical antiquity and the Middle Ages was the sovereign, his maintenance in power, and his rule over peoples and territories—what Foucault calls "advice to the prince" literature—beginning in the sixteenth century we see the emergence of a new kind of political treatise, a genre concerned not with sovereign rule over a population, not with "imposing law on men, but of disposing things." In these works, Foucault argues, "government is defined as a right manner of disposing things so as to lead not to the form of the common good, as the jurists' texts would have said, but to an end which is 'convenient' for each of the things that are to be governed."[40] This shift from exercising rule over a territory and the people who occupy it to the disposition of things, is premised not so much in the opposition of men and things as in the novel conviction that

> what government has to do with is not territory but rather a sort of complex composed of men and things. The things with which in this sense government is to be concerned are in fact men, but men in their relations, their links, their imbrication with those other things which are wealth, resources, means of subsistence, the territory with its specific qualities, climate, irrigation, fertility, etc.; men in their relation to that other kind of things, customs, habits, ways of acting and thinking, etc.; lastly, men in their relation to that other kind of things, accidents and misfortunes such as famine, epidemics, death, etc.[41]

Critical to the operation of governmental rationality then, are two linked shifts in the scope of rule: the move toward viewing populations as aggregate entities, and thus as objects of government, in and of themselves; and toward viewing these populations as themselves aggregated together with a whole variety of other "things," from territory and natural resources to a "range of intrinsic, aggregate effects" of population itself, large scale environmental, economic, and social phenomena such as epidemics, mortality rates, wealth, and poverty. As Foucault writes:

> The population now represents more the end of government than [does] the power of the sovereign. . . . Interest at the level of the consciousness of each individual who goes to make up the population, and interest

considered as the interest of the population regardless of what the particular interests and aspirations may be of the individuals who compose it, this is the new target and the fundamental instrument of the government of population: the birth of a new art, or at any rate a range of absolutely new tactics and techniques.[42]

The emergence of governmental rationality further entails a subtle but important shift in the tenor of ruling, that is, an increased emphasis on what Foucault calls the pastoral model, elaborated by Western Christianity as the care of souls but also picked up and secularized by the modern state as the care of populations.[43] In this sense, the techniques of governmentality take as their object not the rule of law or exercise of force over a subjugated people, but instead the safeguarding and well-being of a citizenry, the improvement of its living conditions, the enhancement of its wealth, and so on. If elements of the former order, like a concern with the rule of law, are never entirely abandoned by the governmentalist enterprise, they are refigured within it less as a means of exercising the sovereignty of rulers than as techniques for generating and optimizing citizens' capacities for autonomy, self-sufficiency, and political engagement. In this sense, "sovereignty is far from being eliminated by the emergence of a new art of government . . . ; on the contrary, the problem of sovereignty is made more acute than ever" as its seat shifts from the person of the Prince to the collection of persons we call citizens.[44] This is to say that the techniques of governmental rationality carry within them a policing function that disciplines citizen-subjects even as it enables and empowers their actions; the state disciplines not in spite of but by virtue of its capacity to enable and empower, not in spite of its benign objectives but as a function and consequence of them.

In light of this new objective of modern government, danger takes on new importance and new meaning. Minimizing danger, whether that issuing from within the populace or from external forces like competing national states or destructive natural phenomena, was always an object of government. With modernity, however, the apprehension of danger and the minute investigation of its causes and its consequences become the necessary conditions of the pastoral. This new focus on danger on the part of government is accompanied, moreover, by a new appreciation of danger on the part of citizens. More precisely, in Thomas Dumm's words, "in the modern era, danger has been internalized as a behavioral imperative,"[45] so much so that we might say that the internalization of danger is central to the structure of modern citizenship itself.[46]

It is this focus on both the means of enhancing citizens' lives and developing their capacities for self-discipline and self-governance that introduces the need for a fully developed political science, Foucault suggests. Our ability to conceive of a population in the aggregate rests upon the comprehensiveness of our knowledge about it; the task of managing a population necessitates the collection of vast amounts of information, information that not only "records" and describes a population, but also constitutes it, inscribing and ascribing characteristics that are to be known, and thus managed and governed.[47] If, by the late twentieth century, the collection and analysis of census data, public opinion polls, and voting records have virtually transformed this political science into a statistical science,[48] the same impulse inspires John Adams' earlier device of the boudoir. In this respect, Adams' meditation on the American boudoir is but one instance in a much larger conversation surrounding the form of government that would best affiliate and aggregate the various states and citizens in the aftermath of the Revolution. This effort to aggregate together a variety of unlike things into the institutions of a federal state, moreover, involved treating the citizen's local body as a conceptual marker of the past once again, but this time as one that was, importantly, no longer to be thought of as a relic or symbol of America's natural past. The effort to break with a republican model that had positioned the citizen's body as the link between American land and local institutions did not entail the abandonment of the local body altogether, but rather it involved integrating these local bodies within explicitly unnatural, national political institutions. In this sense, the body was resignified by framers of the federal Constitution not as a prepolitical past, but as an eminently political symbol of archaic systems of local governance. Even more than Adams' account, however, it is in the pages of *The Federalist Papers* that we can see what Hamilton called this new "science of politics"[49] at work.

One united people

Alexander Hamilton's introduction to the series of essays published originally in the New York *Independent Journal* over a period of ten months beginning in October 1787, and later collected as *The Federalist Papers*, stresses the world historical significance of the constitutional issues confronting the new American nation. "After an unequivocal experience of the inefficacy of the subsisting federal government," he begins, Americans were being called upon to deliberate about the potential advantages posed by an alternative plan, a Constitution of the United States drawn up and debated at length by delegates to the Constitutional Convention that met in Philadelphia from May to September, 1787. For Hamilton, the proposed Constitution represented something greater than the sum of its parts, something more than a plan for simply (re)organizing a government. It offered Americans the opportunity "by their conduct and example, to decide the important question, whether societies of men are really capable or not of establishing good government from reflection and choice, or whether they are forever destined to depend for their political constitutions on accident and force."[50]

Government by "reflection and choice," as the authors of *The Federalist* go on to make clear, involves both the rationalization and the modernization of politics, counterposing, in the words of Sheldon Wolin, "rationality [against] difference . . . , national power based upon what *The Federalist* called 'the new science of politics' and the 'imbecility' of the constitutional system embodied in decentralized systems."[51] In fact, much of the rhetorical force of *The Federalist* lies in its figuring of the Constitution as the very embodiment of reason and modernization. The recent American past, the nation's preexisting national culture, the Antifederalist opposition, and a whole variety of historical examples both ancient and modern, domestic and foreign, are all identified as archaic remnants of a feudal past. When the authors of *The Federalist* look beyond the confines of the Constitution itself to contemporary political life in America, what they apprehend are the dangers of feudalism.

The Federalist's much-noted search for exemplars on which Founders might model the new American state, in fact, turns up a series of counterexamples, not models for the future so much as lessons of the past.[52] These counterexamples, which include the confederacies of Greek antiquity, as well as the more contemporary Germanic empire and the United Netherlands, all point to sources of instability within the form of Confederation itself. Throughout most of the first twenty essays of *The Federalist*, the apprehension of danger in the American republic, along with the analysis of similar instances of "primitive" confederated governance,[53] comes to shape one of the work's central organizing themes, with impending danger a force around which the authors mobilize their readers. At least in the early essays of *The Federalist*, danger figures as a creative force that renders the strategies of governance of the recent American past archaic. Its pervasiveness in the world prompts the authors to call for the development of new techniques of government: institutions and procedures that would not eliminate or transcend, but integrate and redeploy the perceived sources of danger that shape life in the modern world.

Perhaps most notable among these dangers is that of arbitrary rule by powerful individuals. Whatever the perils posed by foreign governments to the loosely associated states of the Confederation, a "still more alarming" threat is posed by the "domestic factions and convulsions" associated with personalized forms of rule.⁵⁴ The authors of *The Federalist* entertained a deeply pessimistic assessment of human psychology ("men are ambitious, vindictive, and rapacious," warns Hamilton),⁵⁵ and they professed skepticism toward any arrangement of public rule that relies on the goodness, the generosity, or the vigor of individual leadership. Even Hamilton's well-known promotion of the importance of an energetic and singular Executive, for example, vests those qualities in the office rather than the officeholder.⁵⁶ For no matter how strong and powerful the leader (and the authors treat Pericles and Cardinal Wolsey directly, and by inference Louis XIV, the Duke of Marlborough, and Louis XV), none is immune to the frailties of human character, frailties that result in "rivalships and competitions of commerce" that "take their origin entirely in private passions; in the attachments, enmities, interests, hopes, and fears of leading individuals in the communities of which they are members."⁵⁷ However petty and personal they may be, these excitements of momentary passions—of private pique, jealousy, petulancy, personal intrigue, misdirected appetite, and perhaps most significant, the vulnerability of great men to power-hungry women (like Aspasia, the Madame de Maintenon, the Duchess of Marlborough, and Madame de Pompadour)—pose the greatest dangers to the body politic, dangers averted (so *The Federalist* argues) by the development of strong, and common, administrative institutions.

Institutions protect the whole against its most powerful parts—self-interested individuals or organized factions—as well as against hostile external forces. They refine and enlarge public views by articulating questions of common concern impartially, resisting the designs of individuals of factious temper, sinister motive, or local prejudice. Writing in Number Ten, Madison was quite explicit in this regard. For Madison, one of the greatest threats to democratic governance was that posed by the "factious spirit" that "has tainted our public administration" under the Articles of Confederation. How might government best cure the mischiefs of faction, he asks. One option, that of eliminating faction whole cloth by legislating into existence a uniformity of interests and points of view, Madison dismissed as tantamount to tyranny, the abolition of the very liberties essential to political life. Another strategy, eliminating the causes of faction, he viewed as impossible at best. "The inference to which we are brought," then, "is that the *causes* of faction cannot be removed and that relief is only to be sought in the means of controlling its *effects*."⁵⁸ Framing institutions that represent broad and diverse constituencies, he argues, will institutionalize rather than eliminate or criminalize conflict, and the more extensive the constituency—the "greater number of citizens and extent of territory which may be brought within the compass" of representative government, and the "greater [the] variety of parties and interests" aggregated together by representative institutions—the more likely that the danger of any particular faction's gaining power will have been minimized.[59] Political differences are not eliminated, but are veiled, sustained institutionally even as they are rendered less visible, less distinct, and less immediate. The dangers posed by the existence of faction are transformed, redirected as forces that protect and maintain rather than undermine representative government and its constituent subjects.[60]

In this sense, the development of representative institutions encourages us to think of their constituencies in new and more abstract ways, as generalized *and* aggregated populations whose interests institutions are designed to represent. Accordingly, *The Federalist*'s project of institution building not only reconceives the whole, but reconceives it as a force to be studied, guarded, administered, and improved. Hamilton sums this up:

> Who [is] so likely to make suitable provisions for the public defense as that body to which the guardianship of the public safety is confided; which, as the center of information, will best understand the extent and urgency of the dangers that threaten; as the representatives of the WHOLE, will feel itself most deeply interested in the preservation of every part; which, from the responsibility implied in the duty assigned to it, will be most sensibly impressed with the necessity of proper exertions; and which, by the extension of its authority throughout the States, can alone establish uniformity and concert in the plans and measures by which the common safety is to be secured?[61]

In short, strong public institutions are preferable to strong leaders insofar as they take account of the "aggregate interests of the community"[62] and are more likely to remain immune to instability, injustice, and confusion, the "mortal diseases under which popular governments have everywhere perished."[63]

Most notably, perhaps, the development of strong national institutions provides a centralized government with more direct access to citizens themselves, access that was obstructed under the Articles of Confederation by the barrier formed of state governments. "The great and radical vice in the construction of the existing Confederation," Hamilton argues in Number Fifteen, "is in the principle of legislation for states or governments, in their corporate or collective capacities, and as contradistinguished from the individuals of whom they consist."[64] With the exception of the rule of apportionment, he explained, national government under the Articles lacked all means of raising armies or money except through the intermediaries of the states, for there were no national institutions that granted the government of the whole access "to the individual citizens of America."[65] The relative inaccessibility of citizens, Madison argues in Number Twenty, lies at the heart of the "imbecility in the government; discord among the provinces; foreign influence and indignities; a precarious existence in peace, and peculiar calamities from war" exemplified by the political instability of a government like that of the United Netherlands.[66] The experience of that confederation, he concludes, should teach us that "a sovereignty over sovereigns, a government over governments, a legislation for communities, as contradistinguished from individuals, as it is a solecism in theory, so in practice it is subversive of the order and ends of civil polity."[67]

The Federalist's answer to these problems born of polycentric government is that the new Constitution, in Hamilton's words, "must extend the authority of the Union to the persons of the citizens—the only proper objects of government."[68] Curiously enough, what is perhaps most conspicuously absent from the text of the 1787 Constitution itself is precisely these "proper objects of government," the persons of the citizens, who do not really make their appearance, at least not in the form of rights-bearing individuals, until the ratification of the Bill of Rights in 1791. However, this is not to say that citizenship itself disappears from the 1787 Constitution, but rather that citizenship is refigured as membership in an aggregate political entity, a national whole, a citizenry. It is this notion of a citizenry that is both the subject and object of the Constitution, the *We* of "We the People of the United States." In the pages of *The Federalist*, this new understanding of citizenship is perhaps most clearly articulated by John Jay.

"Providence," Jay proclaimed in *Federalist* Number Two, "has been pleased to give this one connected country to one united people—a people descended from the same ancestors, speaking the same language, professing the same religion, attached to the same principles of government, very similar in their manners and customs, and who, by their joint counsels, arms, and efforts, fighting side by side throughout a long and bloody war, have nobly established their general liberty and independence." "This country and this people," Jay concludes, "seem to have been made for each other."[69] Jay's proclamation of national unity is more performative than descriptive, that is, along with the essays that follow, it sets out to accomplish the unification it purports to describe. Yet however much the passage seems to echo Jefferson's concern with linking America and Americans together through the inheritance of a common land from a set of common ancestors, there is nonetheless an important difference between them. Where Jefferson works to supply colonials with a common past on which they might build, Jay and the collective Publius more generally were driven by the conviction that consolidating the nation required a vision of the people as one. The authors of *The Federalist* considered a common patrimony alone to be insufficient ground on which to build a nation. Jay's effort to reshape the American imagination as the basis for a national state, then, does not end with the question of population. To the contrary, his concern with establishing a singular entity governed by a single centralized state proceeds by combining the citizenry together with a broad range of other things that will "ensure the safety of the whole."[70] The success of government depends on its ability to "harmonize, assimilate, and protect the several parts and members" of the nation.[71] "If [foreign governments] see that our national government is efficient and well administered, our trade prudently regulated, our militia properly organized and disciplined, our resources and finances discreetly managed, our credit re-established, our people free, contented, and united, they will be much more disposed to cultivate our friendship than provoke our resentment."[72] It is in this horizontal linking of unlike peoples and things—that is, of political principles and commitments, ancestral history, customs, military capacities, natural resources and productive potential, and practices of trade and financial management—that Jay finds both the necessary mechanism of national unity and an all-important source of political permanence and stability.

In this sense, if there are no citizens *per se* described by *The Federalist*, if that work elaborates no explicit formula of citizenship proper, what it does give us is a principle of the citizenry, a citizenry that is, moreover, sovereign of itself and made so by governmentalist techniques of aggregate universalism that sought to incorporate (rather than eliminate or neuter) the properties of local bodies and local political cultures if only to meld them together into a complex, national whole. What phrase, what passage, what expression of the 1787 Constitution is at once more concrete and yet also more abstract than the subject of its Preamble? "We the People of the United States" is made tangible only by the tasks it assigns to government and the practices by which it accomplishes these tasks: "to form a more perfect Union, establish Justice, insure domestic Tranquility, provide for the common defence, promote the general Welfare, and secure the Blessings of Liberty to ourselves and our Posterity . . . "[73] Insofar as "We the People" describes an abstract sovereign, it is a sovereign produced not so much through processes of abstraction and disembodiment as through the aggregation of unlike things. Accordingly, the particularities of both citizens' local bodies and the local political (and household) cultures that produce them are transformed into resources out of which a new federal order is created.

Particularity is neither transcended nor abandoned but incorporated into the national citizenry itself, and if the outlines and particulars of the individual, local body become less distinct under a language of aggregate citizenship, the citizen's body still forms a central and material, if only fleetingly material, element of the national whole. Citizenship, under the 1787 Constitution, is like a veil thrown over the citizen's body, or more precisely, over an amalgamation of bodies, a veil that obscures as much as it reveals, a veil that like Adams' boudoir, "does not link forces together in order to reduce them, [but] seeks to bind them together in such a way as to multiply and use them."[74]

Though *The Federalist* works to transform political differences from dangers to resources for the national state, difference itself retains dangerous qualities. In the next to last essay of *The Federalist*, Hamilton revisits the question of particularity, its place and its function, within this new science of government. Addressing the concern that the proposed Constitution did not contain any specification of the rights of individual citizens, he argues that the very need for a Bill of Rights is anachronistic, a "primitive signification" having "no application to constitutions professedly founded upon the power of the people and executed by their immediate representatives and servants." "Bills of rights are, in their origin, stipulations between kings and their subjects, abridgments of prerogative in favour of privilege, reservations of rights not surrendered to the prince."[75] Using language that echoes Adams, Hamilton insists that "a minute detail of particular rights is . . . far less applicable to a Constitution like that under consideration, which is merely intended to regulate the general political interests of the nation, than to a constitution which has the regulation of every species of personal and private concerns."[76] In the context of this federal Constitution, he goes on to argue, a bill of rights is "not only unnecessary . . . but would even be dangerous."[77] *The Federalist* ends on a note that recalls its earlier analogy between the problems of (the) Confederation and the dangers of feudalism. However, these problems and dangers have been transferred, now, onto different ground. Where the earlier essays had identified polycentric state-based citizenship as a dangerous relic of the old order, here Hamilton tries to do the same for the concept of individual rights. The problem is that Hamilton's argument in *Federalist* Seventy-Four rests on a sort of rhetorical sleight-of-hand. The demand for individual rights was as much a product of the notion of national citizenship inscribed in the Constitution of 1787 as it was a remnant of Whig political thought, and the danger represented by rights was internal to the new constitutional order itself.[78] If this new form of *pluris* threatens to rend the veil that holds together a diverse citizenry, that danger resides not (simply) in the past, but in the present, a danger that takes the form of heresy.

Wildness is a woman

Good government requires effective institutions, not virtuous citizens: so runs the argument of *The Federalist*. Hannah Arendt puts it this way:

> Here . . . we may find the root of the surprising so-called realism of the Founding Fathers with respect to human nature. They could afford to ignore the French revolutionary proposition that man is good outside society, in some fictitious original state, which, after all, was the proposition of the Age of Enlightenment. They could afford to be realistic and even pessimistic in this matter because they knew that whatever men might be in their singularity, they could bind themselves into a community which, even though it was composed of 'sinners,' need not necessarily reflect this 'sinful' side of human nature.[79]

"Men's baser instincts were more dependable than their better ones," as Paula Baker has written, "hence, the framers made self-interest the basis for government."[80] For Baker, the framing of the Constitution in these terms lays the basis not only for the construction of strong national institutions, but also for the development of a bifurcated culture of politics in America, one that entrusted the cultivation of moral order to women in the household and family, and freed men to act in partisan ways in public and "admit that community divisions existed."[81] Barred from owning property and generally unable to support themselves as *femes soles* outside of the households of their fathers, husbands, or other male relatives, eighteenth-century American women nonetheless managed to gain a degree of influence in public life by promoting the importance of the early education and intellectual development of the nation's next generation of democratic citizens. "Much in this momentous department depends on female *administration*," wrote one advocate of republican motherhood, "and the mother, or the woman to whom she may delegate her office, will imprint on the opening mind, characters, ideas, and conclusions, which time, in all its variety and vicissitudes will never be able to erase."[82] By thus marshalling their case that if the new nation's present lay in the hands of men its future had been consigned to mothers, women won a variety of important institutional concessions, such as the development of women's colleges and the publication of journals and readers designed especially for them.[83]

In Baker's analysis, this gendered division of political labor rests on an unstable foundation of public and private spheres, one that is increasingly breached over time as women's "housekeeping" responsibilities took them beyond the limits of the home into public campaigns for moral reform, most notably prohibition, and for social legislation that ranged from establishing limits on child labor and mandating industrial safety to fostering improved education, nutrition, and safe and adequate housing. By the early decades of the twentieth century, Baker argues, American politics had incorporated the concerns of the domestic sphere, as women's reform movements persuaded elected officials of the need for an activist government that would promote the social welfare of its citizens. At women's behest, she suggests, public bureaucracies effectively took over what had once been women's work of social housekeeping by redefining those matters as concerns of public policy, even as women were being admitted to the domain of partisan politics through the extension of the suffrage.

As a synthetic account of the transformation of American politics from the Founding to the Progressive Era, Baker's analysis has much to recommend it, for it not only grants a central place to the too-often overlooked (quasi)political activities of women, but also shows how concerns once considered to lie outside the responsibility of government eventually came to define its purpose. Baker's account of the process she calls the "domestication of American politics," however, does not quite grasp the complicated place of republican motherhood under the Constitution of 1787. Occupying the interspace between family and politics, republican motherhood both challenges that division and remains caught within it. A close reading of one of the representative texts of republican motherhood—a series of political, social, and moral essays collectively entitled *The Gleaner*—can help us understand not only the unstable division between public and private created by the 1787 Constitution, but also the constitutive instabilities that shaped the very notion of an aggregate citizenry itself. Like Machiavelli's *Fortunà*, which symbolized a threat to the Prince embedded in the order of the world, wildness erupted within the order established by *The Federalist*, indeed, within the very terms it articulated. And like Machiavelli's *Fortunà*, this wildness was a woman.

From 1792 to 1794, the *Massachusetts Magazine* published a series of essays (interspersed with a serialized domestic fiction about the education and rearing of a young girl) written by a pseudonymous Mr. Vigillius. Collected in book form as *The Gleaner* in 1798, the work is dedicated to John Adams and it mobilizes a vigorous defense of the principles embodied by *The Federalist*. Decrying the politics of party, faction, and personal ambition, the essays equate the "lineaments of the constitution of the United States" with "the lineaments of liberty."[84] Yet Vigillius' essays do not simply echo the themes of *The Federalist*, but expand on them by seeking to secure a place for women within the new order. In this respect *The Gleaner* articulates what is probably the most thoroughly worked out statement of the ideology of republican motherhood of the early national era. The problem developed thoughout *The Gleaner* series, as one essay put it, was that although women and men were equally capable of enduring hardship, equally brave, equally patriotic, energetic, eloquent, and equally capable of "supporting, with honour, the toils of government,"[85] women were nevertheless "injudiciously exclude[d]" from "conspicuous rewards of merit."

> To man, the road of preferment is thrown open—glory crowns the military hero—the bar, the pulpit, the medical career, the husbandman, the merchant, the statesman, these all have their *points* of *eminence*; and *virtue, blended with first rate abilities, may conduct their possessor even to the Presidential chair of the United States*. But the sex, agreeably, to existing regulations, can enjoy but *secondary or reflected* fame.[86]

To the end of promoting greater equality between women and men, the essays argued for improved education for girls and for the opening of the professions to them. "Marriage should not be represented as [a daughter's] *sumum bonum*, or as a certain or even necessary event" the essayist advised parents. Rather, "girls should learn to respect a single life, and even to regard it as the *most eligible*, except a warm, mutual, and judicious attachment had gained the ascendency in the bosom."[87]

What makes *The Gleaner* most interesting is neither its straightforward support for constitutional government, nor its elaboration of principles of republican motherhood, but the kind of political acrobatics involved in arguing how and why the governance of *unum* boded especially well for women. For in making his case, Mr. Vigillius quite unintentionally discovered the tensions contained within the aggregate universalist language of citizenship promoted by the 1787 Constitution. In the final essay of the series, entitled "The Gleaner Unmasked: throwing aside the veil," the author explained that the pseudonym "Mr. Vigillius" had been chosen in keeping with the conventions of much of the political writing of the day, to emphasize the importance of speaking generally and generically, as a citizen whose public persona veiled all specifying characteristics. The choice of the name "Mr. Vigillius," the author confessed, did not simply disguise the identity of the writer, but also misled readers as to her gender. In her final *Gleaner* essay, Judith Sargent Murray explained the significance of her choice of pseudonym: "Observing in a variety of instances, the indifference, not to say contempt, with which female productions are regarded, and seeking to arrest attention, at least for a time, I was thus furnished with a very powerful motive." Murray was concerned that her writings be taken seriously as a disinterested and rational assessment of the position of women in the new order: "I was ambitious of being considered *independent as a writer*."[88]

Maintaining independence from partisan interests, elevating reason over prejudice and superstition, and thinking institutionally: these are political values held in common by the authors of both *The Gleaner* and *The Federalist*. Yet if Murray remained close to the content of *The Federalist*, she both followed and departed from its authorial conventions. This was not quite the "utopia of self-abstraction" that Michael Warner describes as flourishing in eighteenth-century America, the convention by which the authors of *The Federalist* signed their work as Publius. Adopting a specifically masculine form of address, *Mr. Vigillius*, Murray seems to suggest that the very effort to speak as citizen was, at some level, to inhabit "the white male body [as] the relay to legitimation."[89] Murray's effort to speak politically on behalf of women might remind us of Lauren Berlant's claim that "'the-subject-who-wants-to-pass' is the fiercest of juridical self-parodies as yet authored by the American system." Yet the real irony of Murray's pseudonym of choice is that it is both invited and disallowed by the structure of a political *We* brought into being through the Constitution's aggregation of unlike things. The invocation of *We* invites individual citizens to locate their local bodies within the aggregate body of the citizenry. This connection is not made in the service of emphasizing particularity, but of establishing the equivalence of citizens *qua* citizens. For Murray, women's claim to equal citizenship rested precisely in making this connection. However, Murray's apprehension of the degree to which, in the early republic, sexual difference did make a difference, places her in the paradoxical position of having to invoke the masculine as a means of claiming the authority of the general. In this respect, *The Gleaner*'s effort to secure a place for women as citizens within the new federal system would seem to constitute a carefully calibrated, if quite unintentional, heresy to *The Federalist*'s program, rending the veil and breaking through *unum*'s delicate fabric.

While Wolin is right, then, to suggest that the techniques of the 1787 Constitution place those who would theorize *pluris* in the "paradoxical position of seeking to generalize about difference," we might add that, at least for women, the effort to articulate the general required the embrace of what was most particular about it. This is to say that in the domain of citizenship, the techniques of aggregate universalism did not eradicate republican demands for self-identical citizens so much as they reformulated them. In this sense, *The Federalist*'s new techniques of government, like the perceived sources of danger that they incorporated and redeployed, were anything but abstract. Quite the contrary:

this new science of politics involved not only a whole variety of disciplinary practices that sought out and ordered the material differences evident among both individual citizens and the various states, but incorporated and contained those differences through the techniques of aggregation. Hamilton's ideal of government established by "reflection and choice" neither abstracts from, nor eliminates, the elements of "accident and force" whose influence *The Federalist* would check; rather, it resituates forces of *pluris* complexly within the body politic in the name of *unum* itself.

For this reason, I suggest that the term "aggregate universalism," rather than "abstract universalism," may characterize more accurately the complicated strategies by which the 1787 Constitution effects its institutionalization of a particular model of citizenship, as well as a particular set of distinctions between reason and accident, order and contingency, government and nature. *The Federalist*'s exhaustive review of internal dangers, of natural and institutional resources available to the new nation, of existing institutional arrangements between and among the various states, as well as its detailed considerations of the ideal ratio of representatives to citizens, of the regulation of elections, and of the powers distinct to the legislative, executive, and judicial branches of government—these are all efforts to establish institutional closure around competing forms and symbols of difference. Becoming a citizen in this complex polity thus entailed becoming unnatural, incorporating within a larger national whole, a national citizenry that was both the subject and object of governmental rationality.

The very act of that incorporation generated contingent forces and energies unanticipated, and certainly unintended, by the authors of *The Federalist*. Judith Sargent Murray's complicated pseudonymous act of passing as a man in order to speak as (ungendered) citizen also suggests this, for what is especially significant about her "throw[ing] aside the veil" in the final essay is both the fact of the disclosure itself, and that the disclosure was not an effort to reveal the falseness or superficiality of the aggregate universalist citizen. As Murray's act of eventual self-identification suggests, the deliberate effort to pass as citizen in keeping with the politics of *unum* produces a new form of desire for public self-disclosure: the confession that one is passing. Murray's confessional identification of the writer behind the pseudonym is not an effort to speak truth to power in the sense of disclosing the truth behind, or the real body within, aggregate universalism. It is an effort to demonstrate her commitment to it, an act of good faith in *unum*, and accordingly, an indication that *unum* itself generates new discourses of *pluris* in ways unforeseen by its architects. In this respect, the effects of *The Federalist*'s techniques of government were decidedly nonsimple, for they not only produced new means of thinking about citizenship as general and of the citizen as an adopted persona that is deliberately self-abstracted, but they also produced new, and newly particularizing, public practices of self-confession. Importantly, these practices fostered new kinds of public discourses of and about *pluris*, emphasizing differences and particularities, as citizens began to speak of the particularities associated with the local body *specifically in their capacity as departicularized citizens*, as Murray did in her *Gleaner* essays.

The politics of *unum* produced a new kind of *pluris*, differences generated by *unum* itself but nevertheless uncontainable within its terms. This is to say, with Connolly, that there is wildness in the world that exceeds even our most strenuous, and well intentioned, efforts to contain, suppress, eliminate, or master it; even as this wildness resonates with connotations that we moderns may tend to associate with *nature*, for the constitutional moment associated with the Constitution of 1787, this wildness is better viewed as a property of *politics*, an unintended by-product of the aggregation of unlike things. *E pluribus unum*.

Endnotes

1. William E. Connolly, *The Augustinian Imperative: A Reflection on the Politics of Morality* (Newbury Park, CA: Sage Publications, 1993), 9.

2. Joyce Appleby, "Introduction: Jefferson and His Complex Legacy," *Jeffersonian Legacies*, ed. Peter S. Onuf (Charlottesville: University Press of Virginia, 1993), 3.

3. Jane Bennett, *Thoreau's Nature: Ethics, Politics, and the Wild* (Thousand Oaks, CA: Sage Publications, 1994), 5. See also Michel Foucault, "Governmentality," *The Foucault Effect: Studies in Governmentality*, eds. Graham Burchell, Colin Gordon, and Peter Miller (Chicago: The University of Chicago Press, 1991).

4. See Michel Foucault, *The History of Sexuality, Volume I: An Introduction* (New York: Vintage, 1980), esp. Part Five. See also Foucault's essay on "Governmentality," cited above.

5. As Peter Euben has put it (albeit in a very different context), "the impulse toward tyranny comes not simply from what is basest in us, but from what is most admirable." Thomas Dumm, too, has demonstrated the "gloomy" effects of governmentality in his work on the disciplinary origins of the United States. See J. Peter Euben, *The Tragedy of Political Theory: The Road Not Taken* (Princeton: Princeton University Press, 1990), 37. Also, Thomas L. Dumm, *Democracy and Punishment: Disciplinary Origins of the United States* (Madison: University of Wisconsin Press, 1987).

6. Sheldon S. Wolin, "*E Pluribus Unum*: The Representation of Difference and the

Reconstitution of Collectivity," *The Presence of the Past: Essays on the State and the Constitution* (Baltimore: The Johns Hopkins University Press, 1989), 128.

7. Sheldon S. Wolin, "*E Pluribus Unum*: The Representation of Difference and the Reconstitution of Collectivity," 130.

8. Sheldon S. Wolin, "*E Pluribus Unum*: The Representation of Difference and the Reconstitution of Collectivity," 129.

9. Sheldon S. Wolin, "*E Pluribus Unum*: The Representation of Difference and the Reconstitution of Collectivity," 132.

10. Sheldon S. Wolin, "*E Pluribus Unum*: The Representation of Difference and the Reconstitution of Collectivity," 128.

11. Sheldon S. Wolin, "*E Pluribus Unum*: The Representation of Difference and the Reconstitution of Collectivity," 136.

12. Sheldon S. Wolin, "*E Pluribus Unum*: The Representation of Difference and the Reconstitution of Collectivity," 136.

13. Michael Warner, "The Mass Public and the Mass Subject," *The Phantom Public Sphere*, ed. Bruce Robbins (Minneapolis: University of Minnesota Press, 1993), esp. 236–38, 239. For an earlier but more extensive analysis, see Michael Warner, *The Letters of the Republic: Publication and the Public Sphere in Eighteenth-Century America* (Cambridge: Harvard University Press, 1990).

14. Michael Warner, "The Mass Public and the Mass Subject," 235.

15. This is very much like a nationalist counterpart of what Bruce Robbins characterizes as "feeling global." See Bruce Robbins, *Feeling Global: Internationalism in Distress* (New York: New York University Press, 1999).

16. Charity Clarke to Joseph Jekyll, November 6, 1768. Quoted in Mary Beth Norton, *Liberty's Daughters: The Revolutionary Experience of American Women, 1750–1800* (Boston: Little, Brown, and Company, 1980), 169.

17. In his later work, Gordon Wood indicates that some colonists went so far as to advocate the enactment of sumptuary laws "to coerce people into living within their ranks." See Gordon S. Wood, *The Radicalism of the American Revolution* (New York: Vintage, 1991), esp. 136. For an example of the eighteenth-century vice laws, the case of Pennsylvania is fairly representative. Pennsylvania's law originally passed in 1779 but was regularly amended and expanded. See *The Statutes at Large of Pennsylvania From 1682 to 1801*, comp. James T. Mitchell and Henry Flanders (Pennsylvania: Wm. Stanley Ray, 1903),vol IX (1776–79), 333–37. For the Pennsylvania act that criminalized masquerade (passed February 15, 1808), see *A Digest of the Laws of Pennsylvania, 1700–1818*, ed. John Purdon (Philadelphia: Philip H. Nicklin, 1818), 430.

18. Quoted in Gordon S. Wood, *The Creation of the American Republic, 1776–1787* (New York: W.W. Norton, 1972), 479.

19. For a hint of the scandal that ensued when none other than George Washington

was spotted, in 1778, in attendance at the theatre (accompanied by the Marquis de Lafayette) on the very day that Congress had passed a resolution recommending that states adopt laws "for the suppression of theatrical amusements," see George C.D. Odell, *Annals of the New York Stage* (New York: AMS Press, 1970), I:195.

20. By her own account, Holmes "received no wounds or bruises from [the crowd] only shame and horror of the mind." The story is recounted in Mary Beth Norton, *Liberty's Daughters: The Revolutionary Experience of American Women, 1750–1800*, 175–76.

21. *The Price of Freedom: Tory Writings from the Revolutionary Era*, ed. Catherine S. Crary (New York: McGraw-Hill, 1973), 51.

22. This incident, and numerous similar ones, are recounted in *The Price of Freedom: Tory Writings from the Revolutionary Era*, 81; also 91, 370.

23. "The Closet Companion" is reprinted in *The Rising Glory of America, 1760–1820*, ed. Gordon S. Wood (New York: George Braziller, 1971), 110–16. All emphasis used here appears in original.

24. "The Closet Companion," 112, 114.

25. "The Closet Companion," 110–11 *passim*.

26. "The Closet Companion," 110.

27. "The Closet Companion," 110.

28. Joyce Appleby, "Introduction: Jefferson and His Complex Legacy," 3.

29. Sheldon S. Wolin, "*E Pluribus Unum*: The Representation of Difference and the Reconstitution of Collectivity," 134. I do not mean to suggest that the institution of new techniques of an explicitly national citizenship put an end to republican practices altogether. Indeed, as William Novak has shown, state and local governments continued to enact and enforce public laws regulating or eliminating private liberty for the common good, in the name of promoting public safety, comfort, welfare, morals, or health. See William J. Novak, *The People's Welfare: Law and Regulation in Nineteenth-Century America* (Chapel Hill: The University of North Carolina Press, 1996).

30. Lauren Berlant, "National Brands / National Body: *Imitation of Life*," *Comparative American Identities: Race, Sex, and Nationality in the Modern Text*, ed. Hortense J. Spillers (New York: Routledge, 1991), 112–13.

31. Michael Warner, "The Mass Public and the Mass Subject," 239.

32. Michael Warner, "The Mass Public and the Mass Subject," 237–38.

33. Lauren Berlant, "National Brands / National Body: *Imitation of Life*," 112–13. See also Carole Pateman, *The Sexual Contract* (Stanford: Stanford University Press, 1988); Joan B. Landes, *Women and the Public Sphere in the Age of the French Revolution* (Ithaca: Cornell University Press, 1988); Catharine A. MacKinnon, *Toward a Feminist Theory of the State* (Cambridge: Harvard University Press, 1989). In addition to those cited by Berlant, a more recent and quite sophisticated account is formulated in Joan

Wallach Scott, *Only Paradoxes to Offer: French Feminists and the Rights of Man* (Cambridge: Harvard University Press, 1996).

34. John Adams to James Sullivan (May 26, 1776), in *The American Enlightenment: The Shaping of the American Experiment and a Free Society*, ed. Adrienne Koch (New York: George Braziller, 1965), 185.

35. John Adams to William Cunningham (January 3, 1809), in *The American Enlightenment*, 209–210.

36. Adams to Cunningham, in *The American Enlightenment*, 209–20. At the time, physicians believed that cold baths helped to bring hysterics to their senses.

37. Michel Foucault, *Discipline & Punish: The Birth of the Prison* (New York: Vintage, 1979), 202.

38. Michel Foucault, *Discipline & Punish: The Birth of the Prison*, 170.

39. It is probably the case that, in recent years, the volume of analytic work examining Foucault's elaboration of governmental rationality has come to exceed his own published work on the question. See essays and interviews by Foucault and others collected in *The Foucault Effect: Studies in Governmentality*, eds. Graham Burchell, Colin Gordon, and Peter Miller (Chicago: The University of Chicago Press, 1991). Also *The Later Foucault: Politics and Philosophy*, ed. Jeremy Moss (Thousand Oaks, CA: Sage Publications, 1998); *Foucault and Political Reason: Liberalism, Neo-liberalism, and Rationalities of Government*, eds. Andrew Barry, Thomas Osborne, and Nikolas Rose (Chicago: The University of Chicago Press, 1996). Most recently, Barbara Cruikshank's *The Will to Empower* stands not simply as an elaboration of, and inquiry into, the implications of governmentality, but as an examination of the various strategies of governmental rationality at work in contemporary welfare rights struggles, philanthropic self-help schemes, and the promotion of "self-esteem." See Barbara Cruikshank, *The Will to Empower: Democratic Citizens and Other Subjects* (Ithaca: Cornell University Press, 1999).

40. Michel Foucault, "Governmentality," 95.

41. Michel Foucault, "Governmentality," 93.

42. Michel Foucault, "Governmentality," 99, 100.

43. See Colin Gordon, "Governmental Rationality: An Introduction," *The Foucault Effect*, esp. 8–14; also Michel Foucault, "Governmentality," 87–104.

44. Michel Foucault, "Governmentality," 101.

45. Thomas L. Dumm, *Democracy and Punishment: Disciplinary Origins of the United States,* 8. See also Michel Foucault, "On the Genealogy of Ethics," *Beyond Structuralism and Hermeneutics*, eds. Hubert Dreyfus and Paul Rabinow (Chicago: The University of Chicago Press, 1983), 231–32; Mark Reinhardt, *The Art of Being Free: Taking Liberties with Tocqueville, Marx, and Arendt* (Ithaca: Cornell University Press, 1997), esp. 19.

46. Barbara Cruikshank examines this aspect of governmental rationality in *The Will to Empower: Democratic Citizens and Other Subjects*.

47. Although Foucault began to think and write about governmentality late in his life, it is not difficult to see how his later work built upon and in some ways synthesized the institutional reorganization of power that he had previously identified in the birth (and the object) of the prison, the hospital, and the asylum, to name only a few.

48. Foucault reminds us the term "statistics" names the "science of the state." Michel Foucault, "Governmentality," 96. See also Alain Desrosières, *The Politics of Large Numbers*, trans. Camille Naish (Cambridge: Harvard University Press, 1998).

49. *The Federalist Papers*, ed. Isaac Kramnick (New York: Penguin, 1987), Number IX, 119.

50. *The Federalist Papers*, Number I, 87.

51. Sheldon S. Wolin, "*E Pluribus Unum*: The Representation of Difference and the Reconstitution of Collectivity," 134.

52. Two series of contiguous essays—one near the beginning of the collection, the other closer to its middle—spell out a variety of dangers that threaten the new republic. The first series surveys the threats posed by the influence and military power of foreign governments (Numbers II–V), the potential for war between the various states of the Confederation (Numbers VI–VIII), and the designs of powerful self-interested individuals and factions (Numbers IX–X). Each of these threats to domestic tranquility and effective governance reappears later in the second set, in a series of installments that examine the "defects of the present Confederation" by drawing an explicit analogy between its polycentrism and a variety of feudal confederacies (Numbers XV–XX).

53. The term "primitive" is Madison's, which he attaches to the outlooks of the individual states when he writes that "the immediate object of the federal Constitution is to secure the union of the thirteen primitive States." Madison's use of the term "primitive" is notable for the rhetorical force of its many connotations. Primitive may be read here to mean original and primary (as in the "thirteen original States"); but it also carries important connotations of the archaic, crude, un(der)developed, and/or untutored. See James Madison, "Federalist Number XIV: An Objection Drawn from the Extent of Country Answered," *The Federalist Papers*, 143.

54. As Shklar puts it, as "much as they admired George Washington, the Framers also followed the wisdom of the modern age and planned a political system that did not require great statesmen in order to succeed in its aims." Judith N. Shklar, "A New Constitution for a New Nation," *Redeeming American Political Thought*, ed. Stanley Hoffman and Dennis F. Thompson (Chicago: The University of Chicago Press, 1998), 164.

55. *The Federalist Papers*, Number VI, 104.

56. See *The Federalist Papers*, Number LXX, 402–8.
57. *The Federalist Papers*, Number VI, 104.
58. *The Federalist Papers,* Number X, 125.
59. *The Federalist Papers*, Number X, 127.
60. The metaphor of the veil will be discussed at greater length below.
61. *The Federalist Papers*, Number XXIII, 186. Emphasis in original.
62. *The Federalist Papers*, Number X, 123.
63. *The Federalist Papers*, Number X,122.
64. *The Federalist Papers*, Number XV, 147.
65. *The Federalist Papers*, Number XV, 148.
66. *The Federalist Papers*, Number XX, 170.
67. *The Federalist Papers*, Number XX, 172. Emphasis in original.
68. *The Federalist Papers*, Number XV, 149. The significance of this innovation was by no means lost on those who opposed the Philadelphia Constitution. At the opening of the Virginia Convention, Patrick Henry suggested that "the question turns . . . on that poor little expression, We, the *people*, instead of the *states*, of America. States are the characteristics and the soul of a confederation. If the states be not the agents of this compact, it must be one great, consolidated, national government, of the people of all the states." Quoted in Gordon S. Wood, *The Creation of the American Republic, 1776–1878* (New York: Norton, 1972), 526. Emphasis in original.
69. *The Federalist Papers*, Number II, 91.
70. *The Federalist Papers*, Number IV, 99.
71. *The Federalist Papers*, Number IV, 99.
72. *The Federalist Papers*, Number IV, 100.
73. "The Constitution of the United States of America," *The Federalist Papers*, 491.
74. Michel Foucault, *Discipline and Punish*, 170. My use of the metaphor of the veil in relation to the 1787 Constitution should not be confused with a much later formulation of the principles of liberal governance, John Rawls's classic *A Theory of Justice*, that also relies on the imagery of a veil. In Rawls's case, justice as fairness is formulated by recourse to a "veil of ignorance" that obscures the particularities of individuals and their structural interests in the moment in which they agree upon the basic institutional arrangements that shape the public order. In *The Federalist*, however, the veil operates as an aggregating device within which not ignorance but a comprehensive knowledge of the whole is gathered and produced. This distinction between strategies of carefully acquired ignorance, and comprehensively produced knowledge, is a major factor that differentiates abstract universalism from the aggregate universalist techniques of *The Federalist*. See John Rawls, *A Theory of Justice* (Cambridge: Belknap, 1971).

75. *The Federalist Papers*, Number LXXXIV, 475.
76. *The Federalist Papers*, Number LXXXIV, 476.
77. *The Federalist Papers*, Number LXXXIV, 476.
78. For a more detailed discussion of the debates surrounding the inclusion of a Bill of Rights, see Gordon Wood, *The Creation of the American Republic, 1776–1787*, 536–43; and Stanley Elkins and Eric McKitrick, *The Age of Federalism: The Early American Republic, 1788–1800* (New York: Oxford University Press, 1993), esp. 60–62.
79. Hannah Arendt, *On Revolution* (New York: Penguin, 1981), 174.
80. Paula Baker, "The Domestication of Politics: Women and American Political Society, 1780-1920," *American Historical Review* 89:3 (June 1984), 630–31.
81. Paula Baker, "The Domestication of Politics: Women and American Political Society, 1780–1920," 631.
82. Judith Sargent Murray, *The Gleaner*, 1:XXXV (Boston: I. Thomas and E.T. Andrews, 1798), 6.
83. For more on the historical gains made by women in this era, see Linda K. Kerber, *Women of the Republic: Intellect and Ideology in Revolutionary America* (Chapel Hill: The University of North Carolina Press, 1980); Mary Beth Norton, *Liberty's Daughters: The Revolutionary Experience of American Women, 1750–1800*; Jan Lewis, "The Republican Wife: Virtue and Seduction in the Early American Republic," *William and Mary Quarterly* 44 (October 1987), 689–721; Rosemarie Zagarri, "Morals, Manner, and the Republican Mother," *American Quarterly* 44:2 (1992), 192—215. For accounts that focus specifically on women's reading, see Cathy Davidson, *Revolution and the Word: The Rise of the Novel in the United States* (New York: Oxford University Press, 1988); Bruce Burgett, *Sentimental Bodies: Sex, Gender, and Citizenship in the Early Republic* (Princeton: Princeton University Press, 1998), esp. Chapter 4.
84. Judith Sargent Murray, *The Gleaner* 1:XXVII, 271–72.
85. Judith Sargent Murray, *The Gleaner* 3:LXXXIX, 198.
86. Judith Sargent Murray, *The Gleaner* 2:LIV, 217. Emphasis in original.
87. Judith Sargent Murray, *The Gleaner* 1:XVII, 168. Emphasis in original.
88. Judith Sargent Murray, *The Gleaner* 3:Conclusion, 313–14. Emphasis in original.
89. Lauren Berlant, "National Brands / National Body: *Imitation of Life*," 112–13.

II

Reconstruction and Its Aftermath: The Relocation of the Past

THE PERIOD OF NATIONAL RECONSTRUCTION FOLLOWING THE AMERICAN Civil War entailed far more than just the reconciliation of previously warring states; indeed, the years between the end of the war and the Compromise of 1877 witnessed a fundamental reorganization of the American polity, what Charles and Mary Beard have called a "Second American Revolution."[1] At the center of this revolution were the three Amendments to the Constitution ratified between December 1865 and February 1870. In a number of ways, the Reconstruction Amendments were revolutionary, making a decisive break with the world of *The Federalist*. It might be said that the Amendments remapped power within both the national body politic, by making federal authority definitively superior to state authority, and the individual bodies-politic of citizens, by eliminating slavery, nationalizing citizenship, establishing universal manhood suffrage, and guaranteeing all citizens equal protection under the law. Yet for all that the three Reconstruction Amendments accomplished, it might also be said that they were in some ways of little institutional consequence. While they established a new formula for apportioning representatives to Congress, they did not substantially alter the structure of the legislature, the judiciary, or the executive. While they expanded the compass of Constitutional rights, they articulated no new rights tailored to the needs of a postslavery society. And while they outlawed slavery, which was a significant novelty in federal law, the Reconstruction Amendments largely reiterated the basic assumptions of a prior legal code. Nonetheless, something truly revolutionary had happened, for if the basic institutional structures of American government in the postwar period looked remarkably similar to those of the antebellum years, the content of the form did not. As Richard Bensel has argued, the government established by the Constitutional Convention of 1787 was "not so much overthrown by the Civil War as rendered anachronistic" by it.[2] I explore this process of anachronization as it worked itself out within the American political imagination during the years following the Civil War, a period that can be characterized as a second founding. Reconstruction accomplished a conceptual relocation of a past that Founders had represented, symbolically, in the figure of the citizen's body. Accordingly, the era saw the development of two new and distinct languages of citizenship, one that rendered the body fully visible within politics by articulating race and gender as meaningful categories of citizenship, and another that rearticulated the principles of 1787 through the categories provided by the new Amendments.

General rules and suffrage rights

As I argued in Part I, the Constitution of 1787 succeeded insofar as it was able to produce a unified public through a process of aggregation, (first) by bringing difference into the political as an archaic remnant of the past contained within the present, and (second) by veiling these differences and distinctions under the rubric of a national citizenry. Indeed, the 1787 Constitution succeeded in making citizens identically subject to the rule of law precisely insofar as it succeeded in representing them as a new people ("We the People of the United States"),[3] the aggregate subjects of a *novus ordo seclorum*. While the universalist strategies of "general rule" committed Founders to a departicularizing polity that promised equality by virtue of what Anne Norton has called "color-blind, gender-neutral liberalism,"[4] as we know, the Constitution did not, in fact, treat all citizens identically or equally.[5] How, then, can we understand this failure of the promise of equality, and how can we square that failure with the apparent disembodiment of citizenship that would seem to underwrite its success? If the form of citizenship the Founders envisioned was in the end a largely disembodied one, it may also be the case that "disembodiment" does not quite capture the complex means by which the effacement of the body was accomplished. For the strategy of defining general rules did not eliminate the body, or the particularities of bodies, from American languages of citizenship, as both invoke and then render it archaic. Citizenship was articulated through bodies, but not left with them.

It became possible, for a time, for some to press the ambiguity of "general rules" in the service of promoting radically inclusive interpretations of suffrage rights, especially in an era before the meaning of national citizenship had been definitively established, when admission to the polls was governed largely by local custom. As Frederick Douglass noted in his 1857 commentary on the *Dred Scott* decision, prevailing notions of citizenship had actually enabled free African Americans to participate in the political process:

> The Constitution knows all the human inhabitants of this country as "the people." It makes, as I have said before, no discrimination in favor of, or against, any class of the people, but is fitted to protect and preserve the rights of all, without reference to color, size, or any physical peculiarities. Besides, it has been shown by William Goodell and others, that in eleven out of the old thirteen states, colored men were legal voters at the time of the adoption of the Constitution.[6]

Just as the ideal of the citizen as a "prosthetic person" had made discrimination according to race conceptually (if not practically) impossible, it also made discrimination by gender difficult to justify in Constitutional terms. When, in 1800, a group of New Jersey women petitioned their state legislators to amend the state constitution so as to explicitly ensure women's right to the franchise, they were met with the considered response that doing so was unnecessary: so many women already voted that such an amendment, legislators insisted, was superfluous. As citizens of the state of New Jersey, women were already guaranteed that right.[7]

This relative openness in the practice of suffrage, however, was short-lived. In 1807, New Jersey's legislature passed a new election law that excluded women from the polls.[8] Throughout the Jacksonian and antebellum years, a series of codes enacted by state legislatures made state citizenship contingent upon race, so that by 1857 Frederick Douglass could speak of the potential for freedom suggested by the legal votes cast by "colored men" only in the past tense: "at the time of the adoption of the Constitution." In 1842, the state legislature of Georgia unanimously resolved that free blacks were not United States citizens. Tennessee had preceded Georgia in disenfranchising free blacks in 1834 (though without going so far as to declare them noncitizens of the United States), followed by North Carolina a year later and by Pennsylvania in 1838. By the time of the Civil War, some form of the franchise was guaranteed to free blacks in only six states: Maine, Vermont, New Hampshire, Massachusetts, Rhode Island, and New York. As Rogers Smith points out, much of this state-level disenfranchisement took place in the context of the Jacksonian era's abandonment of property and tax-paying qualifications for the exercise of suffrage rights, qualifications that had, in large part, achieved the same kind of *de facto* disenfranchisement for African Americans that the new legislation now ensured.[9] It is also during this period that we see the growth and popularization of the American school of ethnography which sought the "truth" of (white) racial superiority in physical differences between white and black bodies.[10] Insofar as race—and via race, the question of the body—became increasingly the subject of public discourse over the first six decades of the nineteenth century, it was, like gender, a subject that could not be articulated within the generic language of aggregate universalism. This process through which the body increasingly became the object of legislative and scientific scrutiny was both a consequence of aggregate universalism and a sign of its supercession. Governmental rationality itself had identified the citizen's body as a potential object of legislative, judicial, and administrative scrutiny, and the governmentalist language of aggregate universalism fostered the development of public articulations of *pluris*, of difference. This generation of *pluris* was internal to *unum*, still it threatened to destabilize the constitutional order. The states, and the state, responded with efforts to recontain *pluris* by fixing its meaning through legislation and judicial interpretation.

At the federal level, it was the 1857 Supreme Court decision in *Dred Scott v. Sandford* that highlighted the curious place of the raced body in the federal and antebellum republic, and brought the body into the canons of Constitutional interpretation, if not the Constitution itself. Scott, a slave from Missouri whose master had twice taken him to live for extended periods outside of slave territory, sued in 1846 to gain recognition as a free man and citizen, of both Missouri and the United States. He argued that his return to a slave state could not reinstate a slave status made obsolete by residence in territories where slavery was illegal. The Court's decision concluded that no black person could be a citizen of the United States "within the meaning of the Constitution"[11] and Scott, therefore, was not "clothe[d]" by the privileges and protections afforded by it.[12] Thus divested of the mantle of citizenship on account of race, Scott and African Americans more generally were placed outside the veil of an aggregate citizenry even as they were retained within the ambit of administrative governance. In this respect, the black body came to mark the limits of *The Federalist*'s techniques of government. To recall John Jay's argument in *Federalist* Number Four, the success of government hinges on its ability to "harmonize, assimilate, and protect the several parts and members of the nation."[13] With the *Dred Scott* decision, African Americans were made permanently unassimilable, a juridically constituted faction within the body politic.

It was the Reconstruction Amendments themselves that decisively illuminated the body, brought it into the direct focus of the Constitution, guaranteed for it a permanent and permanently visible place in American languages of citizenship, and by doing so effected a fundamental alteration in the terms by which, since Reconstruction, Americans have imagined the possibilities and conditions for making a common public life. In this sense, while the Amendments effectively overturned the content of the *Dred Scott* decision by extending both equal protection and suffrage to the freedmen and by establishing citizenship as centered in the national state, they also paradoxically accepted and extended its formal innovation, that is, its direct and focused concentration on the place of the body in discussions of national citizenship. Among scholars of constitutional law, the impact of the Reconstruction Amendments on questions of constitutional interpretation and institutional change is a matter of some contention;[14] indeed, how we understand their political significance depends in large part upon whether we focus on their impact in the realm of legal institutions or that of the political imagination. For students of judicial politics and constitutional law, the pressing questions with respect to Reconstruction involve the relative weight granted national and state citizenship by the Amendments,[15] and whether the Amendments' guarantee of equal protection applied to violations of civil rights by individuals and groups (like the Ku Klux Klan) or by the states alone.[16] My concerns here are somewhat different: rather than asking about the intent or scope of the Reconstruction initiatives, I am more interested in considering them as artifacts and indicators of a more general shift in American languages of citizenship, developed in response to the persistent eruption of the body into the domain of the visible, in an arena whereby it had previously been camouflaged, or obscured, by the techniques of aggregate universalism.

Formally, the Amendments made three general accomplishments: they outlawed slavery (Thirteenth Amendment); guaranteed equal protection under the law to all citizens without regard to "race, color, or previous condition of servitude" and revised criteria for the apportionment of representatives, thus eliminating the notorious "3/5 Compromise" of Article I (Fourteenth Amendment); and established the right to vote for all male citizens (Fifteenth Amendment). The Amendments also significantly strengthened the national state, abolishing a specific form of property without compensating owners, articulating a notion of national citizenship established by birthright, establishing the nation as a power superior to the states, declaring equality to be a Constitutional value, and making national rights institutionally enforceable against the states.

The Reconstruction Amendments also represent the Constitutional expression of a fundamental alteration in the terms of the political imagination in the

United States, for they suggest a radical restructuring of the forms and processes of political identification, articulating a new relationship between the citizen, the nation, and the body, and they thereby structured both a new political morphology and a new motif of political time through which citizens could formulate, articulate, and press political claims. In this sense, the Reconstruction Amendments served to secure a permanent and perceptible place for the body within politics by fixing its meaning in American languages of citizenship.

The Reconstruction Amendments and the political imagination

The Civil War and Radical Reconstruction, Mark Brandon has argued, presented the nation with an opportunity to begin anew, a chance to reconstitute national citizenship on more inclusive ground. Doing so would have required the articulation of new languages of citizenship that resonated strongly among citizens themselves. As Brandon writes, "the capacity of a constitution to constitute a *polity*, as opposed to establishing mere government, depends on the success of the constitution in acting on the minds of those who would be citizens."[17] However, for Brandon, both Radical Republicans' insistence that readmission of Southern states to the Union occur within the context of military occupation, and the Republican Party's feeble and short-lived commitment to racial equality in both North and South, effectively squandered this opportunity. "With respect to reconstitution," he writes, "the Radicals' solution denied the possibility of constructing foundational myths, plausible to both North and South, that might have supplied (or obviated the need for) metaphysical props for the new order." In the end, the Radicals "inhibited the capacity of their program to command the respect and attachment of those citizens who most threatened the program's success." Democracy gave way to force, and "in the South, slavery was replaced by sharecropping and other forms of economic organization that tied free blacks in servitude to the soil and to a new aristocracy that eerily resembled the old."[18]

In many ways, Brandon is quite right: there is a world of difference between a constitutional order that can lay claim to the authority and freely given consent of a sovereign people, and one whose power is established through coercion and violence. I am inclined to agree, moreover, with Brandon's conclusion that the Radical Republicans' program ended in a sort of constitutional failure. I am less inclined to grant his reasons for labeling Reconstruction a failure, namely, that it failed to provide a language through which freedmen (and, a century later, other ethnic minorities) might articulate their place within the nation. I would not, therefore, agree with Brandon's conclusions that the "centrifugal tendencies based importantly on race and ethnicity" that plague late twentieth-century American life represent latter-day expressions of this much earlier failure.[19]

I suggest this: first, that the Reconstruction Amendments did provide emancipated slaves with a language of political identity, and one moreover that was (at least in principle) open to *all* citizens; second, and paradoxically, that the openness and malleability of this new language allowed white supremacists to reformulate the grounds of citizenship itself; and finally, that if it is the case that late twentieth-century America has been fraught with "centrifugal" tendencies fostered by what is known as identity politics, then this is a consequence not of the failure of Reconstruction, but of its success, even if that success has taken a form unforeseen and unforeseeable by the architects of the Reconstruction initiatives. What Brandon fails to see is how the Reconstruction Amendments reassembled the components of the 1787 Constitution by shifting the place of the body (and hence the significance of race) within it, reorganizing the place of this symbolic past in the Constitutional politics of the present.

The Reconstruction Amendments fundamentally altered the nature of the American political imagination even if their immediate impact on institutions was minimal by comparison. The Fourteenth Amendment's reference to the specifically "male inhabitants" (and a few lines later to "male citizens") of the states in its formula for the apportionment of representatives (in Section 2) makes the first reference to gender in the text of the Constitution. The Fifteenth Amendment introduces the terms "race" and "color." Together, these two amendments effected a revolution in citizenship not so much by adding new elements to our vocabulary, as by enunciating what had long been present but unspeakable.[20] The Amendments made the body visible, and they recast its meaning: once a figure of the suppressed past of political life, the raced and gendered body became a symbol of its future.

The knotty politics of the post-Civil War suffrage movements can help us get at this new political logic embodied in the Amendments. We are accustomed to thinking about the Reconstruction Amendments as the stewards of women's formal exclusion from the suffrage,[21] but the three Amendments, in fact, effected a far more complex reorganization of the political than we may immediately recognize, for in the end they compounded the ambiguities of Constitutional languages of citizenship, ambiguities that advocates of Woman suffrage were quick to exploit. In a reading of the Reconstruction Amendments that nineteenth-century suffragists promoted as the "New Departure," Victoria

Woodhull suggested to a joint meeting of the Judiciary Committees of both Houses of Congress in 1871, that the Fourteenth and Fifteenth Amendments, if taken literally, actually granted women the franchise, at least by implication. The universal claims, explicit in the extension of equal protection to *all persons* born in or naturalized as citizens of the United States in the first section of the Fourteenth Amendment and in the Fifteenth Amendment's guarantee of the right to vote to *all citizens* regardless of "race, color, or previous condition of servitude," were not attenuated by the grant of the franchise to *male citizens* in the second section of the Fourteenth Amendment. As Woodhull argued:

> If the right to vote cannot be denied on account of race, *how* can it be denied on account of a constituent part of race, unless the power of denial is specially *expressed*. . . . No *inference* can be allowed to determine that *any* part of the citizens covered by the term *race* can be denied the right to vote. . . . A race is composed of two sexes. If you speak of a race you include both sexes. . . .[22]

Women's claims for the franchise could be premised in their status as raced beings, Woodhull argued, and Congress need only pass a Declaratory Act formalizing that fact.[23]

As it happens, women did not wait for a Declaratory Act that would never materialize, but began to vote, claiming the right to do so under the authority of the Fourteenth Amendment.[24] Again, such liberties were short-lived, for in 1875 the Supreme Court ruled on the question of women's enfranchisement in the case of *Minor v. Happersett*. Francis Minor, a St. Louis attorney, sued on behalf of his wife Virginia, whom he argued had been admitted to citizenship by the Fourteenth Amendment, and was therefore entitled to all the rights, privileges, and immunities thereof. Writing for the Court, Chief Justice Morrison Waite concluded that although women are included as citizens under the Fourteenth Amendment, they are granted "membership of a nation and nothing more," and the power to grant the franchise had been retained by the individual states.[25] Extrapolating from Waite's analysis, we might say that the Fourteenth and Fifteenth Amendments did not so much exclude women from politics as effectively silence them within it, enshrining a new and distinct form of citizenship, peculiar to women, that would retain its hold until the ratification of the Nineteenth Amendment in 1920.

The effects of the Amendments rippled even further. As *Minor v. Happersett* suggests, they imposed upon questions of citizenship a grid where axes of race and gender ran in perpendicular directions, and thereby formalized and fixed criteria for the exercise of political rights in specific aspects of what were now the radically differentiated bodies of individual citizens. This new technique of citizenship assigned individuals to particular quadrants of this grid, quadrants that defined their access to the franchise. Political citizenship was thus transformed at the most microscopic of levels. Political identity was now a function of the body, and political time was reordered: the body was no longer just a symbol of a distant, mythic, or archaic past, but also a marker and determinant of the citizen's political future. In this sense, the body, which had long been present if largely invisible on the scene of American politics, supplied a new mythic grounding that bound citizens to specific features of their bodies; the body became the sign of a citizen's qualification to participate in the public order and the mark of political interest.

Political palimpsests

In *Refashioning Futures*, David Scott characterizes the emergence of modernity as the establishment of a new order through a decisive break with the past, "a break beyond which there is no return, and in which what comes after can only be read in, read through, and read against the categories of the modern." Scott quotes Zygmunt Bauman's discussion of the difficulty of understanding premodern ideas and societies *now*, from within the modern era, except by way of contrast with terms provided by modernity itself:

> This world which preceded the bifurcation into order and chaos we find difficult to describe in its own terms. We try to grasp it mostly with the help of negations: we tell ourselves what that world was not, what it did not contain, what it was unaware of. That world would hardly have recognized itself in our descriptions. It would not understand what we are talking about. It would not survive such understandings. The moment of understanding would be (and it was) the sign of its approaching death. And of the birth of modernity.[26]

Both Scott and Bauman suggest that moderns cannot know or understand premodern eras in the same terms by which their inhabitants did. They make it clear that the very effort to do so implicates us in a series of inevitable distortions that not only mark us as moderns but also measure our distance from the premodern. However, if it is the case that as Scott puts it, "there is no return" from the inauguration of the modern, perhaps there is also something valuable to be learned from distortion itself; something that, if it does not recuperate a past in the very terms in which its inhabitants would have recognized it, might nonetheless cast that past in a new light that is critically and intellectually significant for "us," if not for "them." Perhaps these inevitable misunderstandings that inhere in our attempts to comprehend the past can tell us what separates us from the past, and can, therefore, help us understand the unspoken ground of the present.

"The past is a necessity that makes freedom possible," Peter Euben has written. "What is new and innovative must be built on the still-living foundations of what is old and inherited."[27] For Euben, the past is a necessary component of the present, it is (to paraphrase Faulkner) never fully past. To press the matter a bit further, we might think of the political present as a palimpsest that never fully erases or obscures its underlying texts. As Lillian Hellman has characterized the pentimento effect in painting:

> Old paint on canvas, as it ages, sometimes becomes transparent. When that happens it is possible, in some pictures, to see the original lines: a tree will show through a woman's dress, a child makes way for a dog, a large boat is no longer on an open sea. That is called pentimento, because the painter "repented," changed his mind. Perhaps it would be as well to say that the old conception, replaced by a later choice, is a way of seeing and then seeing again.[28]

Our distinctly modern engagement with the past is apt to produce some productive disorientation, for it promises new and different understandings of the past, of the present, and of the intellectual and political relations that differentiate the two, offering to us "a way of seeing and then seeing again."

Of course—to bring the discussion back into the orbit of American Reconstruction—I do not mean to suggest that the constitutional initiatives of Reconstruction effected a break with the 1787 Constitution that was anywhere near so profound as that which distinguishes the modern from the premodern. The new constitutional order did not so much supplant as supplement older forms and practices of citizenship in the American political imagination. Even as Reconstruction established new forms and structures of political identification, it renewed the life and direction of its predecessor; the old order was neither defeated nor retired, but reshaped and put to new purpose.

Gauging shifts in the political imagination of a nation is a tricky business, and especially so when there are few definitive texts that can serve as conceptual or intellectual compasses of the era. There simply is no equivalent canonical text for this second founding that sets out in systematic terms the case for Reconstruction in the way that Jefferson's *Notes on the State of Virginia* laid out the ideals and possibilities opened by the Revolution, or makes the case that *The Federalist Papers* made for the 1787 Constitution. Perhaps this is one of the reasons why political theorists have tended to shy away from this period, leaving it instead to the scrutiny of scholars of Constitutional law or American history. Indeed, in the two chapters that follow, the texts under discussion are produced at what many would consider the margins of politics: events like a late-Reconstruction era scandal, the founding documents of white supremacist fraternities, and a rather unorthodox interpretation of Genesis. On the margins, perhaps, but by no means marginal, for a close reading of these texts can help us both to understand the changes wrought on the American political imagination during Reconstruction, and to see again—in new and different ways—the techniques of citizenship discussed in Part I.

Endnotes

1. Charles A. Beard and Mary R. Beard, *The Rise of American Civilization* (New York, 1933), Chapter 28.

2. Richard Franklin Bensel, *Yankee Leviathan: The Origins of Central State Authority in America, 1859–1877* (New York: Cambridge University Press, 1990), ix.

3. In his famous attack, at the Virginia ratification convention, Patrick Henry emphasized the strangeness of this phrase to both eighteenth-century ears and eighteenth-century politics: "What right had they to say, We, the people? My political curiosity, exclusive of my anxious solicitude for the public welfare, leads me to ask, who authorised them to speak the language of We, the people, instead of We, the States? States are the characteristics and the soul of a confederation. If the states be not the agents of this compact, it must be one great consolidated National Government of the people of all the states." Quoted in the "Editor's Introduction" to James Madison, Alexander Hamilton, and John Jay, *The Federalist Papers*, ed. Isaac Kramnick (New York: Penguin, 1987), 32.

4. Anne Norton, "Engendering Another American Identity," *Rhetorical Republic: Governing Representations in American Politics*, eds. Frederick M. Dolan and Thomas L. Dumm (Amherst: University of Massachusetts Press, 1993), 132. For similar assessments, see Lauren Berlant, "National Brands/National Body: *Imitation of Life*," *Comparative American Identities: Race, Sex, and Nationality in the Modern Text*, ed. Hortense J. Spillers (New York: Routledge, 1991), 110–140; Linda K. Kerber, *Women of the Republic: Intellect and Ideology in Revolutionary America* (Chapel Hill: University of North

Carolina Press, 1980); Mary Beth Norton, *Liberty's Daughters: The Revolutionary Experience of American Women, 1750–1800* (Boston: Little, Brown and Company, 1980). For arguments in this tradition that are developed from other national contexts and/or contemporary social theory, see Joan B. Landes, *Women and the Public Sphere in the Age of the French Revolution* (Ithaca: Cornell University Press, 1988); Iris Marion Young, *Justice and the Politics of Difference* (Princeton: Princeton University Press, 1990).

5. I do not assume that these are the same thing. Indeed, as Chantal Mouffe has put it, "it is clear that, in many cases, to treat men and women equally implies treating them differently." Or, as Kimberlé Williams Crenshaw has argued with respect to the *Plessy v. Ferguson* ruling, "to formalize equality [meant] basically to constitute only symmetrical treatment [of black and white citizens] and then to render the social, material context of segregation as well as its effects . . . private or unknowable." See Chantal Mouffe, "Feminism, Citizenship and Radical Democratic Politics," *The Return of the Political* (London: Verso, 1993), 82; Kimberlé Williams Crenshaw, "Color Blindness, History, and the Law," *The House That Race Built*, ed. Wahneema Lubiano (New York: Vintage, 1998), 282; see also Joan Wallach Scott's discussion of the paradoxes that govern the feminist demands for political equality that themselves *produce* sexual difference in Joan Wallach Scott, *Only Paradoxes to Offer: French Feminists and the Rights of Man* (Cambridge: Harvard University Press, 1996).

6. Frederick Douglass, "Speech on the *Dred Scott* Decision," *African-American Social and Political Thought, 1850–1920*, ed. Howard Brotz (New Brunswick: Transaction Publishers, 1992), 261. Indeed, the dissent authored by Justice Benjamin Robbins Curtis in the *Dred Scott* decision makes much the same point:

> [The] Constitution was ordained and established by the people of the United States, through the action, in each State, of those persons who were qualified by its laws to act thereon, in behalf of themselves and all other citizens of that State. In some of the States, . . . colored persons were among those qualified by law to act on this subject. These colored persons were not only included in the body of "the people of the United States," by whom the Constitution was ordained and established, but in at least five of the States they had the power to act, and doubtless did act, by their suffrages, upon the question of its adoption.

See *Dred Scott v. Sandford*, 60 U.S. (19 How.) 393 (1857), Curtis dissenting, at 576.

7. Mary Beth Norton, *Liberty's Daughters: The Revolutionary Experience of American Women, 1750–1800*, 188–94.

8. For further discussion, see Linda K. Kerber, "'Ourselves and Our Daughters Forever': Women and the Constitution, 1787–1876," *One Woman, One Vote: Rediscovering*

the Woman Suffrage Movement, ed. Marjorie Spruill Wheeler (Troutdale, OR: NewSage Press, 1995), 21–36.

9. See Rogers Smith, *Civic Ideals: Conflicting Visions of Citizenship in U.S. History* (New Haven: Yale University Press, 1997), esp. 213–217, 258.

10. Rogers Smith, *Civic Ideals*, esp. pp. 203–06. See also Stephen Jay Gould, *The Mismeasure of Man* (New York: W.W. Norton, 1981); Thomas F. Gossett, *Race: The History of an Idea in America* (New York: Oxford University Press, 1963), esp. Chapter Four; W. E. Burghardt Du Bois, *Dusk of Dawn: An Essay Toward an Autobiography of a Race Concept* (New Brunswick, NJ: Transaction Books, 1984). For a more synthetic analysis of the ideological nature of the concept of "race" and its consequences for Reconstruction-era American politics, see Barbara J. Fields, "Ideology and Race in American History," *Region, Race, and Reconstruction: Essays in Honor of C. Vann Woodward*, eds. Morgan Kousser and James M. McPherson (New York: Oxford University Press, 1982), 143–77.

11. *Dred Scott v. Sandford*, 19 How. 393, 416 (1857). For a more extended discussion of the implications of the *Dred Scott* decision for constitutional interpretation and for citizenship law more generally, see Rogers M. Smith, *Civic Ideals: Conflicting Visions of Citizenship in U.S. History*, ch. Eight and Nine.

12. *Dred Scott v. Sandford*, 19 How. 405, 422 (1857).

13. *The Federalist Papers*, ed. Isaac Kramnick (New York: Penguin, 1987), 99.

14. Bruce Ackerman, for example, challenges what he calls the "dominant professional" (lawyer's) view that these Amendments represent little more than opportunities to clarify rather than fundamentally reformulate the principles of law established in the 1787 Constitution. In his view, the Reconstruction Amendments—and the whole of the interpretive efforts of the Supreme Court during the period of Republican ascendency from 1869–1932 that Ackerman calls the "middle republic"—effected changes far more creative and innovative than the professional view has allowed. If we dismiss these innovations as trivial, Ackerman suggests, we vastly oversimplify both their meaning and their effects, and we impoverish our understanding of the "multigenerational synthesis" that Ackerman calls for as a means of understanding the richness of American constitutional traditions.

More recently, Mark Brandon has contested Ackerman's interpretation, not by reiterating the "standard lawyer's" whole cloth dismissal of the era, but by arguing instead that Ackerman's assessment of the Reconstruction Amendments' innovative character is overstated on two counts. First, Brandon argues, the Amendments "failed to achieve their ostensible purpose of establishing a fundamentally new set of normative and institutional arrangements in the United States" insofar as they failed to "establish for the postbellum order a new mythic ground that was largely invisible to both federalist and antifederalist myths before the war." Second, where Ackerman views Reconstruction itself—most particularly the ratification process which required that the states of the former Confederacy approve the Amendments as a condition for readmission to the union—as a new and creative means of accomplishing constitutional change, Brandon suggests that the coerciveness of the process failed to establish the *authority* of the Amendments as well as of the Constitution itself. My argument falls somewhere between these two, suggesting ways in which the Reconstruction Amendments both did, and did not, effect significant changes in practices of, and means of conceptualizing, citizenship during the period; my focus, moreover, is different from each, for I am less concerned with the Constitution per se than I am with the kinds of political practices it sets into motion. See Bruce Ackerman, *We the People: Foundations* (Cambridge: Belknap Press, 1991), esp. 61–67 and Chapter Four; also, Mark E. Brandon, *Free in the World: American Slavery and Constitutional Failure* (Princeton: Princeton University Press, 1998), esp. Chapter Eight.

15. The first, and the classic, case that posed the question in this way before the Supreme Court is known as the *Slaughter-House Cases*, 83 U.S. (16 Wall) 36 (1873). Walter F. Murphy argues (by reference to *Slaughter-House*) that the Reconstruction Amendments perfected and completed the political values of the 1787 Constitution; Mark Brandon (discussed at greater length below) makes the opposite case. Pamela Brandwein provides an excellent bibliographic mapping of this dispute in the legal literature. See Walter F. Murphy, "*Slaughter-House, Civil Rights,* and Limits on Constitutional Change," 32 *American J. Jurisprudence* 1 (1987); Mark E. Brandon, *Free in the World: American Slavery and Constitutional Failure*, esp. Chapter Eight; Pamela Brandwein, *Reconstructing Reconstruction: The Supreme Court and the Production of Historical Truth* (Durham: Duke University Press, 1999).

16. The classic case here is *U.S. v. Cruikshank* 92 U.S. 542 (1875). For discussion of the implications of the *Cruikshank* decision, see Robert J. Kaczorowski, *The Politics of Judicial Interpretation: The Federal Courts, Department of Justice and Civil Rights, 1866–1876* (New York: Oceana Press, 1985), 205–16; Pamela Brandwein, *Reconstructing Reconstruction: The Supreme Court and the Production of Historical Truth*, Chapter Four.

17. Mark E. Brandon, *Free in the World: American Slavery and Constitutional Failure*, 35.

18. Mark E. Brandon, *Free in the World: American Slavery and Constitutional Failure*, 202, 209, 210, 214.

19. Mark E. Brandon, *Free in the World: American Slavery and Constitutional Failure*, 226.

20. Relevant passages of the Fourteenth and Fifteenth Amendments are quoted below:

Amendment XIV.

Section 1. All persons born or naturalized in the United States and subject to the jurisdiction thereof, are citizens of the United States and of the State wherein they reside. No State shall make or enforce any law which shall abridge the privileges or immunities of citizens of the United States; nor shall any State deprive any person of life, liberty, or property, without due process of law; nor deny to any person within its jurisdiction the equal protection of the law.

Section 2. Representatives shall be apportioned among the several States according to their respective numbers, counting the whole number of persons in each State, excluding Indians not taxed. But when the right to vote at any election for the choice of electors for President and Vice President of the United States, Representatives in Congress, the Executive and Judicial officers of a State, or the members of the Legislature thereof, is denied to any of the male inhabitants of such State, being twenty-one years of age, and citizens of the United States, or in any way abridged, except for participation in rebellion, or other crime, the basis of representation therein shall be reduced in the proportion which the number of such male citizens shall bear to the whole number of male citizens twenty-one years of age in such State.

Amendment XV.

Section 1. The right of citizens of the United States to vote shall not be denied or abridged by the United States or by any State on account of race, color, or previous condition of servitude.

Quoted from ed. Boorstin, *An American Primer*, pp. 183–84. For a concise discussion of the congressional debates surrounding the passage of the Reconstruction Amendments, and the political strategies regarding the terms of Southern readmission to the Union entailed, see Eric Foner, *Reconstruction: America's Unfinished Revolution, 1863–1877* (New York: Harper & Row, 1988), esp. pp. 251–261.

21. This is the view presented by much of the second wave feminist scholarship on the nineteenth century suffrage movement, shaped largely by its focus on Stanton and Anthony. See, especially, Ellen Carol DuBois, *Feminism and Suffrage: The Emergence of an Independent Women's Movement in America, 1848–1869* (Ithaca: Cornell University Press, 1978); Elizabeth Cady Stanton, *Eighty Years and More: Reminiscences, 1815–1897*, ed. Ellen Carol DuBois (Boston: 1993).

22. Victoria Claflin Woodhull, "Constitutional Equality: A Lecture Delivered At Washington, February 16, 1871," *The Human Body The Temple of God; or, The Philosophy of Sociology* (London, 1890), 158–60 passim. Emphasis in original. For Woodhull's Memorial to Congress, see 90–99.

23. For further discussion of suffragists' activities in the immediate aftermath of the ratification of the Reconstruction Amendments, and of the New Departure, see Andrea Moore Kerr, "White Women's Rights, Black Men's Wrongs: Free Love, Blackmail, and the Formation of the American Woman Suffrage Association," and Ellen Carol DuBois, "Taking the Law Into Our Own Hands: *Bradwell, Minor,* and Suffrage Militance in the 1870s," both in *One Woman, One Vote: Rediscovering the Woman Suffrage Movement*, 61–79, 80–98.

24. Ellen Carol DuBois, "Taking the Law Into Our Own Hands," esp. 86–88.

25. For a fuller discussion of the legal ramifications of *Minor v. Happersett*, see Rogers Smith, *Civic Ideals*, 337–42.

26. Zygmunt Bauman, "Modernity and Ambivalence," *Theory, Culture & Society* 7 (1990), 163. See also David Scott, *Refashioning Futures: Criticism after Postcoloniality* (Princeton: Princeton University Press, 1999), 34.

27. J. Peter Euben, *The Tragedy of Political Theory: The Road Not Taken* (Princeton: Princeton University Press, 1990), 76.

28. Lillian Hellman, *Pentimento* (New York: Signet, 1973), 1.

4

Sexual Reconstruction: Gender, Political Friendship, and the New Techniques of Citizenship

>Once friendship disappeared as a culturally accepted relation, the issue arose: "What is going on between men?"
>
>Michel Foucault[1]

In 1875, HENRY WARD BEECHER WAS AT THE HEIGHT OF HIS CAREER AS minister and public speaker when he was brought to trial on the charge of "criminal conversation," or adultery, based on accusations made by Theodore Tilton. Tilton, twenty-two years Beecher's junior and a former member of the prominent Plymouth Church in Brooklyn where Beecher had been pastor since 1848, served as Beecher's assistant, and later his successor, as editor of *The Independent*, the leading religious-political journal in the United States. As they edited the paper in the early 1860s, Tilton and Beecher developed a close friendship and professional partnership, and together they were active in the major political campaigns of the period, including the antislavery and women's suffrage movements. In 1851 Tilton became engaged to Elizabeth Richards, a member of Beecher's congregation, and when Theodore and Elizabeth married not long afterward, it was Henry Ward Beecher who presided over the ceremony.[2]

Beginning in 1864, Theodore Tilton had been in demand as a public speaker for the causes of abolition and women's rights, and his national lecture tours kept him away from home for several months each year. At Tilton's request, Beecher paid regular visits to Elizabeth and the Tilton children during Theodore's absences. By 1866, Beecher had begun writing a novel, *Norwood; or Village Life in New England*, and he used his visits with Elizabeth to read aloud to her from the drafts of individual chapters, drinking in what he later characterized as her "uncritical praise."³ Over time, the two became confidantes and Elizabeth called upon Beecher to intervene in her behalf when her marriage to Theodore became episodically unbearable. At other times, however, the three formed what Elizabeth would later characterize as "a mutual admiration party."⁴ According to the affadavits Tilton filed with the Brooklyn Court in 1874, his wife Elizabeth had confessed to him as early as July 1870, that she had had an affair with Henry Ward Beecher two years earlier.

Tilton's charges against Beecher came as little surprise to the Brooklyn social and political circles in which the Beechers and the Tiltons moved. Rumors about an affair between a prominent Brooklyn clergyman and the wife of one of his parishioners of nearly equal prominence had abounded since 1870, when letters to that effect from Victoria Woodhull were published in *The Times* and *The World*.⁵ Woodhull's charge was intended, she confessed later, to jar Beecher into taking seriously the doctrine of free love, which she claimed he practiced privately even as he denounced it from the pulpit. When Beecher's attacks against Woodhull's advocacy for sex reform only intensified, she and her sister Tennessee Claflin publicized the details of the affair in a special issue of their journal, *Woodhull and Claflin's Weekly*, in late 1872.⁶

Beecher's trial packed the courtroom every day from January to June 1875. Its progress was reported regularly in major newspapers from New York to St. Louis and Chicago. The full transcript was published and sold serially by news vendors in cities throughout the nation. A parade of celebrity witnesses, including Susan B. Anthony and other leaders of the Woman suffrage movement, were called to testify about the specific charges leveled against Beecher, and to shed some light on the nature of the friendship between Beecher and his accuser that had come to such an abrupt, and public, end. When the jury returned with its verdict in June, its conclusion shocked those who had followed every development for the duration of the trial: the jury could not agree. Beecher was acquitted. Plymouth Church celebrated its own *de facto* vindication by voting to increase Beecher's salary by $100,000 so that he could pay his legal fees.⁷

Over the past three decades, American historians have focused repeatedly on the Beecher-Tilton scandal as a means of tracing important shifts in American social life, using it as a model that helps paint a complex picture of a whole variety of tensions and anxieties characteristic of the American middle class in the immediate aftermath of the Civil War. Its personalities have been interpreted as representative figures of an era confronting a sea-change in social conventions; its hold over the public mind a barometer of conflicting norms and shifting values in middle-class America; its very scandalousness an opportunity to probe central issues confronting liberal Protestantism during the period; and the pettiness of the rivalries it unleashed a simulacrum for confronting more profound political rifts in the Woman suffrage movement.[8] In this chapter, I pursue another reading of the trial, one that traces within these events the complex changes in the nature of citizenship wrought by Reconstruction.

"Quite a different state of affairs"

The first of many books published about Tilton's accusations against Beecher, Leon Oliver's 1873 work entitled *The Great Sensation*, opens on a note of hesitation:

> In presenting this book to the reading public, neither the Author, or Publishers, have any desire, or intention to pander to prurient or depraved tastes, or to violate the sanctity of private lives.
>
> They fully recognize and acknowledge the principle that the private lives and acts of private individuals are matters which concern themselves alone, and that it is a prostitution of journalism or authorship, to glean and blazon forth to the world the domestic affairs of any family.
>
> But in this case it seems to them quite a different state of affairs. First the parties are public characters, and have for years been prominently before the public as professed pioneers in political, moral and social reform, and from the Press, the Pulpit and the Platform have sent out broadcast their peculiar doctrines and theories. In addition to this, they by *their own acts,* have made this most notorious scandal of the age, and themselves as connected with it, *public property*, and we therefore submit that it is not only competent, but legitimate, to canvass their actions, and inquire how far *their own lives* conform to the rules they so zealously prescribe for the guidance of others.[9]

Whatever his reluctance to publicize the "lives and acts of private individuals," Oliver's hesitation is balanced by another consideration: something that has long been private has suddenly become public, and he writes to mark that fact, to mark his discomfort with it, but also to exploit it, or at least to see what can be done, and what can be said, in light of this change. In the end, Oliver reduces these events to scandal, an opportunity to moralize about the hypocrisy of public figures who have broken the "rules they so zealously prescribe" for others. But perhaps there is more to these events than Oliver's sensationalism, the prurient interest that he both disowns and promotes, admits. Perhaps the "rules" themselves have changed.

What Leon Oliver confronts as a concern about "violat[ing] the sanctity of private lives" is a marker of a much larger transformation of public and private than his disclaimer acknowledges, a transformation that does not so much eliminate or attenuate the public sphere, but remakes it. The Beecher-Tilton scandal can be read as one instance in a much larger transformation of the public sphere, where what had once been veiled within public life, or relegated to the ground of the private, became the very model of public governance, and where, conversely, the relations among citizens fostered by the 1787 Constitution came to appear as something quite other. Briefly put, the Reconstruction Amendments ushered the gendered body onto the scene of politics and, as a consequence, the public order itself came to mimic the structure of the heterosexual dyad. Moreover, the very success of this sea-change in the symbolic content and structure of citizenship tends to make what Lauren Berlant has called "an erotics of political fellowship"[10] that obtained in the early republic appear incomprehensible as politics, at least to twenty-first-century eyes.

Feminist historians of Reconstruction, particularly Southern historians, have in recent years begun to point to an increasing sexualization of politics during the era, a "conflation of politics and sex [as] interlocking elements."[11] What I am suggesting is that the Beecher-Tilton episode can help us to see the consequences of this sexualization of politics in the lives of citizens, in the practices of politics, and in the institutional structure of citizenship itself. Insofar as the inquiry it sparked involved the excavation of the pre-Civil War era's understanding of political friendship, the scandal can also give us a new purchase on the more informal practices of political friendship fostered by the techniques of citizenship established under the 1787 Constitution.

A crisis in friendship, a scandal among friends

In the summer and fall of 1863, Beecher toured Europe delivering lectures about the social and political crises confronting Americans who were at the time in the midst of civil war. Tilton's letters to Beecher during the period are peppered throughout with news of the war and of debates within the antislavery movement, with advice about whether Beecher should speak publicly in Britain about the American antislavery cause, and also with expressions of affection far more sentimental than Tilton addressed to his own wife. "I have just come into the house from watering my Wax Plant . . ." he wrote to Beecher in mid-June, "and the leaf on which you scratched your initials held itself up to me as green as the memory in which I hold your lordship."[12] "I am in constant bereavement at your absence," he continued two weeks later, "and think of taking to drink, and to reading the Bible. . . . [M]y day's work [is] done, and the thought stealing into my mind that there is no man in America whom I love as much as one man out of it."[13]

Tilton's warmth increased with the length of Beecher's absence. "Your private letters have been like so many kisses and handshakes. Send some more," he wrote in early August, continuing, "My love multiplies for you every day."[14] From his office at *The Independent*, Tilton wrote in September that

> Mr. H—— [name is illegible] unexpectedly came in this morning, & I looked to see you follow him through the doorway—until the blood leaped into my face with expectation. . . . Had I known that you received letters & papers with considerable regularity, I would have written oftener. But to draw the arrow without knowing when it would reach the mark discouraged me; & I wrote less often than my love prompted. When you come home, I will put my arms around your neck & kiss you on both cheeks! . . . I toss to you a bushel of flowers & a mouthful of kisses![15]

In his final letter before Beecher's return, Tilton confessed that "I never knew how much I loved you till your long absence. I am hungry to look into your eyes."[16]

Two years later, at midnight on November 30, 1865, Tilton wrote to Beecher what he called his "last will and testament of reciprocated love," seeking reconciliation in light of their political differences over the terms of Southern readmission to the Union. In this letter, Tilton reminded Beecher that

> from my boyhood up, you have been to me what no other man has been—what no other man can be. While I was a student, the influence of your mind on mine was greater than all books and all teachers. The intimacy with which you honored me for twelve years has been (next to my wife and family) the chief affection of my life. By you I was baptized—by you married. You are my minister, teacher, father, brother, friend, companion. The debt I owe you I can never pay. My religious life; my intellectual development; my open door of opportunity for

labor; my public reputation; all these, my dear friend, I owe in so great a degree to your own kindness that my gratitude cannot be written in words, but must be expressed only in love.[17]

In his testimony before the Court ten years later, Beecher recalled this dispute with Tilton, characterizing it as a "kind of lovers' quarrel."[18] Their friendship, he suggested, had been a complex one, nurtured by acting together in the public world over the course of more than a decade. As he recollected, "it was common employments, companionship, and downright loving on my part."[19] As Tilton himself had written of their daily work habits:

> . . . [W]hat hours we have had together! What arm in arm wanderings about the streets! What hunts for pictures and books! What mutual revelations and communings! What interchangings of mirth, of tears, of prayers!
>
> The more I think back upon this friendship, the more am I convinced that, not your public position, not your fame, not your genius, but just your affection has been the secret of the bond between us; for whether you had been high or low, great or common, I believe that my heart, knowing its mate, would have loved you exactly the same![20]

Given the intimacy and intensity of the friendship disclosed by these letters and testimony, what readers of the early twenty-first century may find most striking about Beecher's trial is the nature of the "criminal conversation" with which he had been charged. Unlike Oscar Wilde, brought to trial across the Atlantic two decades later under another euphemistic criminal charge—the "gross indecency" of homosexuality—Henry Ward Beecher stood accused of heterosexuality, specifically, of having seduced not Theodore Tilton but his wife, Elizabeth.

A "sacred wedding that knows no sex"

"The whole subject of friendship has been much in my mind this winter," Theodore Tilton remarked in a letter to Elizabeth early in 1867. That the start of the era known as Radical Reconstruction should be so marked by Tilton is significant, for that period consolidated a decided shift in the forms, qualities, and practices of political life as well as the nature of relations between citizens that political theorists since Aristotle have referred to as political friendship. In his letter, Tilton captured the spirit of this bond among public persons, even as he sentimentalized it:

> I am satisfied that whoso makes no intimate or confidential friends, both among men and among women—friends with whom he girdles himself round about as with a halo—friends who are props to keep him lifted perpetually toward his highest life—friends whose friendship is a kind of sacred wedding that knows no sex—such a man neglects one of the greatest of human opportunities for intellectual, moral, and spiritual growth.[21]

Tilton's letter retains traces of a tradition of friendship (*philia*) that for the ancient Greeks denoted a much broader range of relationships than is conveyed by the contemporary sense of the term, even as it departs from that tradition.

Aristotle distinguished among three forms of friendship, classifying them according to the kind of activity associated with each: utility friendship, or that which prevails between partners to a commercial enterprise or exchange, or between those who travel together to the same destination; pleasure friendship, which involves those who experience happiness in common pursuits;[22] and perfect friendship, in which "each loves the other for what he is, and not for any incidental quality."[23] While this third sense, and to some degree also the second, comports most fully with the modern connotations of friendship, and while it invokes both the moral goodness and the similarity-in-goodness of those who are party to it, in its broadest sense the ancient meaning of friendship did not necessarily involve either goodness or similarity, but names more generally the publicly manifest relationship established between individuals who work together in common.[24] The particular type of friendship developed depended on the kind of activity in which partners to that friendship engaged. Friendship was produced as the effect of an activity, and different kinds of friendship the effect of different kinds of activities, not understood as an essential relationship among persons nor as the expression of any organic attribute intrinsic to those who were party to it. For Aristotle, political friendship is a form of utility friendship,[25] a "kind of partnership" between men "that becomes necessary in their life together."[26] The modern understanding of friendship is so saturated with connotations of personal affection and likeness that it bears emphasizing that while the ancient sense of a distinctly political friendship did assume some form of common interest (*koinonia*) shared by those who were party to it, it did not necessarily entail a shared virtue, agreement in disposition or opinion, or ontological sameness.[27] Indeed, political friendship constituted the ground on which conflict and discord might be articulated. As Bernard Yack has put it, it was "a source of conflict as well as a means of promoting greater cooperation."[28] If the term *polis* names the complex of meanings, practices, and institutions formed by common action in the name of public things, the political form of *philia* is the relationship formed between and among those who work together to construct a polis, even if in doing so they find themselves sometimes working at cross-purposes, inspired by different and conflicting motivations.

Given Tilton's emphasis on intimacy and confidentiality as essential properties of the friendship he prizes, however, it is clear that when he speaks of political friendship it is not in this ancient sense. To understand his thinking on friendship, we need to turn to Henry Ward Beecher. In a series of sermons he delivered during 1874, Beecher elaborated a typology of friendship that both recalls and departs from Aristotle's in significant ways, ways that can help us understand the dynamics of political friendship under the legacy of the 1787 Constitution. Echoing Aristotle, Beecher argues that the "elective affinities" of friendship ("elective" insofar as they are distinct from blood relations) are occasioned by the "common exigencies and common necessities" that obtain among neighbors, commercial partners, those who are "united together under the same government, in the same state, and in the same country," and those who are joined by their "moral similarities and attractions."[29] However, he departs from Aristotle by maintaining that the different forms and stages of affinity are neither confined to particular arenas of public activity, nor are they the products of that activity. Where Aristotle views political friendship as the product of public action, Beecher understands it as the precursor to public action, an organic function of the human heart.[30] But if friendship originates in corporal life, it does not end there, he suggests, for "a man who lives in these relationships of the body and of the physical globe, lives in the meagerest and poorest elements of his nature."[31] For Beecher, friendship in its highest form is love, a "soul-relationship" that "survive[s] time and the grave."[32] While this "translation" from the heart as source of friendship to the soul as its ultimate destination seems to place Beecher's concept of friendship outside the political altogether, he goes on to turn soul-relationship to worldly rather than (exclusively) other-worldly ends. The function of love, and the purpose of the biblical injunction "Thou shalt love" is to "subjugate the passions" and thus press us beyond our selves, to inspire us to make a world in common with others. Love, for Beecher, is "the great architectural force by which the world is to be reconstructed in wisdom, in doctrines, in rules, in regulation. It is to develop in the souls of men the greater divine element . . . until its force is such that out of it shall be evolved all elements of truth, of justice and of liberty."[33] Where Aristotle positioned utility friendship as the lowest form of friendship developed between men as they establish their highest life together in the polis, Beecher equates public action with love.

Beecher's notion of soul-relationship marks an important shift in the theological and social ground of late-Victorian America. As Ann Douglas has argued, Beecher is part of the American "domestication" of the Christian concept of heaven. In his hands, heaven was transformed from an other-worldly to a worldly place, and the Christian God recast from a wrathful and punitive disciplinarian to a gentle, loving, even "therapeutic" enabler of worldly spiritual life.[34] Significantly, this rejection of theological convention was also a break with an American tradition that runs from Jonathan Edwards to Beecher's own father, Lyman Beecher. In this sense, "love and affinity," as Altina Waller argues, helped "to justify new social class alignments" emerging in the aftermath of the Civil War.[35] Beecher counseled the rejection of tradition—whether family background or conventions of thought and religious precept—if tradition turned out to restrain social mobility. He stressed the importance of forgiving occasional moral lapses if those lapses were committed in the course of maneuvering creatively in, through, and beyond established social hierarchies. "Beecher's religion," as Richard Wightman Fox has put it, "was countercultural not in being antibourgeois, but in being an embourgeoisement of the Romantic assault on bourgeois convention."[36]

Yet if Beecher's philosophy of love marks a break with American theological tradition, it could also be said that his concept of public friendship maintains continuity with an older tradition of American political thought, offering a mature articulation of a form of public life that was becoming untenable at the very moment Beecher gave expression to it. In fact, the sentimental republic promoted in Beecher's sermons represents an understanding of citizenship, fostered by the terms of the 1787 Constitution, that proved incompatible with the new place of the body established during Reconstruction. This statement may strike the reader as odd, given my discussion of this prior Constitutional moment in Chapter 3. In that chapter, I was concerned primarily with the ways in which the aggregation of unlike things embodied by the 1787 Constitution not only produced an aggregate citizenry, but also produced as heresies those things which were not, according to its schema, the proper objects of government. My point here, however, is to highlight the nature of the bonds developed between and among citizens within this aggregate citizenry.

Beecher's articulation of a sentimental public sphere describes the almost ritualistic culture of intimacy among public citizens that obtained from the

Revolutionary era through the Civil War. As Bruce Burgett has argued, America prior to Reconstruction was the site of a flourishing public culture that relied upon affective, passionate, and embodied responses to the ferment of public life. "As such, sentimentalism located [citizens'] bodies as both pre-political sources of personal authenticity *and* as public sites of political contestation."[37] This coincidence of attachment and agonism may look strange to modern eyes, for it seems to run counter to our received understandings of politics in a democracy. Arendt characterizes well the dangers of some forms of fraternity in her discussion of pariah peoples under totalitarianism:

> Humanity in the form of fraternity invariably appears historically among persecuted peoples and enslaved groups. . . . This kind of humanity is the great privilege of pariah peoples. . . . [but] the privilege is dearly bought . . . In this as it were organically evolved humanity it is as if under the pressure of persecution the persecuted have moved so closely together that the interspace which we have called world (and which of course existed between them before the persecution, keeping them at a distance from one another) has simply disappeared.[38]

There are important democratic reasons to resist the higher or more affective forms of friendship in public life, for intimacy may introduce into politics expectations of sameness and personal closeness that cannot, and perhaps should not, be satisfied by public activity or political institutions.[39] The sentimental public sphere that flourished under the 1787 Constitution, however, should not be equated with the collapse of the "interspace" between citizens. Rather, it has much more in common with Jill Frank's recent interpretation of the Aristotelian concept of *homonoia*, where the "sameness of mind" that obtains among friends is conceptualized not as a "simple harmony" but "a harmony requiring difference, [which] will be an ongoing coming to terms—an ongoing refounding of the polity, if you will—through speech and self-governing activity."[40]

Even the military heroes of the Revolutionary generation, Jonathan Ned Katz has suggested, prided themselves "not upon the hard-boiled avoidance of sentiment but upon the cultivation of the finer feelings."[41] Consider, in this regard, an excerpt from a 1779 letter from a young Alexander Hamilton to John Laurens, written when both were members of the close circle of officers surrounding George Washington to whom Washington referred as his "family." In April, shortly after Laurens had returned to his home in South Carolina to organize battalions of slaves to fight for the Revolutionaries' cause, Hamilton wrote:

Cold in my professions, warm in [my] friendships, I wish my Dear Laurens, it m[ight] be in my power, by action rather than words, [to] convince you that I love you. I shall only tell you that 'till you bade us Adieu, I hardly knew the value you had taught my heart to set upon you. Indeed, my friend, it was not well done. You know the opinion I entertain of mankind, and how much it is my desire to preserve myself free from particular attachments, and to keep my happiness independent on the caprice of others. You sh[ould] not have taken advantage of my sensibility to ste[al] into my affections without my consent. But as you have done it and as we are generally indulgent to those we love, I shall not scruple to pardon the fraud you have committed, on condition that for my sake, if not for your own, you will always continue to merit the partiality, which you have so artfully instilled into [me].[42]

This intimacy, the frequent and passionate expression of affection and longing, was not uncommon among public men in the pre-Civil War republic. A similar erotics of political fellowship gave structure to the American abolitionist movement, and to Southern proslavery intellectual culture as well. Both Katz and Donald Yacavone have documented a number of similar friendships among men in antebellum America, relationships that "by employing the 'language of fraternal love' [enabled these men to] express their personal commitment to the cause and to one another."[43]

To readers of the early twenty-first century, this language of fraternal love would seem to betray its speakers' homosexual desire, to name a desire that is more private than public, more personal than political, and more libidinal than social. A somewhat richer understanding of the bonds that obtain between and among citizens in this period can be developed by reference to what Eve Kosofsky Sedgwick has called male homosocial desire. That term, Sedgwick writes:

is intended to mark both discriminations and paradoxes. "Homosocial desire," to begin with, is a kind of oxymoron. "Homosocial" is a word occasionally used in history and the social sciences, where it describes social bonds between persons of the same sex; it is a neologism, obviously formed by analogy with "homosexual," and just as obviously meant to be distinguished from "homosexual." In fact, it is applied to such activities as "male bonding," which may, as in our society, be characterized by intense homophobia, fear and hatred of homosexuality. To draw the "homosocial" back into the orbit of "desire," of the potentially erotic, then, is to hypothesize the potential unbrokenness of a continuum between homosocial and homosexual.[44]

The concept of male homosocial desire illuminates the ways in which bonds formed between men (and explicitly political bonds between public men figure prominently in her analysis)[45] express themselves as passionate and demand that we reappraise our understanding of both desire and the texture of public life. If the term calls to mind a notion of homosexual desire, this reminder is both deliberate and deliberately obscured, for as Sedgwick insists, "how far this force is properly sexual (what, historically, it means for something to be 'sexual') will be an active question."[46]

Sedgwick's deliberate ambiguation of the nature of these bonds between men has been criticized for its "depend[ence] on the repression of the homosexual into the homosocial."[47] The emphasis she places on their social character, that is, seems to deny the very possibility that they might, in fact, be sexual. I want to suggest, however, that the value of Sedgwick's analysis lies in its ability to help us grasp the complex interconnection between the personal and the political. Her project consists not so much in making precise empirical claims about the nature of relations between and among men, as in developing strategies of reading that help us to see how distinctions between what is sexual and what is not, and between the hetero- and the homo-, give shape and substance to modern thought even as they bring to crisis certain central structures and features of knowledge itself.[48] While it is tempting to dichotomize public and private life as (respectively) politics and sexuality, Sedgwick's work counsels us to resist this temptation and look at the ways in which practices and meanings overlap and intermingle, at once muddying and reaffirming boundaries and distinctions between them. The obvious difficulty in analyzing this process lies in the fact that our own tools of analysis are formed in and through this dichotomy. Our criteria for distinguishing the "properly sexual" from what we might call the "properly political" tend to replicate this divide. The concept of male homosocial desire helps us to bridge these two domains without collapsing distinctions between them. It helps us to understand the complex place of desire within the political.

Letters such as Hamilton's to John Laurens, or those that passed between Beecher and Theodore Tilton, can tell us something important about the nature of public friendship in the era between the Revolution and Reconstruction, a period characterized by a structure of desire that both linked citizens and guaranteed their autonomy through the fleeting materiality of the citizen body. As a way of getting at this operation of desire within the political, let me turn briefly to John Adams' classic discussion of the "passion for distinction" in his 1790 *Discourses on Davila*, a formulation that takes on new meaning when reread in light of Sedgwick's work. For Adams:

> As nature intended [men] for society, she has furnished them with passions, appetites, and propensities, as well as a variety of faculties, calculated both for their individual enjoyment, and to render them useful to each other in their social connections. There is none among them more essential or remarkable than the *passion for distinction*. . . . Wherever men, women, or children are to be found, whether they be old or young, rich or poor, high or low, wise or foolish, ignorant or learned, every individual is seen to be strongly actuated by a desire to be seen, heard, talked of, approved, and respected, by the people about him and within his knowledge.[49]

There are three elements in particular that I'd like to highlight in Adams' meditation on citizenship. The first involves the precise form of distinction that, Adams suggests, individuals achieve only by virtue of their participation in public life. In this regard, Adams counterposes distinction, understood in its most public and productive sense as "industry in the search of truth, and the practice of virtue" or as "the great principle of activity for the good of others," to other forms of personal self-promotion that require a public audience but which are fundamentally *self*-interested projects: ambition, the desire of attaining power for its own sake; jealousy, the "fear . . . that another, who is now inferior, will become superior;" envy, the desire to "bring [another] down to our level, or to depress him below us;" and vanity, "a belief of false professions of esteem or admiration, or . . . a false opinion of [one's] importance in the judgment of the world."[50] As Arendt has argued, the difference between distinction and self-promotion is what differentiates democracy from tyranny: "It is precisely because the tyrant has no desire to excel and lacks all passion for distinction that he finds it so pleasant to rise above the company of all men; conversely, it is the desire to excel which makes men love the world and enjoy the company of their peers, and drives them into public business."[51] This "desire to excel" is but the individual expression of a collective aspiration and collective project, and for this reason it is a public-minded enterprise. For Adams, the passion for distinction is not only a public virtue, but a form of desire that can be satisfied only by virtue of the public-mindedness and public engagement of individual citizens with other citizens as they pursue a common life together.

Moreover, for Adams, the activities by which citizens achieve distinction are not simply public duties, but practices that promote distinct forms of public pleasure. This is not so much a matter of contentment with one's earned distinction, that is, not so much a matter of seeking individual pleasure in public life, as it is a particular form of pleasure born of what Jefferson called the "pursuit of public happiness."[52] The work of citizens fostered certain kinds of enjoyment as distinctive pleasures *of* public life. In Adams' words, "the desire of the esteem of others is as real a want of nature as hunger; and the neglect and contempt of the world as severe a pain as the gout or stone."[53] "The point," as Arendt put it, "is that Americans knew that public freedom consisted in having a share in public business, and that the activities connected with this business by no means constituted a burden but gave those who discharged them in public a feeling of happiness they could acquire nowhere else."[54]

It is at just this point, though, that we might discern a number of ways in which the passion for distinction encounters the complications of Adams' own pragmatics of "general rules." Public pleasures depend upon the apprehension of a public as necessarily composed of unlike things with competing interests and perspectives; of "men, women, [and] children, rich or poor, high or low, wise or foolish, ignorant or learned . . . ." The performance of this "activity for the good of others" requires a notion of the public as an aggregate entity, a comprehensive and comprehensible, if complex, whole. It is in these terms that we might consider in slightly different light Adams' concern with the necessity of general rules, without which "there will be no end of [contest]. New claims will arise; women will demand a vote; lads from twelve to twenty-one will think their rights not enough attended to; and every man who has not a farthing will demand an equal voice with every other, in all acts of state." In the presence of an aggregate citizenry, public law cannot recognize in complex, nuanced terms the unlikeness of the things and peoples it links together. Under the terms of the constitutional moment defined by the 1787 Constitution, the aggregate citizenry produced through the articulation of these general rules was identifiably (if generically) masculine: the passion for distinction, therefore, was formed as an instance of male homosocial desire. It is precisely this element of an erotics of public citizenship that could not survive, or more precisely could not survive without substantial modification, the new status and new visibility granted the body in Reconstruction-era America. With the human body not only present but now quite visible in the public lives of citizens, this language of fraternal love seemed to articulate not a disembodied erotics of public life, but suggested instead a newly sexualized form of citizenship. It is in light of these changes that we can begin to see the specifically political significance of the disintegration of the friendship between Henry Ward Beecher and

Theodore Tilton. The relatively short span of years that separates their "kisses and handshakes" of the early 1860s from the definitive break occasioned by the 1875 trial belies the enormity of the conceptual distance traversed. Under the reign of the new constitutional moment represented by the Reconstruction Amendments, public friendship was refashioned and the structure of public desire was transformed, as Woodhull's analysis presented to Congress had hinted, as a distinctive form of public heterosexuality.

"God bless this trinity"

The transformation of citizenship from homosocial to heterosexual had the effect of casting suspicion on the nature of the particular kind of friendship enjoyed by Henry and Theodore, and the accusations leveled against Beecher provided an occasion for a sustained retrospective reexamination of their relationship, and of Elizabeth's place within it. It is significant that this whole episode coincided with what historians of sexuality have demonstrated is the invention of the figure of the homosexual, an invention that, Jonathan Ned Katz maintains, preceded the construction of a notion of self-conscious heterosexuality; and with the emergence of a new, silent female citizenship under the terms of the Reconstruction Amendments. Indeed, the Beecher-Tilton scandal, with its careful inquiry into the relationships between and among the three principals, might be read as mirroring this larger ongoing process, and it also shows us how these developments were central to Reconstruction's reshaping of political life.[55]

From the moment the first rumors of an affair began to circulate, after Victoria Woodhull's letters were published in *The Times* and *The World*, all three had maintained a public silence on the issue. Privately, however, they exchanged a flurry of notes and letters, ostensibly clarifying to one another what had, and what had not, happened between and among members of the triangle.[56] Under duress, Elizabeth Tilton confessed the affair to her husband, retracted the confession in a letter written for Beecher, and retracted her retraction in a letter to her husband—all in a single night in late 1870. Throughout the course of the dispute, Elizabeth changed her story several times, as did her husband, whose charges against Beecher grew in intensity as Tilton himself revised and reordered what he thought Elizabeth had confessed. Initially, Tilton claimed only that his wife had admitted to harboring an undue affection for Beecher; later, Tilton accused Beecher of having made untoward advances to Elizabeth, and by the end of the imbroglio, Tilton had charged him with "criminal conversation." Indeed, over time, what had begun as a friendship between Theodore and Henry expanded to include Elizabeth in a mutual companionship of the three. It then intensified, in Theodore's mind at least, into an affair between his wife and his friend, a connection from which he had been notably excluded.

Even after these private confessions, there were moments of reconciliation in which Beecher and Theodore Tilton revisited their former intimacy. Three accounts of a single incident—one given by Beecher in his testimony at the trial, one provided in an affadavit by Elizabeth, and one offered by Theodore—demonstrate the complicated mnemonics of recasting the past in light of the developments of the present. From the witness stand in 1875, Beecher recalled a visit he had paid to the Tilton household around May 1871:

> . . . when I went in Mr. Tilton received me moodily, and then after a little conversation and explanation which took place, he became gracious, and we fell into an easy and unbusinesslike chat, and that in the course of it, sitting there in the old-fashioned way in his house, I went up and argued—sat down on his knee, as it were to make the appeal closer, and when I was sitting there, Mrs. Tilton came into the room and burst out laughing. I recollect that interview, and I think when she came into the room she came up and kissed me very cordially.[57]

In a memorandum that made its way into Beecher's papers, but which was never entered into evidence at the trial, Elizabeth Tilton recalled the same incident:

> I was first aware of Mr. Beecher's presence at our house by coming into the parlor & finding Mr. Beecher on Mr. Tilton's lap—both apparently in the pleasantest of moods—Mr. Beecher rose as I entered—I met him with a kiss—he then sat down upon Theodore's knee—they were talking about the "Sermon on the Mount"—I did not sit down with them, nor enter into their Conversation—but walking [sic] in & out during his visit.[58]

Theodore Tilton's testimony, by contrast, does not recall an intimate friendship with Beecher, betrayed by Beecher's seduction of Elizabeth. Rather, his recollection is of a relationship more formal and detached than his letters to Beecher of a decade earlier suggest. Under reexamination, Theodore Tilton was asked by his lawyers to offer his own version of the May 1871 conversation in the library. "The interview" in which Beecher had perched on Theodore's lap the better to make his point, he recalled:

> though not correctly described [in Beecher's testimony], rose vividly in my mind as having occurred about ten years ago. I remember a scene of that sort, except the kissing all round—I don't remember that circumstance—but about ten years ago there did occur a little incident of that sort, growing out of a pleasant little discussion that we had over the construction of a sentence in a little book that I had then published called "Golden Haired Gertrude."[59]

If Tilton's account of the incident inserts, retrospectively, a degree of distance between himself and Beecher, let me suggest that this distance was not empty but came to be filled, at least by the late 1860s, by the figure of Elizabeth, and for this reason I want to turn for a moment to examine Elizabeth's place in what she characterized as a "mutual admiration party" of three.[60] In late December 1867, well before her husband's suspicions surfaced, Elizabeth Tilton meditated in a letter to Theodore about her place in his friendship with Beecher:

> Why I so mysteriously was brought in as actor in this friendship, I know not yet. No experience of all my life has made my soul ache so keenly as the apparent lack of Christian manliness in this beloved man [Beecher] . . . I do love him very dearly, and I do love you supremely, utterly—believe it. Perhaps, if I, by God's grace, keep myself white, I may bless you both. I am striving. God bless this trinity.[61]

We might ask, along with Elizabeth, what precisely *was* her place in the trinity? This was, after all, the question formally under investigation at Beecher's trial. Given the intensity of the inquiry into the matter, it is significant that Elizabeth herself was never called to testify.[62] Although she attended the trial daily (as did Eunice Beecher, Henry's wife), she made no public statement about it. Instead, her guilt and complicity were asserted, her innocence defended; her letters were read, her guilelessness postulated; her actions were related and dissected, her good intentions affirmed, but Elizabeth's own testimony seemed irrelevant, unnecessary, or perhaps even dangerous.

In light of the larger events of Reconstruction, we might read Elizabeth's positioning in both the "trinity" and the inquiry more politically, as an example of the type of silent female citizenship established as law by *Minor v. Happersett*.

Indeed, evidence from the trial testimony suggests just that. Beecher's trial hinged on the question of the nature of the relationship he developed with Elizabeth during the months that Theodore had been away on lecture tours and Beecher had visited nightly to read to Elizabeth from the draft of his manuscript and drink in her "uncritical praise."[63] On the witness stand, Theodore Tilton was asked to speculate about how his wife's insight may have benefitted Beecher:

> Tilton: . . . [Elizabeth] is not a critique [sic] in the sense that she can take a particular phrase and change the language of it; but she could tell whether a little speech put into Rose Wentworth's mouth was one a woman would be likely to say.
> Q: He [Beecher] took those chapters to read to her for that purpose, having a high regard for her opinion in that matter—not as high regard for her opinion in a strictly critical sense?
> Tilton: No; but in the sense whether it was womanly, and larger than that, whether it touched human sympathy or not.[64]

Elizabeth's critical capacities, it seems, were more a function and a measure of her womanliness than anything else, valuable to Beecher and Tilton alike (at least according to Tilton) as a positive authenticator of (what they already knew to be) the truth of her sex. In this sense what both Beecher and Tilton heard when Elizabeth opened her mouth to speak—regardless of what she may actually have said—were their own thoughts, and their own assumptions about the nature of gender, echoing back at themselves.

Elizabeth Tilton's image of a trinity formed of her husband, herself, and Beecher is at least in retrospect quite insightful, for it marks a break in the public bonds established between men in the era prior to the outbreak of the Civil War. Significantly, Elizabeth's image suggests a new triangulation of desire, a (re)channeling of the bonds that linked Theodore and Henry through a woman, Elizabeth herself. Thus it recharacterizes public desire as heterosexual even as it retains at, and as, its stabilizing base the masculine personages of Beecher and Theodore Tilton. Elizabeth's letter to her husband calls to mind what Sedgwick refers to in *Between Men* as the "folk-wisdom of erotic triangles." For Sedgwick, "in any erotic rivalry, the bond that links the two rivals is as intense and potent as the bond that links either of the rivals to the beloved: . . . the bonds of 'rivalry' and 'love,' differently as they are experienced, are equally powerful and in many senses equivalent."[65] The erotic triangle composed of two men vying for the affections of the same woman reencodes male homosocial desire as heterosexual by redirecting desire through the figure of a woman, even as it remakes patriarchal power on new ground. To suggest a kind of continuity to patriarchal power that survives the shift from homosocial to heterosexual public sphere risks glossing too quickly over the profundity of this transformation of the shape and meaning of social space itself, a transformation in meaning that not only affects the future of public life in America, but is also enacted retrospectively to evaluate and assign new and different meanings to the pre-Civil War practices of citizenship.

Scandalous!

If we understand the study of politics to concern itself primarily with the examination of norms, of public behaviors and commonly held priorities that gain institutional stature, then we might be inclined to view scandal as being at best marginally significant to that enterprise. Scandals do not promote so much as they upset established orders, they do not confirm and secure institutions, but imperil the illusion of stability itself. Yet for precisely these reasons I would suggest that scandal offers important resources for the study of political life, for scandalous events open to scrutiny the very things we are most wont to take for granted, render them problematic, and, accordingly, offer us important opportunities to begin to view sedimented practices in new and different light. Scandals dramatize to us that what we consider to be norms may not be quite as hegemonic or as universally shared as we might like to think they are, and that institutions may be formed of ultimately unsustainable combinations of ideals, intentions, and practices.[66]

Scandals are, after all, extraordinary happenings. They are unpredictable and ultimately uncontainable phenomena, formed by the confluence of a chain of circumstances brought together under conditions that are themselves highly contingent. Only in retrospect—that is, once a scandal has broken and its details have been poured into the media, absorbed, and digested—are events reassembled and given the appearance of having been determined by fate or human conspiracy. Scandals may be contingent then, but they are not arbitrary. Events become scandalous when they capture the public imagination in a particular moment and in a particular way, when they touch on some common preoccupation or simmering tension that has operated just beneath the surface of everyday life for some time.

Paradoxically enough, scandals seem both to disrupt our collective life and to promote it, albeit on somewhat different grounds. They interrupt our routine, day-to-day activities; they command our attention, and draw us into their universe of rumor, innuendo, and detail, and yet by doing so they make it possible for us to feel that these rumors are somehow our own; they are something we hold in common, even if "we" position ourselves contentiously around them. Scandals thus produce the very publics that consume scandalous events, and produce them more often than not as differentiated rather than unitary entities.[67] Moreover, scandal not only promotes multiple interpretations of the same events, but is a consequence of the coexistence of radically dissonant worldviews. More precisely, scandal develops in response to attempts to deny or efface the presence of this dissonance in the public order.[68] Our understanding of a particular scandal, and our response to it, may be thus conditioned by our receptiveness to the world, a world that scandal might, in turn, open us to or enclose us against. We may respond conservatively; we may be inspired to promote further scandal; or we may be prompted to something altogether different. Scandals can invite us to pass judgment quickly, to repeat a litany of received moral standards, to retreat—scandalized—into the complacency of the given; or they can incite us and excite us, making us scandalmongers who celebrate the violation of outmoded moral codes. Yet scandals may also prompt us to something more studied and (self-)reflective, an opportunity to engage their pleasures critically, and to find cautious inspiration in their dangers. For if scandals may confirm us in our preexisting orientation toward the world, they may also disorient us in productive ways and to radical effect. They can prompt us to return to the form and structure of events themselves, to rethink the past not as a definitive answer, but as an openended question, awaiting new interpretation and taking on new meaning in light of the events of the present and the new challenges they pose.

Returning to the particular scandal at hand, that of Beecher and the Tiltons, it is precisely the new prominence given the body within citizenship during Reconstruction, a constitutional order we inherit but which was unknown, or at least altogether new, to the world they inhabited, that differentiates us and our grasp of the scandal from its actors and their experience of it. To take another look at their world in light of what is distinct about our own may set into motion something of a scandal in our own understanding of the Founding and its political effects. The forms of friendship possible in a given state, Aristotle suggests, are linked to the form of constitution that organizes it.[69] As we know, constitutions establish and order the administrative structures of government, and they provide stable institutional frameworks for the interpretation of laws. They also participate in a far more ambitious project, namely, in generating or fostering a mode of collective life that itself produces the institutional, legal, and cultural structures that we call a polity.

If it is the case, then, that practices of political friendship are related to forms of constitution, it follows that a constitutional shift as profound as that effected by the Reconstruction Amendments would also mark a turn away from older forms of citizenship and political action. Indeed, the transformations of Reconstruction—including the decommodification of the African-American body suggested by the abolition of slavery, the complicated politics of race and gender implicated in the Fourteenth and Fifteenth Amendments, and the new techniques of formal political identification that followed—wrought important changes in the meanings Americans would attach to citizenship as well as to the practices that comprised it. Paradoxically, if the language of citizenship fostered by the 1787 Constitution rendered the citizen's body impalpable in public life, the newly embodied motifs of citizenship enshrined in the Reconstruction Amendments promoted far greater physical and sentimental circumspection among citizens than did its predecessor. If, today, we inhabit the aftermath of that shift, nineteenth-century abolitionists and women's rights activists like Beecher and the Tiltons straddled it, struggling to come to terms with a subtle but important change in public meanings of political action, changes of which they were, at most, only vaguely conscious.

In an era when the body was overtly acknowledged for the first time in constitutional languages of citizenship, when women were admitted explicitly (in the words of Chief Justice Morrison Waite) to "membership [in] a nation and nothing more" and on that basis denied the vote,[70] politics itself came to be structured along the lines of heterosexuality, with women made dependent upon husbands' votes to convey their dispositions on matters of public importance. This new structure of suffrage rights worked in much the same way as what feminist economists and social historians have called the family wage, in which male breadwinners were paid wages adequate (in theory if rarely in practice) to the support of a family, and particularly a wife, who performed the necessary but otherwise uncompensated domestic labor that made possible her husband's productivity in the workplace. Like the family wage, the new structure of suffrage rights formalized women's inequality with men by institutionalizing their dependence on them.

Endnotes

1. "Self, Power, and the Politics of Identity," *Michel Foucault: Ethics, Subjectivity, and Truth*, ed. Paul Rabinow (New York: The New Press, 1997), 171.

2. In general, my account of the events surrounding Beecher's trial is drawn from

collected newspaper accounts as well as the trial transcripts, published as *Theodore Tilton against Henry Ward Beecher, Action for Crim. Con.* (New York: McDivitt, Campbell & Co., Law Publishers, 1875), 3 vols. Many of the newpaper accounts, as well as letters and affadavits entered as evidence in the trial, were republished in a variety of venues, including *The Beecher-Tilton Investigation: The Scandal of the Age* (Philadelphia, 1874; *The Beecher-Tilton Scandal: Complete History of the Case from November 1872 to the Present Time* (Brooklyn, 1874); John E.P. Doyle, *Plymouth Church and Its Pastor, or Henry Ward Beecher and His Accusers* (Hartford, 1874); Edmund Fairfield, *Wickedness in High Places* (Mansfield, Ohio, 1874); *The Great Brooklyn Romance: All the Documents in the Famous Beecher-Tilton Case, Unabridged* (New York: Paxon's, 1874); Leon Oliver, *The Great Sensation* (Chicago, 1873); Joseph Treat, *Beecher, Tilton, Woodhull: The Creation of Society* (New York, 1874); Francis P. Williamson, *Beecher and His Accusers* (Philadelphia, 1874); Charles F. Marshall, *The True History of the Brooklyn Scandal* (Philadelphia, 1874). A variety of secondary works, from which I have drawn as well, explore the scandal with considerably more detailed and complex analyses than I have presented. The two most comprehensive of these are Richard Wightman Fox, *Trials of Intimacy: Love and Loss in the Beecher-Tilton Scandal* (Chicago: The University of Chicago Press, 1999), and Altina L. Waller, *Reverend Beecher and Mrs. Tilton: Sex and Class in Victorian America* (Amherst: The University of Massachusetts Press, 1982); see also Richard Wightman Fox, "Intimacy on Trial: Cultural Meanings of the Beecher-Tilton Affair," *The Power of Culture: Critical Essays in American History,* eds. R.W. Fox and T.J. Lears (Chicago: The University of Chicago Press, 1993), 103–34; Robert Shaplen, *Free Love and Heavenly Sinners* (New York: Alfred A. Knopf, 1954); William G. McLoughlin, *The Meaning of Henry Ward Beecher: An Essay in the Shifting Values of Mid-Victorian America* (New York: Alfred A. Knopf, 1970); Clifford E. Clark, Jr., *Henry Ward Beecher: Spokesman for a Middle-Class America* (Urbana: University of Illinois Press, 1978); Paxton Hibben, *Henry Ward Beecher: An American Portrait* (1927) (New York: Press of the Readers Club, 1942). See also two "Beecher family" biographies: William C. Beecher and Rev. Samuel Scoville, *A Biography of Henry Ward Beecher* (New York: Charles L. Webster & Company, 1888); Lyman Beecher Stowe, *Saints, Sinners, and Beechers* (Indianapolis: Bobbs-Merrill & Co., 1934).

3. *Theodore Tilton against Henry Ward Beecher, Action for Crim. Con.*, vol. 2, 735.

4. Undated memorandum by Elizabeth Tilton, Beecher Family Papers, Sterling Memorial Library, Yale University, Group 71, Series I, Box 45, Folder 2021.

5. *The Great Brooklyn Romance: All the Documents in the Famous Beecher-Tilton Case, Unabridged,* 105.

6. The sisters were imprisoned under the authority of the Comstock laws for distributing this putatively obscene material though the U.S. mail. *Woodhull and Claflin's*

Weekly, November 2, 1872. See also "Victoria C. Woodhull. A Glance behind the Scenes in her own and Sister's Lives. To the Editor of 'The Standard.'" (1873) in Victoria Woodhull Martin Papers, Southern Illinois University Archives, Carbondale, IL.

7. Altina Waller, *Reverend Beecher and Mrs. Tilton: Sex and Class in Victorian America*, 11.

8. These interpretations are offered, respectively, by William G. McLaughlin, *The Meaning of Henry Ward Beecher: An Essay in the Shifting Values of Mid-Victorian America*; Clifford E. Clark, Jr., *Henry Ward Beecher: Spokesman for a Middle-Class America*; Altina L. Waller, *Reverend Beecher and Mrs. Tilton: Sex and Class in Victorian America*; Richard Wightman Fox, "Intimacy on Trial: Cultural Meanings of the Beecher-Tilton Affair," *The Power of Culture: Critical Essays in American History*, 103–34; and Barbara Goldsmith, *Other Powers: The Age of Suffrage, Spiritualism, and the Scandalous Victoria Woodhull* (New York: Alfred A. Knopf, 1998). For additional discussions, see Paxton Hibben, *Henry Ward Beecher: An American Portrait*; William C. Beecher and Rev. Samuel Scoville, *A Biography of Henry Ward Beecher*; and Lyman Beecher Stowe, *Saints, Sinners, and Beechers*.

9. Leon Oliver, *The Great Sensation: A Full, Complete and Reliable History of the Beecher-Tilton-Woodhull Scandal* (Chicago: The Beverly Company, 1873), 3. Emphasis in original.

10. Lauren Berlant, "National Brands/National Body: *Imitation of Life*," *The Phantom Public Sphere*, ed. Bruce Robbins (Minneapolis: University of Minnesota Press, 1993), 176.

11. Martha Hodes, "The Sexualization of Reconstruction Politics: White Women and Black Men in the South after the Civil War," *Journal of the History of Sexuality* 3:3 (1993), 412. See also Robyn Wiegman, "The Anatomy of Lynching," *Journal of the History of Sexuality* 3:3 (1993), 445–67; Diane Miller Sommerville, "The Rape Myth in the Old South Reconsidered," *Journal of Southern History* LXI:3 (August 1995), 481–518; Laura F. Edwards, "The Disappearance of Susan Daniel and Henderson Cooper: Gender and Narratives of Political Conflict in the Reconstruction-Era U.S. South," *Feminist Studies* 22:2 (Summer 1996), 363–386.

12. Letter from Theodore Tilton to Henry Ward Beecher, Beecher Family Papers, Sterling Memorial Library, Yale University, Group 71, Series I, Box 15, Folder 615.

13. Letter from Theodore Tilton to Henry Ward Beecher, July 3, 1863, Beecher Family Papers, Sterling Memorial Library, Yale University, Group 71, Series I, Box 15, Folder 615.

14. Letter from Theodore Tilton to Henry Ward Beecher, August 7, 863, Beecher Family Papers, Sterling Memorial Library, Yale University, Group 71, Series I, Box 15, Folder 615.

15. Letter from Theodore Tilton to Henry Ward Beecher, September 18, 1863, Beecher Family Papers, Sterling Memorial Library, Yale University, Group 71, Series I, Box 15, Folder 615. Emphasis in original.

16. Letter from Theodore Tilton to Henry Ward Beecher, September 24, 1863, Beecher Family Papers, Sterling Memorial Library, Yale University, Group 71, Series I, Box 15, Folder 615.

17. *Tilton v. Beecher,* vol. 2, 738.

18. Quoted in *Tilton v. Beecher,* vol. 2, 738.

19. *Tilton v. Beecher*, vol. 2, 735.

20. Theodore Tilton to Henry Ward Beecher, November 30, 1865, in *Tilton v. Beecher*, vol. 2, 738.

21. Theodore Tilton to Elizabeth Tilton, February 12, 1867. Quoted in *Tilton v. Beecher,* vol. 2,14.

22. Significantly, for Aristotle happiness is not a state of being but "a kind of activity; and an activity clearly is developed and is not a piece of property already in one's possession." "To be" happy is, in Aristotle's terms, the effect of prior actions, not an organic, permanent, or natural state. There is nothing passive or given about happiness; happiness is fabricated, brought into being in and through action, not invoked or evoked as an organic emotion or harmonic state. See Aristotle, *Ethics*, 1098a7, 16; 1169b11–35. I am using J. A. K. Thomson's translation, published as Aristotle, *Ethics* (New York: Penguin, 1986).

23. Aristotle, *Ethics,* see 1156b2–23.

24. Hence, Aristotle distinguishes the types of friendship according to the purposes for which they are formed, not by those who are parties to them. See his *Ethics*, trans. J. A. K. Thomson (Harmondsworth: Penguin, 1986), esp. Books Eight and Nine. For fuller dicussions of Aristotle's understanding of friendship than can be undertaken here, see Susan Bickford, "Beyond Friendship: Aristotle on Conflict, Deliberation, and Attention," *Journal of Politics* 58:2, 398–421; Bernard Yack, *The Problems of a Political Animal* (Berkeley: University of California Press, 1993); Bernard Yack, "Community and Conflict in Aristotle's Political Philosophy," *Review of Politics* 47, 92–112; John M. Cooper, "Aristotle on Friendship,"*Essays on Aristotle's Ethics*, ed. Amelie Oksenberg Rorty (Berkeley: University of California Press, 1980); John M. Cooper, "Aristotle on the Forms of Friendship," *Review of Metaphysics* 30:4, 619–48.

25. This is what Yack calls friendship based on "shared advantage." See Yack, *Problems of a Political Animal*, Chapter Four.

26. Aristotle, *Ethics*, 1172a6.

27. Aristotle's criticism of Plato's *Republic*, for example, took that work to task for promoting a form of political intimacy so close, and so enclosed, that it rendered difference impossible, reduced the polis to the singular, and hence annihilated politics. In

Aristotle's words, Plato's polis "attempted as far as possible to be entirely one. . . . And yet it is evident that as it becomes increasingly one it will no longer be a polis. For the polis is in its nature a certain sort of multitude (*plēthos*), and as it becomes more a unity it will be an *oikos* instead of a polis and [then] a human being instead of an *oikos*. . . . So even if one were able to do this, one ought not to do it, as it would destroy the polis. Now the polis is made up not only of a number of human beings, but also of human beings differing in kind; a polis does not arise from persons who are similar (*ex homoiōn*)." See Aristotle, *Politics*, 1261a15–24. This translation is by Josiah Ober, and can be found in Josiah Ober, "The Polis as a Society: Aristotle, John Rawls, and the Athenian Social Contract," *The Athenian Revolution: Essays on Ancient Greek Democracy and Political Theory* (Princeton: Princeton University Press, 1996), 171. For further discussion, see also Bernard Yack, *The Problems of a Political Animal*, 118–21.

28. Yack, *Problems of a Political Animal*, 110. More recently, Susan Bickford has suggested that Aristotle's language of friendship and community is at odds with his emphasis, elsewhere, on the kind of discord and disagreement that requires citizens to engage in political deliberation. "What governs and makes possible . . . adversarial communicative interaction," she writes, "is not, for Aristotle, friendship or concord, but rather a quality of *attention* inherent in the very practice of deliberation" (399). For Bickford, Aristotle's reliance on political friendship to establish a bond between citizens promotes a "unitary polity, one in which a sense of common interest underlies interaction" (408). By contrast, his concern with the process of deliberation, Bickford argues, makes possible a richer and more "adversary democracy [which] understands citizen interests to be in conflict" (398). While I agree with Bickford that there is a tension within Aristotle between an emphasis on community and a willingness to promote a more discordant democracy, and while I am sympathetic with her desire to promote a means of enriching political contest, it seems to me that Bickford's tendency to occasionally conflate friendship with concord (in spite of her efforts to distinguish between them) leads to too-rigid dichotomies of friendship and conflict, and a deeply problematic assumption about "unitary" (as opposed to "adversary") democracy. At issue is the degree to which we freight "friendship" with modern qualities that deny it its more explicitly plural and political connotations. In this respect, doesn't the very concept of unitary democracy deny the irreducibly *plural* nature of politics and the difference that plurality entails? In this sense, is not a "unitary democracy" somewhat of an oxymoron? See Susan Bickford, "Beyond Friendship: Aristotle on Conflict, Deliberation, and Attention," 398–99, 408.

29. Henry Ward Beecher, "Soul-Relationship," *Plymouth Pulpit: Sermons Preached in Plymouth Church* (New York: Fords, Howard, & Hulbert, 1892), II:148–49.

30. Henry Ward Beecher, "The Primacy of Love," *Plymouth Pulpit: Sermons Preached in Plymouth Church*, II:50.

31. Henry Ward Beecher, "Soul-Relationship," *Plymouth Pulpit*, II:151.
32. Henry Ward Beecher, "Soul-Relationship," *Plymouth Pulpit*, II:150.
33. Henry Ward Beecher, "The Primacy of Love," *Plymouth Pulpit*, II:51.
34. Ann Douglas, *The Feminization of American Culture* (New York: Knopf, 1977). The term "therapeutic" is Richard Wightman Fox's, in "Intimacy on Trial: Cultural Meanings of the Beecher-Tilton Affair," 120.
35. Altina L. Waller, *Reverend Beecher and Mrs. Tilton: Sex and Class in Victorian America*, 109.
36. Richard Wightman Fox, "Intimacy on Trial: Cultural Meanings of the Beecher-Tilton Affair," 121.
37. Bruce Burgett, *Sentimental Bodies: Sex, Gender, and Citizenship in the Early Republic* (Princeton: Princeton University Press, 1998), 3.
38. Hannah Arendt, "On Humanity in Dark Times: Thoughts about Lessing," *Men in Dark Times* (New York: Harcourt Brace & Company, 1983), 13.
39. For extended discussion of why the "weaker" form of friendship fosters democratic politics better than the stronger, more affective types, see Yack, *Problems of a Political Animal*, esp. 110–27. For a similar argument framed in terms of feminism, see Martha A. Ackelsberg, "'Sisters' or 'Comrades'? The Politics of Friends and Family," *Families, Politics, and Public Policies: A Feminist Dialogue on Women and the State*, ed. Irene Diamond (New York: Longman, 1983), 339–56; also Mary G. Dietz, "Citizenship With A Feminist Face: The Problem With Maternal Thinking," *Political Theory* 13:1 (February 1985), 19–37.
40. Jill Frank, "A Unity of the Different," paper presented at the Annual Meeting of the American Political Science Association, September 1998, 14.
41. Jonathan Ned Katz, *Gay American History* (New York: Thomas Y. Crowell, 1976), 453.
42. This, and more, quoted in Jonathan Ned Katz, *Gay American History*, 453–454.
43. Donald Yacovone, "Abolitionists and the 'Language of Fraternal Love,'" *Meanings for Manhood: Constructions of Masculinity in Victorian America*, eds. Mark C. Carnes and Clyde Griffen (Chicago: The University of Chicago Press, 1990), 85–95. Yacovone bases his analysis on relationships that developed, among abolitionists, between Charles Stuart and Theodore Weld, William Lloyd Garrison and Samuel May, and Ralph Waldo Emerson and Martin Gay, and among proslavery intellectuals including William Gillmore Simms, Nathaniel Beverley Tucker, and William H. Hammond. For a compelling account of the ways that this "fraternal love" is reconfigured during the Gilded Age in accord with the demands of monopoly capitalism, see Michael Moon, "'The Gentle Boy from the Dangerous Classes': Pederasty, Domesticity, and Capitalism in Horatio Alger," *Representations* 19 (Summer 1987), 87–110.

44. Eve Kosofsky Sedgwick, *Between Men: English Literature and Male Homosocial Desire* (New York: Columbia University Press, 1985), 1.

45. Here is Sedgwick's effort to suggest the ways in which "men-promoting-the-interests-of-men" fosters a complex form of homosocial desire: "When Ronald Reagan and Jesse Helms get down to serious logrolling on 'family policy,' they are men promoting men's interests. (In fact, they embody Heidi Hartmann's definition of patriarchy: 'relations between men, which have a material base, and which, though hierarchical, establish or create interdependence and solidarity among men that enable them to dominate women.') Is their bond in any way congruent with the bond of a loving gay male couple? Reagan and Helms would say no—disgustedly. Most gay couples would say no—disgustedly. But why not?" (3). Elsewhere, she suggests that "the example of the [ancient] Greeks demonstrates . . . that while heterosexuality is necessary for the maintenance of any patriarchy, homophobia, against males at any rate, is not. In fact, for the Greeks, the continuum between 'men loving men' and 'men promoting the interests of men' appears to have been quite seamless. It is as if, in our terms, there were no perceived discontinuity between the male bonds at the Continental Baths and the male bonds at the Bohemian Grove or in the board room or Senate cloakroom" (4). Both passages are from Eve Kosofsky Sedgwick, *Between Men: English Literature and Male Homosocial Desire*.

46. Eve Kosofsky Sedgwick, *Between Men: English Literature and Male Homosocial Desire*, 2.

47. See, for example, Christopher Castiglia, "Rebel Without a Closet," *Engendering Men: The Question of Male Feminist Criticism*, eds. Joseph A. Boone and Michael Cadden (New York: Routledge, 1990), 207–21.

48. See also Eve Kosofsky Sedgwick, *Epistemology of the Closet* (Berkeley: University of California Press, 1990).

49. John Adams, "Discourses on Davila," *Works*, ed. Charles Francis Adams (Boston: Little, Brown, 1851), VI:232–33. Emphasis in original.

50. John Adams, "Discourses on Davila," *Works*, VI: 233–34.

51. Hannah Arendt, *On Revolution* (New York: Penguin), 120.

52. Notably, the term "the pursuit of public happiness," which Jefferson used in his *Summary View of the Rights of British America, 1774*, was abbreviated two years later to "the pursuit of happiness" in the Declaration of Independence. See Thomas Jefferson, *The Life and Selected Writings of Thomas Jefferson*, ed. Adrienne Koch and William Peden (New York: Modern Library, 1944), 293.

53. John Adams, "Discourses on Davila," *Works*, VI: 234.

54. Hannah Arendt, *On Revolution*, 119.

55. Jonathan Ned Katz, *The Invention of Heterosexuality* (New York: Penguin,

1995). Of course, the psycho-scientific inquiry into homosexuality did not really reach full flower until a few decades later, but as Michel Foucault has established, the initial identification of the homosexual took place around 1870. See Michel Foucault, *The History of Sexuality, Volume I: An Introduction* (New York: 1980), 43. There is some dispute about this precise date, circulating mostly around questions of technical distinctions in medical use of the terms "sexual invert" and "homosexual." For my purposes here, however, these distinctions are less significant than is the larger emerging public concern with what Foucault calls "a certain quality of sexual sensibility." See David M. Halperin, *One Hundred Years of Homosexuality and Other Essays on Greek Love* (New York: Routledge, 1990); also George Chauncey, Jr., "From Sexual Inversion to Homosexuality: Medicine and the Changing Conceptualization of Female Deviance," *Salmagundi* 58–59 (Fall 1982–Winter 1983), 114–45. See also Eve Kosofsky Sedgwick's discussion of this dispute in *Epistemology of the Closet*, 44–48.

56. These notes and letters were entrusted to a mutual acquaintance, Frank Moulton, who was instructed to destroy them all. Moulton did not destroy the letters, but produced them as evidence before the committee convened by Plymouth Church to investigate the charges, and he later distributed copies of these letters to newspapers.

57. *Tilton v. Beecher*, vol. II, 796.

58. Memorandum from Elizabeth Tilton (May 20, 1871), Beecher Family Papers, Sterling Memorial Library, Yale University, Group 71, Series I, Box 45, Folder 2021.

59. *Tilton v. Beecher*, vol. I, 501–2.

60. Undated memorandum by Elizabeth Tilton, Beecher Family Papers, Sterling Memorial Library, Yale University, Group 71, Series I, Box 45, Folder 2021.

61. *Tilton v. Beecher*, vol. 1, 499.

62. According to historian Richard Wightman Fox, Elizabeth asked to testify on Beecher's behalf but his lawyers opposed her doing so on the grounds that common law prevented a woman from testifying against her own husband. See Richard Wightman Fox, "Intimacy on Trial: Cultural Meanings of the Beecher-Tilton Trial," 107.

63. *Tilton v. Beecher*, vol. II, 735.

64. Quoted in *The Great Brooklyn Romance: All the Documents in the Famous Beecher-Tilton Case, Unabridged* (New York: Paxon's, 1874), 67.

65. Eve Kosofsky Sedgwick, *Between Men: English Literature and Male Homosocial Desire*, 21.

66. For a very interesting discussion of how much of the twentieth-century historiography of pre-Revolutionary France has trivialized and ignored the political implications of a whole variety of that era's putatively private scandals, and a demonstration of the ways our understanding of the crises of state in the Old Regime is enriched by attending more carefully to them, see Sarah Maza, *Private Lives and Public Affairs: The*

Causes Célèbres of Prerevolutionary France (Berkeley: The University of California Press, 1993).

67. I recall, for example, having dinner with a friend in a large and impersonal Greenwich Village restaurant in 1991, only days after Anita Hill testified before the Senate Judiciary Committee. In the middle of our conversation (guess what and who we were talking about), we realized that the people at tables all around us—strangers, all of them—were having variations on the same discussion. Occasionally, the diners at one table would acknowledge their neighbors by agreeing with, or taking exception to, the perspectives being offered on workplace sexual harassment at another table, or would simply pause to listen to their neighbors relating their own experience of harassment in the workplace. On the occasion of the Hill-Thomas scandal, Manhattan—that fabled protector of privacy and guarantor of anonymity—had been transformed, if only for a week, into something of a common world where strangers talked to one another, disagreed publicly and sometimes loudly, and most important, learned from others who were unlike them as they argued and offered counterinterpretations of the stories they were consuming from the media and from one another.

68. Consider, in this respect, the variety of scandals that have plagued the Clinton presidency ever since reports about Clinton's (now acknowledged) affair with Gennifer Flowers, or his use of drugs as a student (also acknowledged, though with the important qualification that he never inhaled), surfaced during the 1992 campaign. Widely touted by pundits as a member of the Woodstock Generation, Clinton has come to represent the ascent of a new generation—the one that came of age in an era of sex, drugs, and rock n' roll—to national office. If Clinton himself has courted the image by, among other things, choosing a Fleetwood Mac song as his campaign's theme (hence dignifying the rock n' roll element of the trinity even as he betrayed questionable taste in music), he has also sought repeatedly to distance himself from it. If he has made repeated gestures in an effort to appeal to feminists, he has also signed into law numerous bills that damage, defer, or withdraw hard-won institutional gains on behalf of women, particularly poor women; if he courts queer votes with talk of dignity and public acceptance, he is also the father of "Don't Ask, Don't Tell" and the defender of (exclusively) heterosexual marriage now formalized in federal law through the Defense of Marriage Act he endorsed; if he spoke proudly and nostalgically of his support for the Civil Rights movement, he also peremptorily withdrew his nomination of Lani Guinier for the office of Assistant Attorney General in charge of the Civil Rights Division, denouncing her work in terms that were at least as vicious as those pronounced by columnist Clint Bolick or Senator Alan Simpson. In short, if Clinton courted the image of Woodstock and that segment of his generation that sought to liberate what was once (and is now again) called private life, he has also persistently appealed to the New

Right—formed, as it happens, by members of his own generation as well. By denying the tensions between his own (past?) commitments to some branch of the Left, and his (present? simultaneous?) affinity with the "traditional family values" of the Right, Clinton has refused rather than accepted the challenge of engaging politically with two competing sets of his own "generational" constituents, with (at least) two competing visions held by his national constituents, and perhaps with competing tendencies within his own political vision. Is it any wonder, then, that his administration would be plagued so persistently by the scandal that comes of an effort to live and play on one side of a massively divided generation—indeed, of a massively divided nation—but work on and for the other? This is not hypocrisy, as has often been charged, so much as the raw material for national scandal.

69. See in this regard, Aristotle's discussion of the forms of friendship, and the cycle of constitutions, in Book Eight of the *Nicomachean Ethics*. A somewhat different formulation of this point is suggested, as well, in the *Politics*, when Aristotle argues that the good citizen can be a good man only under the best of constitutions: ". . . the excellence of the citizen must be an excellence relative to the constitution. It follows from this that if there are several different kinds of constitution [the excellence of the citizen must also be of several different kinds, and] there cannot be a single absolute excellence of the good citizen." Aristotle, *Politics*, trans. Ernest Barker (London: Oxford University Press, 1958), at 1276b20.

70. Quoted in Rogers Smith, *Civic Ideals: Conflicting Visions of Citizenship in U.S. History*, (New Haven: Yale University Press, 1997), 341.

5

In the Beginning Was a Crime: Lynching, Rape, and the Reconstruction of the Political Imagination

> Being obliged to forget becomes the basis for remembering the nation, peopling it anew, imagining the possibility of other contending and liberating forms of cultural identification.
> Homi K. Bhabha[1]

> Supposing "antiquity" were, at a certain historical juncture, the *necessary consequence* of "novelty"?
> Benedict Anderson[2]

IF RECONSTRUCTION SAW THE SEXUALIZATION OF POLITICS, IT WAS ALSO marked by a commensurate tendency to rethink the shape of the political realm in familial terms. A variety of initiatives promoted during Radical Reconstruction, beyond the structure of the compromise on suffrage, sought explicitly to reshape the black family—once a realm of, in the words of Eric Foner, "the rough 'equality' of powerlessness"[3]—as a patriarchal institution dominated by a father/husband. The Freedman's Bureau, for example, summarily designated the husband as the sole head of his family and granted him, and him alone, the authority to contract for the labor of his entire family. The Freedman's Bureau Act of 1865 specified that every *male* freedman would be granted land; similarly, the Southern Homestead Act a year later indicated that women would be alloted land only if they were unmarried.[4]

Beyond this, the era saw the beginnings of a rhetoric of reconciliation that depicted the nation itself as a family whose sections were (re)joined as if in marriage by the initiatives of Reconstruction. As Nina Silber has documented extensively, Northerners adopted a set of increasingly gendered metaphors for imagining the nation, reunited after the Civil War, as a house(hold) undivided: Northerners' image of the South "conformed to their image of the idealized feminine sphere; in northern eyes, the South became a region of refined domestic comfort, and the union of North and South restored the sense of domestic harmony that northern society no longer possessed."[5] If this was at first a rocky marriage, with the passage of time came increasing stability. As Silber puts it: "Many [northerners] apparently felt that the emotional attachment of northerners and southerners was of much greater importance than sectional politics; in this way, it became much easier to forget the history and lessons of the Civil War. It also became easier to overlook the South's present-day problems, especially the poverty of many southern whites and the social and economic oppression suffered by southern blacks. These, in effect, became lesser concerns which the South, as junior partner, had won the right to manage on its own."[6] This restructuring of the nation as family suggests a complex and distinctly modern conceptual innovation central to the politics of Reconstruction, namely the (re)emergence of an archaic force held in reserve within the American political imagination. The family, long suppressed by liberal modernism as a principle of political organization (if not as an economic unit), returned in precisely that capacity in, during, and as Reconstruction.

(Re)birth of a nation

D.W. Griffith's 1915 film classic, *The Birth of a Nation*, depicts the founding of the Ku Klux Klan during Reconstruction in response to the attempted rape of a white woman by a recently emancipated slave. In the film's final scene, a group of white citizens dressed in Roman togas gathers in a meeting hall in what Patricia Williams has described as "an apparent state of fraternal bliss." The final subtitle reads, "Liberty and Union, One and Inseparable, Now and Forever!"[7] If the film's lynching scenes and its racial and sectional divisiveness sit uneasily alongside its evocation of civic republicanism, its language of unity and national indivisibility, and its celebration of fraternal citizenship, it is tempting to resolve these tensions too easily by attributing them simply to the romanticized racism of the Progressive Era. However, a closer look at the way the film promotes, and in the end apparently disavows, racial hatred and sectional conflict complicates our desire for neat divisions, symmetrical distinctions, and fluid, continuous, and uninterrupted chronologies.

Asked to explain the logic behind his film's title, Griffith himself offered a somewhat garbled account of America's founding. The film was entitled *The Birth of a Nation*, he explained in 1915, "Because it is. . . . The Civil War was fought fifty years ago. But the real nation has only existed in the last fifteen or twenty years . . . The birth of a nation began . . . with the Ku Klux Klans."[8] As Michael Rogin has suggested, the "floating 'it'" in Griffith's response makes it unclear what, precisely, Griffith meant to identify as the immediate catalyst of national (re)birth: the political climate of Reconstruction during which the Klan was originally organized, that of the Progressive Era which coincides with what Griffith describes as the "existence of the real nation," or the film itself.[9] To these possibilities, I would like to suggest an even stranger interpretation of Griffith's understanding of his film. If the "birth of a nation began . . . with the Ku Klux Klans," perhaps we might view that "floating 'it'" as a sort of fabulous transposition of the Klan back to America's *original* founding, that of 1776 or 1787. In the pages that follow, I explore the ways that white supremacist fraternal organizations of the Reconstruction era did indeed construct an elaborate national genealogy, one that claimed a direct line of descent from this original founding. This genealogy, replete with national fathers, prodigal sons, and unwelcome cousins, was articulated in light of the effect of the Reconstruction Amendments on the meaning of national citizenship.

Southern proslavery thought, which Louis Hartz has called America's "Reactionary Enlightenment," occupies a somewhat anomalous place in the American political imagination. For Hartz, Southern antebellum defenses of slavery represent a "remarkable twist coming out of America's odd relationship to modern political thought. A nation built in the liberal image and yet without the feudalism that liberalism destroyed, once it challenged the liberal formula, it began to reproduce the philosophy of a feudal world it had never seen."[10] In spite of this fantastic adaptation of patriarchal thought for plantation life, in spite of the "sweat that had to go into making the South medieval,"[11] and in spite of its efforts to articulate a romantic "theory of blood and solid nationalism,"[12] Hartz argues, "the political thought of the Civil War symbolizes not the weakness of the American liberal idea but its strength, its vitality, and its utter dominion over the American mind."[13] "This is exactly the pathos of Southern 'feudal' thought: the old liberal and the old bourgeois preoccupation kept sticking out all over it, betraying it, contradicting it."[14]

However, it may well be the case that, contra Hartz, the peculiarity of "Southern feudal thought" consists not in its absolute otherness to the larger tradition of political thought in the United States, but instead in its remarkable resurrection and restatement of it. This is especially true of the transubstantiation of Southern proslavery thought accomplished during Reconstruction. As I have argued, feudalism is not so alien to the liberal tradition in America as Hartz would have us think, for remnants of feudal tradition lived on, first as the local body of feudal-republicanism, and then as an archaic force within the body politic established by the liberal revolution of 1787. The crisis of citizen fraternity occasioned by the sudden visibility of the body in American languages of citizenship during Reconstruction prompted Southerners to return to and reembrace this complex heritage. In doing so, they did not simply reinhabit and rearticulate the traditions of 1776 or 1787, but instead developed their own distinctive—even fantastic—visions of national fraternity.

In the hands of Southerners concerned with shaping national reunification to their own purposes, the fantasy of national fraternity was also a fantasy of white fraternity. It is Hartz who asked why we need to attend to the strange and archaic tradition of Southern proslavery thought (which, I would argue, includes Reconstruction-era as well as antebellum thought): "If the episode [imagined by slavery's advocates] was fantastic, why worry about fantasy? If behind [the] elaborate feudal façade lay the vicious institution of slavery, why lament the fate of the façade?" Hartz himself offered one answer: "Fantasy may serve a curious purpose for the American political mind, for it may well be the only technique whereby it can seize any kind of perspective other than the liberal perspective which has governed throughout its history."[15] Let me offer another: perhaps fantasy is the only technique whereby the American liberal tradition can come to terms with itself.

As Rogers Smith has pointed out, Reconstruction both opened up and closed down possibilities for wide ranging political and economic reforms. The successes were real, of course. Reconstruction guaranteed the constitutional rights of freedmen; it accomplished the (admittedly limited) redistribution of property; and the efforts undertaken by the Freedmen's Bureau enabled former slaves to negotiate work contracts as free laborers. Nonetheless, it remains the case that many of the former Confederate states initiated legal efforts designed to constrain the legal rights of freedmen, to restrict them from renting land, and to force them into signing exploitative labor contracts that fostered working conditions little better than what they had known as slaves. This ambiguous legacy of Reconstruction, Smith argues, is best explained by what he calls the "multiple traditions approach," which recognizes the persistent and contemporaneous influence of doctrines of racial, ethnic, and gendered supremacy alongside competing doctrines of liberal egalitarianism throughout the course of American political development. In this respect, Smith attributes Reconstruction's thwarted efforts at reform to virulent racism on the part of most Southerners and many Northerners, a racism grounded in pseudo-scientific theories of racial hierarchy and black inferiority, and one that fomented hatred based in anxieties about racial difference.[16]

Smith is surely right to attribute white Americans' obstructionism at least in part to their investments in theories of racial hierarchy and black inferiority, and to the anxieties about racial difference they fostered. His emphasis on the various tensions circulating around the question of racial difference, however, runs the risk of obscuring an important, novel element of the Reconstruction initiatives themselves, and of white supremacists' response to them. For what is distinctive about the politics promoted by the Amendments is not the heightened legal salience of racial difference, but instead the dissolution of formal legal, political, and institutional markers of racial difference. The rhetorical structure of the Amendments works to guarantee freedmen's political standing not as a consequence of their race, but despite it: "the right of citizens . . . to vote *shall not be denied or abridged* . . . on account of race, color, or previous condition of servitude." Insofar as constitutional Reconstruction heightened the visibility of the raced body in American languages of citizenship, it did so, paradoxically, by (re)positioning race as a difference that makes no difference. The Amendments did not eliminate racial categories but retained them as empty signifiers within the political. However, if the law was formally indifferent to race, it was conspicuously not blind to gender. Freedmen's explicit claim on the rights of citizenship was grounded in their status as men, not their status as former slaves, a fact that became especially notable in light of the simultaneous and explicit denial of suffrage rights to women, both black and white. It is this legal identity of black men and white men that Smith's analysis obscures. As Robyn Wiegman has argued, the perceived "threat" posed by the admission of African-American men to national citizenship comes out of "the frightening possibility of a masculine sameness and not simply from a fear of racial difference."[17]

This is by no means to deny the extralegal, often forthrightly illegal, and undeniably brutal responses to the formal admission of black men to American citizenship on the part of recalcitrant white citizens, but rather to suggest a slightly different framework by which we might understand these responses. The fantasy of (re)building an exclusively white nation—a fantasy committed to celluloid decades later in D.W. Griffith's film, but enacted and theorized on a regular basis during the Reconstruction years—is founded as much in a terror of sameness as it is in the loathing of difference. In Reconstruction, these two complementary dynamics energized the process of imagining a newly reconciled

American nation that would be rent no longer by sectional tensions, family disputes, or civil wars.

Foundings and forgetting

In her meditation on Southerners' efforts to rethink gender and nation in the aftermath of the war, LeeAnn Whites brings to light a curious trick of nationalist memory at work in white Southern efforts to memorialize Confederate soldiers killed in battle. At an elaborate ceremony in April 1875, the residents of Augusta, Georgia laid the cornerstone of their memorial to the war dead. The Reverend General C.A. Evans explained in his dedicatory address that the monument symbolized not a declaration of continued adherence to the secessionist cause, but an opportunity to move beyond the "many distressing humiliations which we have suffered," and to ensure that as sectional animosities faded, only "the heroism, devotion and patriotism of all [would be] remembered." The memorial bore witness to the "honesty" and "valor" of Confederate soldiers' motives, another speaker insisted, even as it acknowledged that "men cannot always choose the right cause, but when, having chosen that which their conscience dictated, they are ready to die for it, if they justify not their cause, they at least ennoble themselves."[18] Whites's analysis is worthy of quoting here at some length:

> Once completed, [the monument] would mark the death of the Confederate cause, even as it indicated that the Confederate Dead continued to live. Indeed as the bearers of a new tradition in the making, they would grow larger in memory than they had been in life.
>
> Sectional reconciliation was therefore based on the abandonment of the causes of the war and focused instead on the common sacrifice of the individual soldier, whatever his political affiliation, whatever his "cause." There was, however, a hierarchy of abandonment here. The cause of Confederate independence could be articulated by the memorial movement as "lost," while the cause of the defense of the institution of slavery was either never mentioned or actively denied. The very silence and denial of the Confederate Memorial movement on the issue of slavery as a cause of sectional conflict revealed the way in which it was the cause that was truly lost. For although the Confederate nation was defeated, the political prerogatives of white men, which it had been designed to represent, were only lost insofar as ex-Confederates persisted in clinging to

the particular political form that they had taken in the drive for Confederate nationalism, and perhaps more critically, as long as they persisted in asserting their rights to slaveownership or some legal replication of it, as in the Black Codes.

What sectional reconciliation required of ex-Confederates was nothing less than a reconstructed understanding of what it meant to be a free white man.[19]

In Whites's analysis, the monuments and rituals that memorialized the Confederate dead represent efforts not to glorify the past or reanimate old antagonisms, but instead to clear a space in the national future for southerners killed in the war. These memorials performed a collective cleansing of both past and present, and forged a new vision of the vanquished Confederacy itself. This is not an effort at historical revisionism on the part of those defeated in the war, at least not in any simple sense, for what I understand Whites to be suggesting is that as they dedicated their memorials to the Confederate dead, white southerners produced two sets of memories. The first set, which recalled slavery and sectional conflict, comprised those memories that were to be forgotten in the name of Southern reconciliation and reconstruction. The second, which Whites only hints at in the passage quoted above, but elaborates in greater detail elsewhere, provided the conceptual resources for resignifying the meaning of both whiteness and manhood in the new South and in the reunified United States more generally. Briefly though perhaps not so simply put, ex-Confederates enacted a complex process of renunciation and recuperation of their "lost causes" through efforts at national reconciliation, and they did so by virtue of a complicated allegory of race, gender, and sexuality that remembered the aims and ideals of the Confederacy in new terms and thus tailored the project of national reconciliation to a distinctly (ex-)Confederate set of resolves.

Ernest Renan's 1882 meditation, "What Is a Nation?," poses the problem of the founding of nations as a complex question of memory and forgetting: "Forgetting, I would even go so far as to say historical error, is a crucial factor in the creation of a nation, which is why progress in historical studies often constitutes a danger for [the principle of] nationality." Historical enquiry into the founding acts by which nations define themselves as unities, he goes on to suggest, often brings to light the nature of the events romanticized as foundings, events that are themselves difficult if not impossible to pacify and idealize. "Historical enquiry brings to light deeds of violence which took place at the origin of all political formations, even of those whose consequences have been altogether beneficial. Unity is always effected by means of brutality. . . ."[20] For this very reason, nations find it necessary to produce, in retrospect, their own accounts of the past that do not simply elide brutal acts or erase the elements of violence that attend their founding, but produce odd forms of quasi-amnesiac rememberings. Nationals do not simply remember, nor do they simply forget, the deeds that they cite as founding events; instead, they reconstitute what it means to remember and forget in order to establish a kind of past that they can hold in common:

> The essence of a nation is that all individuals have many things in common, and also that they have forgotten many things. No French citizen knows whether he is a Burgundian, an Alan, a Taifale, or a Visigoth, yet every French citizen has to have forgotten the massacre of Saint Bartholomew, or the massacres that took place in the Midi in the thirteenth century. There are not ten families in France that can supply proof of their Frankish origin, and any such proof would anyway be essentially flawed, as a consequence of countless unknown alliances which are liable to disrupt any genealogical system.[21]

In Renan's terms, then, the nation is formed in the point and counterpoint between memory and forgetting, where forgetting stands importantly as anterior to, and formative of, memory itself. Nationals are "obliged already to have forgotten"[22] the past, and it is this forgetting (as opposed to the vagaries of descent) that binds them together in and as a nation. Homi Bhabha glosses this complex form of forgetting as "a minus in the origin that constitutes the *beginning* of the nation's narrative."[23] While I appreciate Bhabha's effort to preserve and exploit the complexity of Renan's formulation, I am uncertain that he renders that complexity as accurately as he might. To call forgetting "a minus in the origin" misses what I see as Renan's point: forgetting is not so much a void at the heart of memory as it is the necessary starting point of national memory. We are obliged to forget *before* we can remember, in order that we can remember a nation not as it once was but as we need it to have been, as we need it to be. Forgetting, then, is not only prior to national memory, but also contains the content from which that memory will be fashioned.

Novel antiquities and the war between the (e)states

One thing that is particularly notable about the foundings of 1776 and 1787, at least from the vantage point of the early twenty-first century if not from that of two centuries earlier, is Founders' failure to refer to their own forebears, or at least to others who, like the signatories to the Mayflower Compact, the Pilgrim Fathers, Sir Walter Raleigh, or even Christopher Columbus might also be construed as prior founders.[24] Founders' conviction about the unprecedented nature of their actions and their desire to cast off the ancestor worship they perceived as characteristic of European tradition throws into relief the novelty of Southerners' distinctive vision of reconciliation and reunion. White southerners, in fact, embraced the past, but in the process of remembering they created something wholly new.

White supremacist fraternities, including the Klan, the Knights of the White Camelia, the state White Leagues, and an organization named significantly, if ambiguously, the '76 Association, self-consciously positioned themselves as heirs to the political and constitutional thought of the American founding. The '76 Association committed itself to "uphold[ing] the principles of the United States Constitution as established and interpreted by its framers."[25] Similarly, the Klan's 1868 creed celebrated the "supremacy of the Constitution, the Constitutional Laws thereof, and the Union of States thereunder," a union the organization pledged to "protect and defend."[26] As Allen Trelease notes in his history of the founding and early years of the Ku Klux Klan, this stated commitment to constitutional principles seems, at best, disingenuous when compared to the Klan's forthrightly unlawful behavior:

> It would be hard to imagine a greater parody than this on the Ku Klux Klan as it actually operated. It frequently pandered to men's lowest instincts; it bullied or brutalized the poor, the weak, and the defenseless; it was often the embodiment of lawlessness and outrage; it did almost nothing to succor Confederate widows and orphans; and it set at defiance the Constitution of the United States.[27]

While Trelease is certainly right to emphasize the lawlessness of Klan activities, I think that something valuable can be gained, nonetheless, by taking the white supremacist fraternities at their word, and that something important can be brought to light by attending to the contrast in rhetorical styles of these nineteenth-century "sons" and their putative "Fathers." The white supremacist fraternities promoted a language of national reconciliation by positioning themselves as the political sons of the nation's fathers, and thus as brothers to their Union counterparts. In this sense, white Southerners can be said to have "read nationalism *genealogically*, as the expression of an historical tradition of serial continuity,"[28] invoking "Founding Fathers" as authorities for the (re)instatement of a past constitutional order that would defeat the innovations of the present. Explicitly framing themselves as the sons of Revolutionary fathers, the Knights of the White Camelia declared in their constitution that "Radical legislation is subversive of the principles of Government of the United States, as originally adopted by our fathers."[29] This genealogical nationalism effectively recast the war between the states as fratricide, an eruption of violence between citizen-brothers.[30] In laying claim to a national tradition common to both Southerners and Northerners, moreover, these former Confederates recast Reconstruction as a war between the *e*states, that is, as a struggle over competing interpretations of the national patrimony.

For these former Confederates, resurrecting the Founders as fathers entailed producing them anew, this time as the venerated relics of a constitutional order, new antiquities barely a century old, celebrated less for their (rhetorical) universalism than for their attendant inability to speak of race, and their failure to outlaw slavery. In the hands of the white supremacist fraternal organizations, the 1787 Constitution was remembered as much for what it had palpably not accomplished as for what it had. It is also the case that the white supremacist fraternities promoted an account of Constitutional history that was profoundly dependent on the categories of political identification made possible by the Reconstruction Amendments. In resurrecting the Founders in support of their cause, they mobilized a vision of the past that was, at best, anachronistic to, if not wholly incoherent within, this earlier constitutional moment. Echoing Lincoln at Gettysburg, and apparently unaware of the irony of doing so, the Knights of the White Camelia proclaimed in their charge to initiates that "the government of our Republic was established by white men, for white men alone, and it was never in the contemplation of its founders that it should fall into the hands of an inferior and degraded race." Any effort, like that represented by the initiatives of Radical Reconstruction, "to wrest from the white race the management of its affairs in order to transfer it to control of the black population is an invasion of the sacred prerogatives vouchsafed to us by the Constitution . . . [and] subversive of the established institutions of our Republic."[31] If the Knights accurately recalled the homogeneous racial demographics that described the Founders, their very mobilization of racial categories in the name of national ideals and institutions suggests a memory based on something that is not old but new, specifically, the ability to speak of citizenship in distinctly racial terms. White supremacist efforts at reconciliation through the invention of a shared legacy of North and South in the 1787 Constitution produced as memories new things, most notably an essential whiteness that defined what was common to Northern and Southern citizens in their newly traced national genealogy.

In this production of whiteness as new memory and new legacy, the fraternities also produced new significations of the blackness of the newly enfranchised freedmen. The 1874 platform of the Louisiana White League cast a nostalgic eye on their activities in the early years of Reconstruction:

> From the time that the right of suffrage was . . . accorded too hastily to a race in the infancy of freedom, we firmly resolved that it was our duty, and a wise expediency, to accept the policy of the reconstruction laws in their full scope. We endeavored at once to address ourselves to the intelligence of the negro, to explain to him that slavery having been forever abolished, he, as a citizen possessing all the rights of white citizens, had the same interests, and the same duties as the white men. . . . We invited him to our meetings, we called him to our platforms, we placed some of them upon our tickets.

This complicated account, where conclusions regarding freedmen's putative inability to govern themselves becomes entangled with self-congratulatory reminiscences of the League's willingness to cooperate in black enfranchisement, places on display ex-Confederates' apprehension of the complex sameness that equated and related all free men in the wake of Reconstruction. As the League's account of its own recent history continues, however, the attempt to include black men in White League activities is pronounced a failure. The freedmen, it seems, would not accept the mantle offered them and, at least as the White League recalled the events, they repeatedly rebuffed the brotherhood's attempts at cooperation and inclusion. "Election after election," the platform continues, freedmen "turned a deaf ear to us; treated all our advances with distrust and suspicion; unhesitatingly followed the leadership of men whom they knew to be unworthy and dishonest, and, with scarcely an exception invariably voted like a body of trained soldiers obeying a command."[32] This language of blind obedience invoked by the White League serves both to identify the freedmen as a threat, and to recall a different kind of obedience to a different set of masters. The fiction of an attempt at biracial brotherhood in early Reconstruction comes to stand in for the racial tyranny of slavery, and the failure of that attempt becomes the basis for a new kind of brotherhood linking North and South:

> Any one who has been to [negroes'] meetings, or overheard their private conversations, knows that they dream of the gradual exodus of the whites, which will leave Louisiana to their exclusive control, like another Hayti. The increasing spirit of caste founded on the most absurd inver-

sion of the relations of race, shows itself in every form. Their incessant demands for offices from the State, city, and Federal Government, for which they are unfit, and to which they have no title other than the color of their skins; the development in their conventions of a spirit of proscription against white radicals and even against honorable republicans who fought in the northern armies for their liberation; their increasing arrogance, which seems to know no bounds; their increasing dishonesty, which they regard as statesmanly virtue; their contemptuous scorn of all the rights of the white man which they dare to trespass upon, all these signs warn us that the calamity which we had long apprehended is now imminent, and that we must prepare for all its consequences. Disregarding all minor questions of principle or policy, and having solely in view the maintenance of our hereditary civilization and Christianity menaced by a stupid Africanization, we appeal to the men of our race, of whatever language or nationality, to unite with us against that supreme danger."[33]

The Platform reminded readers of the juridical sameness by which white and black men were now defined as equal citizens, and it mobilized fears of highly organized freedmen as justification for the organization of "a league of the whites [against] that formidable, oath-bound, and blindly obedient league of the blacks which, under the command of the most cunning and unscrupulous negroes in the State, may at any moment plunge us into a war of races."[34] Representing politically organized freedmen as a threat to a brotherhood that consisted not only of Southern whites but the whole of the reunited (white) nation, the League called for

> a timely and proclaimed union of the whites as a race, and their efficient preparation for any emergency, [to] arrest the threatened horrors of a social war, and teach the blacks to beware of further insolence and aggression, . . . we call upon the men of our race to leave in abeyance all lesser considerations; to forget all differences of opinions and all race prejudices of the past, and with no object in view but the common good of both races, to unite with us in an earnest effort to re-establish a white man's government in the city and the State.[35]

The complicated interplay, and manipulation, of sameness and difference in the White League's platform, its reflection upon a (biracial) brotherhood lost and a (white) brotherhood regained, suggests an important point about genealogy—a point that is as indebted to Renan as it is to Nietzsche (whose *Genealogy of Morals* was published but five years after Renan's talk at the Sorbonne) and to Foucault's reading of Nietzsche not quite a century later. Renan's skepticism about the value of conventional genealogy, that is, about the tracing of lineage and the geographic origins of ancestors in the quest to determine one's true nation (a project that "would anyway be essentially flawed, as a consequence of countless unknown alliances which are liable to disrupt any genealogical system"), suggests that the conventional genealogical project offers either one of two outcomes. Either genealogy gives way to its post-Nietzschean form which, as Foucault characterized it, finds "at the historical beginning of things not the inviolable identity of their origin [but] the dissension of other things,"[36] or it suppresses a complex network of disparate lineages (the "dissension of other things") in order to establish identity. The dis*covering* of ancestors entails the production of memories best forgotten, indeed, memories that must be forgotten *if* the aim of genealogy is to establish purity of lineage. For what genealogy uncovers, Renan suggests, is not the purity and identity of origin and endpoint, but the accidental and contingent process of mongrelization that stretches out between the two. It is precisely the contingency of "countless unknown" and disruptive alliances, exhumed by the national subject of genealogical inquiry, that a nation-in-becoming is "obliged already to have forgotten" if it is to establish uninterrupted links to its putative origin. Genealogy names the process by which a nation in search of something that will stand as its origin produces accounts of the past that both exhume and reinter lost facts, unknown and (perhaps) unknowable truths, and inconvenient and disruptive ancestors.

This is to say that the White League and other white supremacist fraternities produced a white genealogy for a mongrel nation by representing freedmen as disruptive figures in the American (re)union who would have to be suppressed if the reunification of white brothers as sons of common fathers was to proceed. To this end, these organizations articulated new languages of political universalism that forgot the 1787 Constitution's techniques of aggregation, even as they remembered, and revalued, its failure to incorporate—or, at least, to incorporate successfully—blacks and women into national citizenship. *This* would become a language of truly *abstract* universalism, for it proceeded by abstracting whiteness, that element common among founding "fathers," in order to treat a white "nation" as the whole of the nation, hence extracting freedmen from the citizenry. In this sense, if aggregation was the technique of government in the early national era, it could be said that abstraction constituted the technique of government promoted by white Southerners' efforts at national reunification during the Reconstruction era. Like that earlier era,

Reconstruction produced memories that its citizens were obligated almost immediately to forget in order that they might reimagine a white nation.

Castrating men, dis-membering citizens, and the new American imaginary

Totems—the symbolic figures that represent the common ancestry of a particular clan and function, as Freud put it, as "their guardian spirit and helper"—suggest taboos.[37] If the "Founding Fathers" embraced by the Southern fraternal organizations as the common ancestors of (white) southerners and northerners alike can be said to have functioned as something of a national totem, they served also as the foundation for the elaboration of certain taboos. By contrast with totemic prohibitions against tribal endogamy that Freud identifies as the forerunner of the incest taboo, the new fraternal orders founded in the South during Reconstruction required not exogamy but endogamy, marriage within the racial group. Insofar as Southern efforts to participate in the project of national reconciliation proceeded in terms of reimagining the nation as family linked through the sign of a common whiteness, the matter of interracial marriage came to be viewed as a distinctly political threat to the integrity of the national future; and related questions about how to ensure a racially pure reproduction crystallized racial anxieties while aligning them with concurrent tensions about gender and sexuality. As Martha Hodes has demonstrated, Reconstruction marks a sudden and significant adjustment in white southerners' willingness to tolerate liaisons that crossed the color line: "only with black freedom," she writes, "did such liaisons begin to provoke a near-inevitable alarm" among whites throughout the South.[38] However, if racial intermixture came to be newly threatening to white Southerners during Reconstruction, it was hardly newly imaginable to them. Quite the contrary. The enduring consequences of miscegenation produced reminders, in the form of offspring—inconvenient relatives—whose existence disrupted the South's fantasies of an unbroken whiteness. As it happens, the complicated politics of gender and race that lay at the heart of Reconstruction, formulated in the Reconstruction Amendments as relevant and irrelevant differences, provided an extensive trove of symbolic possibilities for reimagining a political order that dis(re)membered disruptive alliances and their progeny.

Absent judicial or legislative clarifications that indicated otherwise, the "social equality" that Southerners perceived as mandated by the Reconstruction initiatives licensed racial intermixture—or so they feared. An 1869 opinion by the Supreme Court of Georgia expressed this anxiety even as it sought to provide the grounds for racial separation:

> Have white persons and persons of color the right under the constitution and laws of Georgia, to intermarry, and live together in this State as husband and wife? The Code of Georgia, as adopted by the new [state] constitution . . . forever prohibits the marriage relation between the two races, and declares all such marriages null and void. . . . Government has full power to regulate civil and political rights, and to give to each citizen of the State . . . equal civil and equal political rights. . . . But government has no power to regulate social status. Before the laws the Code of Georgia makes all citizens equal, without regard to race or color; but it does not create, nor does any law of the State attempt to enforce moral or social equality between the different races. . . . Such equality does not in fact exist and never can.[39]

The Georgia Supreme Court, in this ruling, offers a carefully delimited vision of what government can, and what it cannot, accomplish, of those arenas of national life where government can and should make a difference, and those where it simply cannot. The Court declared politically untouchable what it called "social status," using language that recalls the spirit (without acknowledging the authority) of the Fifteenth Amendment's naming of race as a difference that does not make a difference. Thus, the Court interpreted the Code of Georgia as legitimately prohibiting, or at least legitimately denying the claim of a right to, racial intermarriage insofar as the state, it asserted, cannot be in the business of enforcing an impossible "moral or social equality between the different races."[40]

Whatever solace the Georgia ruling may have offered, the specter of "social equality" continued to call to mind the threat of racial impurity born of fears of untrammeled sexual access to white women by freedmen. In his 1871 testimony before the Joint Select Committee to Inquire into the Conditions of Affairs in the Late Insurrectionary States, Klan Grand Wizard Nathan Forrest evoked an increasingly recurrent image of freedmen, exhilarated and emboldened by their new status as citizens, leaving political meetings to rape white women: "The negroes were holding night meetings; were going about; were becoming very insolent, and the southern people all over the State were very much alarmed. . . . Ladies were ravished by some of these negroes, who were tried and put in the penitentiary, but were turned out in a few days. . . . "[41] This evocation of the specter of interracial rape capitalized upon anxieties surrounding the sudden dissolution of legal and constitutional differentiations between white and black men insofar as it suggested that, absent institutional markers of difference in "social status," freedmen might in fact be expected to desire lives—and wives—identical to those of their white fellow citizens. Indeed, as numerous historians have documented, the efforts of freedmen to exercise their newly-won Constitutional rights, activities like voting or insisting upon fair payment for their labor, were treated not only as criminal acts throughout the Reconstruction-era South, but as criminally and violently sexual. Political participation by blacks was translated, under the juridical purview of the lynch mob, into the crime of interracial rape.[42]

White hysteria surrounding the possibility of interracial rape, state statutes prohibiting interracial marriage, and racial loyalty oaths like that required of initiates to the Knights of the White Camelia to "promise never to marry any woman but one who belongs to the white race,"[43] all attest to the degree to which white Southerners responded to the formal equality among men provided for in the Reconstruction Amendments as threats of a specifically sexual nature. As I argued in Chapter 4, the sudden visibility granted the body by Reconstruction-era languages of citizenship confronted longstanding traditions of male public homosociality and were resolved by recourse to rethinking politics in explicitly heterosexual, though not heterosocial, terms. Nonetheless, the very excessiveness of southern white supremacists' response to the transposition of heterosexuality onto public life can tell us something about the ways that traces of a masculine homosocial desire survived Reconstruction and suffused the new terms within which fraternal association was refigured during the era. For indeed, Southerners did not simply rely upon legislative prohibitions to discourage interracial marriage, but took recourse as well in the disciplinary effects of lynching and castration rituals.

The sudden proliferation of lynchings of freedmen throughout the South in the years immediately following the war is well documented (Ida B. Wells-Barnett, for example, counted 10,000 lynchings by 1895).[44] Equally well documented, though less carefully analyzed for its distinctly political significance, is the ritual castration of freedmen that frequently accompanied these lynchings.[45] As Trudier Harris discusses in some detail, the notion of mob violence associated with lynching—with its evocation of angry, unruly, and disorganized vigilante action—tends to obscure the degree to which lynch mobs also routinely engaged in highly organized, systematic, and stylized rituals of judgment, punishment, and collective purification. Lynching rituals often involved the conduct of some sort of mock trial during which accusers recited detailed accounts of the crime alleged, usually the sexual assault of a white woman, then tortured, dismembered, and eventually executed the accused, and finally arranged for both public display and private collection of the relics (one might even go so far as to call them trophies) removed from their victims' bodies. "In some accounts," Harris writes, "the lynchers were reputed to have divided pieces of the black man's genitals among themselves."[46]

The symbolic weight with which these souvenirs were invested is suggestive. As Robyn Wiegman has argued, the significant increase in lynching and castration of freedmen during the final three decades of the nineteenth century suggests an increasing reliance on the discourse of sexual difference to negotiate race; and served, moreover, as a complex disciplinary mechanism that did not simply remind freedmen of the lines they must not cross, but also "sever[ed] the black male from the masculine, interrupting the privilege of the phallus, and thereby reclaiming, through the perversity of dismemberment, his (masculine) potentiality for citizenship."[47] Castration performed a double task. First, in the most literal sense, it emasculated freedmen and thus undermined their ability to realize the physical threat they were perceived to embody. In this regard, the literal gives way to the symbolic and merges with it, for castration reinstated a distinction between white and black men by calling into question their eligibility for inclusion into the collective specified by the Fourteenth Amendment as "male inhabitants."

The ritual nature of these castrations, moreover, dramatized and even heightened whites' anxieties about black manhood by converting accusation and fantasy into conviction and public spectacle.[48] Insofar as these events publicized white anxieties about masculine sameness and escalated the freedman's manhood to the status of hypermasculine threat, lynching and castration rituals worked to dramatize, mobilize against, and vanquish rampant (white) anxieties provoked by the dissolution of the markers of legal difference that had distinguished white men from black prior to Reconstruction. If castration symbolically feminized the freedmen on whose bodies it was performed, it also quite literally undermined their ability to realize the threat they embodied—not simply the threat of rape, but that of free and equal citizenship in a multi-ethnic polity. Dis-membered from the body politic, freedmen were recast as "inconvenient relatives" that white citizens of both North and South were obliged already to have forgotten.

Even as this analysis suggests the centrality of castration rituals to the disenfranchisement of freedmen in the wake of Reconstruction, castration's significance has not yet been fully exhausted by it, nor has the significance of the freedman's place in Southerners' fantasy of Reconstruction as family reunion been fully analyzed. For the nature of the event—organized lynching by members of white fraternal organizations—suggests both the endurance of male homosocial practices and the reorganization and rechanneling of male homosocial desire in the period. However much male homosociality may have been brought to crisis by Reconstruction, these castrations point to traces of male homosocial desire that survived that crisis by taking new form in violence and sadistic ritual. Insofar as the terms of freedmen's admission to the rights of citizenship emphasized their status as men, the Reconstruction Amendments maintained and even confirmed the public sphere as a male preserve. While the Beecher-Tilton scandal demonstrates one means by which the crisis of homosocial desire was resolved, that is, by (re)channeling it through women, lynching and castration rituals suggest another. These practices refocused male homosocial desire and its attendant anxieties onto freedmen; hence, "the heterosexuality of the black male 'rapist' is transformed into a violently homoerotic exchange"[49] through the vehicle of fraternal rituals devoted not to the pursuit of public life *per se* (as in Adams' passion for distinction), but to the violent instantiation of relations of authority and terror within it. As Wiegman puts it, "in the image of white men embracing—with hate, fear, and a chilling form of empowered delight—the same penis they were so overdeterminedly driven to destroy, one encounters a sadistic enactment of the homoerotic at the very moment of its most extreme disavowal."[50]

This is to say that the figure of the hypersexualized black man was not only just a fantasy, but a fantasy borne of a specific set of anxieties about manhood and fraternal citizenship, made especially acute by Southern efforts to reimagine national reunification as familial reconciliation. We might view the (lynched) freedman—in turn hypermasculinized, then feminized, but vested throughout with a threatening sexuality—as a figure formed of Southerners' complex and often contradictory ambivalence about the project of national reunion. In light of the complicated, sadistic enactment and disavowal of homoeroticism involved in the castration ritual, moreover, we might read prohibitions on interracial marriage as doubly prohibitive: most explicitly as taboos against interracial liaisons, but also as prohibitions against homoerotic fraternity. The symbolically feminized freedman came to represent precisely that which was being expunged from both the American public sphere and its new national genealogy. In this sense, if it is the case that as Benedict Anderson has written, "from citizen fraternity everything sexual is removed,"[51] in post-Reconstruction America, that asexuality is a consequence of both the ritual purging and collective disavowal of male homosocial desire, and the institutionalization of the heterosexual form within politics established initially through the inauguration of silent female citizenship.

Violence, the state, and the origins of sexual difference

As Renan suggests, national states are founded in and through acts of violence. Even if the violent origins of the state must be elided and erased from memory in order that nationals may identify themselves with and through it, the complicated mnemonics of nationalism never fully eliminates from the legacy of foundings the consequences of founding acts, but instead recharacterizes them as myths archaic to the state itself. One lesson suggested by the events of Reconstruction is that the federal state's efforts to rebuild the South's political and economic institutions fostered not a national peace but instead novel forms of both state and extrastate violence.

The aftermath of Reconstruction left a political landscape that looked, particularly in the South, startlingly similar to that of the antebellum years, if not in some ways even more bleak. This is not to minimize the profound importance of the elimination of chattel slavery, but rather to recognize that for blacks the replacement of slavery by sharecropping left freedmen in bondage to white capitalist landowners,[52] and that the emergence of the Black Codes effectively transferred the enforcement of "plantation discipline" from slaveholders to the state itself.[53] In a different register, the long military occupation of the South by the North established a legacy of embitterment that maintained sectional identification and exacerbated sectional resentment, and ultimately called into question for Southerners the desireability of the white fraternity they initially sought with their Northern counterparts. It is in this light that we might read a curious artifact of the post-Reconstruction era: Victoria Woodhull's interpretation of the biblical myth of origins as told in the book of Genesis.

Written in 1876, "The Garden of Eden; or, Paradise Lost and Found" was one of Woodhull's most popular speeches, and it marked a turning point in her career. Throughout the previous year, her newspaper, *Woodhull & Claflin's Weekly*, had begun to introduce biblical themes, replacing the words of John Stuart Mill, which had once run just beneath the masthead, with Bible verses.[54] Along with the closing of the newspaper in June 1876, "The Garden of Eden" has been read as the marker of Woodhull's retreat from radical politics into organized religion.[55] However, while it is certainly true that Woodhull was distancing herself from politics at this point, the speech nonetheless has important political implications. In fact, the work is an effort to recuperate the violent origins of the state through an allegory that identifies sexual difference as a central political fact of state power.[56]

Woodhull's analysis is especially interesting insofar as it repeats a familiar tale of crime, disorder, and the consolidation of the law, only to turn that tale in surprising directions. Her reading echoes her earlier analysis of the democratically expansive potential suggested by the Reconstruction Amendments, but it does so in light of Congress' failure to pass the Declaratory Act that she had deemed necessary to ensure women's right to the franchise. Accordingly, her analysis this time is markedly pessimistic, bitter, and even apocalyptic. Read against other modern political interpretations of the Garden of Eden (the one I have foremost in mind here is that of Locke), Woodhull's analysis helps us understand the problematic political consequences of the new visibility of the body, and the description of the nation in familial terms, in post-Reconstruction America.[57]

Woodhull begins her analysis in "The Garden of Eden" by suggesting that the inhabitants of the Garden occupied a moment prior to the development of both law and moral order, "a time . . . when man did not know good and evil." Their lives and activities were governed not by moral considerations, nor by the dictates of a law external to themselves, but by the demands and desires of their own bodies, "and it is easy to conceive that the whole face of the earth may have been occupied by human beings who were nothing more than animals." Like animals, the humans in the tale were sexually dimorphic, but sexual difference had not yet been assigned social meaning, nor had it been freighted with moral content. The male and female inhabitants were not yet distinguishable from one another in the terms by which moderns are accustomed to describing them—as Adam and Eve: "These were the male and female whom God created according to the first chapter of Genesis. It does not mean at all that they were a single male and female. They were not Adam and Eve then. They were simply male and female man, or Adam; for in chapter v. verse 2, we are told 'Male and female created he them and called *their* name Adam;' that is, the human animals that inhabited the earth were called Adam."[58]

Woodhull's account is organized by the same moment of crisis that structures Genesis: a single act brings this era to its close, necessitating the articulation of a set of rules by which we govern our common life in a postlapsarian world. However, by contrast with the dominant Christian interpretation of the Fall, Woodhull argues that the precipitating event could not have constituted a violation of a moral injunction (the Old Testament deity's "ye shall not . . ."),[59] coming as it did prior to the emergence of morality and the law:

> At the time when knowledge began to find root in the brain of man, it is pretty evident that the human animal, man, was pure and perfect physically; that is, that they were like the other animals, and that they are to

be judged of as we judge of animals now. Considered in this light, what are the differences between man and the animals? This is a question of the most vital importance, since, if there was a fall of man from the original state of purity, it is necessary that we know of what that fall consisted before we can provide intelligently for an escape therefrom. It was not a moral fall certainly, since morality is not an attribute of animals, unless physical purity is morality. This view of ethics is not legitimate, since morals are the last development in the growth of man, are an outgrowth of, or a building upon, intellect. Nor could that fall have been intellectual, since as there had then been no knowledge of good and evil, there was no intellect; there had been no power of comparison in the human brain. We are obliged to conclude, therefore, that that sin committed by man was a physical sin.[60]

"Now what," she continues, "was this sin?" For Woodhull, the only possible conclusion is that the sin that precipitated the Fall was the act of rape: male Adam raped his female companion.

Rape, then, brings political order into being, Woodhull suggests, and endows that order with a particular organization of power that establishes sexual difference as politically meaningful. In this respect, Woodhull's argument in "The Garden of Eden" recalls her 1871 speech before the National Woman's Suffrage Convention in the months following Congress' refusal to pass the Declaratory Act confirming women's enfranchisement by the Reconstruction Amendments:

> Women have no Government. Men have organized a Government, and they maintain it to the utter exclusion of women. Women are as much members of the nation as men are, and they have the same human right to govern themselves which men have. Men have none but an usurped right to the arbitrary control of women. . . . Men fashioned a government based on their own *enunciation* of principles: that taxation without representation was tyranny; and that all just government exists by the consent of the governed. . . . And yet men deny women the first and greatest rights of citizenship—the right to vote.[61]

Woodhull's stress here on the constitutive power of language and the consolidation of that power in the hands of men finds its corollary in "The Garden of Eden," where the Old Testament god's grant to Adam of the sovereign power of naming "every living creature" (in Genesis 3:20)[62] is extended after the Fall to the naming of woman herself: "and Adam called his wife's name Eve."[63]

Woodhull's identification of a form of political power that both requires the presence of women on the scene of politics and necessitates their subjugation at the hands of men, recalls the incarnation of a silent female citizenship discussed earlier. What Woodhull gives us is an account of a single violent act that produces a particular form of sovereign power and a newly recognizable form of sexual difference. But her account of the events surrounding the Fall does not end there, for it offers a narrative of a violation around which women might mobilize, and from which new forms of feminist politics and feminist political identification might be imagined. This new feminist imagination coalesces around the place of the human body as a conceptual origin of political order, an insight that Woodhull develops in her treatment of the Garden of Eden itself. Addressing herself to the numerous expeditions that sought to determine the geographic location of the Garden, Woodhull gestures to the absurdity of these endeavors. The book of Genesis, she points out, indicates that Eden covered a territory through which the rivers Pison, Gihon, Hiddekel, and Euphrates ran, but of these four rivers, only one, the Euphrates, is known to modern geography. Similarly, the mapping given in Genesis that locates the rivers with respect to particular territories (Havileh, Ethiopia, and Assyria), Woodhull points out, turns out to be impossible as well. "The Garden of Eden," she concludes, "is something altogether different from a vegetable patch, or a fruit or flower garden."[64]

The Garden of Eden, she maintains, is "wholly allegorical . . . [and] we are [now] ready to inquire what the subject is which this allegorical picture represents."[65] Turning to the popular *Cruden's Concordance* as a key to understanding the meaning of the place names associated with the Garden, Woodhull elaborates:

> In that learned work we read thus: "Pison—changing or doubling, or extension of the mouth."
>
> "Gihon—The Valley of Grace, or breast, or impetuous." In other authorities this word is held to mean "Bursting forth as from a fountain, or from the womb."
>
> "Hiddekel—a sharp voice or sound;" other authorities say, "Swift, which refers to the swiftness of the current."
>
> "Euphrates—that makes fruitful or grows." Now we may inquire into the meaning of the names of the countries in which these rivers were situated.
>
> "Havileh—that suffers pain, that brings forth."
>
> "Ethiopia—Blackness—[Darkness]—heat, burning."

> Assyria is the country of, and signifies, Ashur, "One that is happy," which would make the meaning of Assyria to be, the land of the happy; or the land in which the happy dwell.
> And the whole of these rivers and countries combined form the Garden of Eden, which, as we learn, means: "Pleasure or delight."[66]

The mouth, the breast, the womb, and the voice; pain, heat, happiness, pleasure: for Woodhull, the evidence was conclusive. "Where should the Garden of Eden be found if not within the human body? Is there any other place or thing in the universe more worthy to be called an Eden?"[67]

Woodhull's analysis in "The Garden of Eden" might prompt us to recall Renan's insight that historical inquiry poses a threat to national stability. In recuperating an original violation (albeit one that is fictive rather than historical in any strict sense), Woodhull seeks both to remind the reader of the violent means by which political order gained its foothold, and to use that memory as a vehicle for a kind of emancipation. The Garden of Eden represents a past that need not remain forever lost to us, but one to which a justly ordered society might return. It is the memory of this "very much despised place" that serves as a resource for the development of a liberatory imagination:

> The despised parts of the body are to become what Jesus was, the Savior conceived at Nazareth. The despised body, and not the honored soul, must be the stone cut out of the mountain that shall be the head of the corner though now rejected by the builders. There can be no undefiled or unpolluted temple of God that is not built upon this corner-stone, perfectly.[68]

Speaking here at her most prophetic, Woodhull exhorts us to see that it is only by virtue of revaluing that which has been reviled that human freedom—and with it, women's equality—might be accomplished.

Between the period during which Woodhull delivered "The Garden of Eden" on the lecture circuit in 1876 and its publication as the opening essay in her book, *The Human Body, The Temple of God* in 1890, Woodhull abandoned her earlier free-love doctrines, immersed herself in a devout if also somewhat idiosyncratic Christianity,[69] married the heir to a British banking fortune, and resettled in London as Mrs. John Biddulph Martin. As published in 1890, "The Garden of Eden" bears within it the traces of both Woodhull's complicated politics and her complicated embrace of Christian moralism. It is a difficult text that promotes a potentially scandalous reading of Genesis, and exerts itself to subdue that scandal. This capacity of the text to defy our desires to reduce it to a single reading that delivers a simple or straightforward message is, perhaps, indicative of the complicated legacy of Reconstruction itself. Perhaps Woodhull's political thought and her Christian moralism are not so much separate commitments held serially, as they are complementary, if also competing, aspects of the American political imagination that she inherits, inhabits, and refigures.

This is to say that what is most imaginative in Woodhull's interpretation of Genesis may be what is also most startling, even unsettling about it, and this not simply for those who are discomfited by the prophetic tone she adopts. Woodhull is uncertain that the prelapsarian god is a moral god, for it is on his watch that the physical violation of rape is committed, that sexual dimorphism is vested with political and moral significance, and the ensuing need for law and order designed, perhaps, to protect women, but which also maintains their subjugation, is established. In this sense, Woodhull's account can be read as another founding narrative that figures the human body as a remnant of the old world that initiates the new. Insofar as her fable offers powerful commentary on the political insufficiencies of Reconstruction, Woodhull counters the various narratives of origins that celebrated a reunified America (whether that of the South's self-annointed heirs of 1787, or that of northern Republicans as redeemers of American unity) by deromanticizing them. In her dystopic account of the genesis of political life, Woodhull identifies another principle by which life in common might be governed. For Woodhull's fable is not simply another founding narrative but also a morality play that finds in the figure of Eve herself the resources for the development of a new common order in which "the despised body" is finally vindicated.

Insofar as Woodhull's allegory is formed of perhaps equal parts of rancor for the past and hope for a different future, her account suggests another means of achieving freedom, promoting a morality of freedom that would redeem women's subjugation in the very origins of a political world. For Woodhull, the woman-who-would-be-citizen is a body haunted by the specter of politics, by the very fact that her subjectivity is formed in and of the fact of political subjugation. American public life is in turn haunted by the specter of Woman, of the figure whose original violation made political life possible. The language of political morality that Woodhull's narrative offered to women—one that could be adapted by others who, like the freedmen, found themselves placed in more or less analogous positions by the events of Reconstruction—is one that finds the sources for redemption in the fact of originary injury itself. It is a language that, whatever its nineteenth-century provenance, should be familiar to those who have witnessed the American culture wars of the late twentieth century.

Endnotes

1. Homi K. Bhabha, "DissemiNation," *Nation and Narration*, ed. Homi K. Bhabha (New York: Routledge, 1990), 311.

2. Benedict Anderson, *Imagined Communities: Reflections on the Origin and Spread of Nationalism* (London: Verso, 1991), xiv.

3. Eric Foner, *Reconstruction: America's Unfinished Revolution, 1863–1877* (New York: Harper & Row, 1988), 87. Foner's characterization is supported by the work of others who, like Angela Davis, argue that "the salient theme emerging from domestic life in slave quarters is one of sexual equality." See Angela Y. Davis, *Women, Race & Class* (New York: Vintage, 1981), 18. See also Michele Wallace, *Black Macho and the Myth of the Superwoman* (New York: Dial Press, 1979).

4. Eric Foner, *Reconstruction: America's Unfinished Revolution, 1863–1877*, 87.

5. Nina Silber, *The Romance of Reunion: Northerners and The South, 1865–1900* (Chapel Hill: The University of North Carolina Press, 1993), 9–10. Silber's argument represents an interesting counterpart to Anne Norton's depiction of the gendered metaphors that governed antebellum sectionalism, namely, a feminized, even maternal, South and a patriarchal North. See Anne Norton, *Alternative Americas: A Reading in Antebellum Political Culture* (Chicago: The University of Chicago Press, 1986).

6. Nina Silber, *The Romance of Reunion: Northerners and the South, 1865–1900*, 10.

7. Patricia J. Williams, "The Ethnic Scarring of American Whiteness," *The House that Race Built*, ed. Wahneema Lubiano (New York: Vintage, 1998), 258.

8. Quoted in Michael Rogin, "'The Sword Became a Flashing Vision: D.W. Griffith's *The Birth of a Nation*," *Ronald Reagan, The Movie, and Other Episodes in Political Demonology* (Berkeley: University of California Press, 1987), 192.

9. Michael Rogin, "'The Sword Became a Flashing Vision': D.W. Griffith's *The Birth of a Nation*," 192. For further discussion of this film and its place in American mass culture, see Michael Rogin, *Blackface, White Noise: Jewish Immigrants in the Hollywood Melting Pot* (Berkeley: University of California Press, 1996).

10. Louis Hartz, *The Liberal Tradition in America* (New York: Harcourt Brace & Company, 1955), 150.

11. Louis Hartz, *The Liberal Tradition in America*, 149.

12. Louis Hartz, *The Liberal Tradition in America*, 164.

13. Louis Hartz, *The Liberal Tradition in America*, 177.

14. Louis Hartz, *The Liberal Tradition in America*, 155.

15. Louis Hartz, *The Liberal Tradition in America*, 175.

16. Rogers M. Smith, *Civic Ideals: Conflicting Visions of Citizenship in U.S. History* (New Haven: Yale University Press, 1997), esp. Chapter Ten. See also Thomas F.

Gossett, *Race: The History of an Idea in America* (New York: Oxford University Press, 1963), Chapter XI; David M. Chalmers, *Hooded Americanism: The History of the Ku Klux Klan* (Durham: Duke University Press, 1987).

17. Robyn Wiegman, *American Anatomies: Theorizing Race and Gender* (Durham: Duke University Press, 1995), 14.

18. Quoted in LeeAnn Whites, *The Civil War as a Crisis in Gender: Augusta, Georgia, 1869–1890* (Athens: The University of Georgia Press, 1995), 161–62.

19. LeeAnn Whites, *The Civil War as a Crisis in Gender: Augusta, Georgia, 1860–1890*, 163.

20. Ernest Renan, "What is a nation?," trans. Martin Thom, *Nation and Narration*, 11.

21. Ernest Renan, "What is a nation?," 11.

22. This is Benedict Anderson's rendering of a portion of Renan's passage, quoted above. Here is Renan's original, with the passage in question italicized: "Or, l'essence d'une nation est que tous les individus aient beaucoup de choses en commun et aussi que tous aient oblié bien des choses. . . . Tout citoyen français *doit avoir oblié* la Saint-Barthémy, les massacres du Midi au XIIIe siècle." See Benedict Anderson, *Imagined Communities: Reflections on the Origin and Spread of Nationalism* (2nd edition), 199–201.

23. Homi Bhabha, "DissemiNation," 310. Emphasis in original.

24. A similar point is also made by Benedict Anderson, *Imagined Communities: Reflections on the Origin and Spread of Nationalism*, 193.

25. "Constitution of the '76 Association," *Documentary History of Reconstruction*, ed. Walter L. Fleming (Cleveland, OH: The Arthur H. Clark Company, 1907), vol. II, 355.

26. "Organization and Principles of the Ku Klux Klan," *Documentary History of Reconstruction*, vol. II, 347.

27. Allen W. Trelease, *White Terror: The Ku Klux Klan Conspiracy and Southern Reconstruction* (Westport, CT: Greenwood Press, 1971), 17.

28. The quoted passage is from Benedict Anderson, who is referring to the second-generation nationalist movements of Europe and the Americas (primarily Latin America) from around 1815–1850. Benedict Anderson, *Imagined Communities: Reflections on the Origins and Spread of Nationalism*, 195. Emphasis in original.

29. "Constitution and Ritual," *Documentary History of Reconstruction*, vol. II, 349.

30. This is the phenomenon that Benedict Anderson calls "the reassurance of fraticide." See Benedict Anderson, *Imagined Communities: Reflections on the Origin and Spread of Nationalism*, 199–203.

31. "Constitution and Ritual," *Documentary History of Reconstruction*, vol. II, 352.

32. "Louisiana White League Platform," *Documentary History of Reconstruction*, vol. II, 359.

33. "Louisiana White League Platform," *Documentary History of Reconstruction*, vol. II, 358–59.

34. "Louisiana White League Platform," *Documentary History of Reconstruction*, vol. II, 359.

35. "Louisiana White League Platform," *Documentary History of Reconstruction*, vol. II, 359.

36. Michel Foucault, "Nietzsche, Genealogy, History," *Language, Counter-memory, Practice: Selected Essays and Interviews*, ed. Donald F. Bouchard (Ithaca: Cornell University Press, 1977), 142.

37. Sigmund Freud, *Totem and Taboo*, trans. James Strachey (New York: W.W. Norton & Company, 1950), 2.

38. Martha Hodes, *White Women, Black Men: Illicit Sex in the Nineteenth-Century South* (New Haven: Yale University Press, 1997), 1–2.

39. "Intermarriage of Races in Georgia," *Documentary History of Reconstruction*, vol. II, 288. This ruling was overturned, but not until 1967 when, in *Loving v. Virginia*, the U.S. Supreme Court declared state laws prohibiting interracial marriage to be in violation of the Constitution. Hodes reports that, over time, 41 states have had such laws on their books; in the nineteenth century, thirty-eight states prohibited interracial marriage, of which nine repealed their prohibition during the Civil War. See Martha Hodes, *White Women, Black Men: Illicit Sex in the Nineteenth-Century South*, 213, n. 1. See also Harvey M. Applebaum, "Miscegenation Statutes: A Constitutional and Social Problem," *Georgetown Law Review* 53 (1964), 49–91.

40. Most of the white supremacist fraternities prohibited their members from marrying African American women. The Knights of the White Camelia articulated the stakes this way: "This Order proscribes absolutely all social equality between the races. If we were to admit persons of African race on the same level with ourselves, a state of personal relations would follow which would unavoidably lead to political equality. . . . [But] there is another reason, Brothers, for which we condemn this social equality. Its toleration would soon be a source of intermarriages between individuals of the two races: and the result of this *miscegenation* would be gradual amalgamation and the production of a degenerate and bastard offspring." "Constitution and Ritual," *Documentary History of Reconstruction*, vol. II, 353–53. Emphasis in original. See also the oath not to marry "any woman but one who belongs to the white race" required of candidates for membership in the Knights of the White Camelia, on p. 350.

41. *Report of the Joint Select Committee to Inquire into the Conditions of Affairs in the Late Insurrectionary States* (13 vols), 42nd Cong., 2d sess., 22 (Washington, DC, 1872), vol. XIII, 6–32 *passim*.

42. See, in this regard: Martha Hodes, "The Sexualization of Reconstruction Politics: White Women and Black Men in the South after the Civil War," *Journal of the*

History of Sexuality 3:3 (1993), 401–17. As historian Diane Miller Sommerville has argued, there is a distinct expansion of white Southern sexual paranoia in the years following the Civil War, traceable by comparison with the relative leniency with which black men known to be sexually involved with white women were treated during the antebellum years. See Diane Miller Sommerville, "The Rape Myth in the Old South Reconsidered," *Journal of Southern History* LXI:3 (August 1995), 481–518. In a similar vein, see Laura F. Edwards, "The Disappearance of Susan Daniel and Henderson Cooper: Gender and Narratives of Political Conflict in the Reconstruction-era U.S. South," *Feminist Studies* 22:2 (Summer 1996), 363–86. See also Tilden G. Edelstein, "*Othello* in America: The Drama of Racial Intermarriage," *Region, Race, and Reconstruction: Essays in Honor of C. Vann Woodward*, eds. Morgan Kousser and James M. McPherson (New York: Oxford University Press, 1982), 179–97. On mob violence and lynching during the era, see National Association for the Advancement of Colored People, *Thirty Years of Lynching in the United States, 1889-1918* (New York: Arno, 1969); James E. Cutler, *Lynch-Law: An Investigation into the History of Lynching in the United States* (New York: Longmans, Green, and Co., 1905); Ida B. Wells-Barnett, *On Lynchings: Southern Horrors; A Red Record; Mob Rule in New Orleans* (New York: Arno, 1969); Jacquelyn Dowd Hall, *Revolt against Chivalry: Jessie Daniel Ames and the Women's Campaign against Lynching* (New York: Columbia University Press, 1979); Joel Williamson, *The Crucible of Race: Black-White Relations in the American South Since Emancipation* (New York: Oxford University Press, 1984).

43. "Constitution and Ritual," *Documentary History of Reconstruction*, vol. II, 350.

44. Statistics on lynchings during this period vary widely, probably because the legal authorities responsible for collecting data chose to ignore violent crimes against African Americans, and groups like the National Association for the Advancement of Colored People began collecting their own records in an effort to provide documentation. The count of 10,000 lynchings is offered by Ida B. Wells-Barnett, *On Lynchings: Southern Horrors; A Red Record; Mob Rule in New Orleans* (New York: Arno, 1969). See also National Association for the Advancement of Colored People, *Thirty Years of Lynching in the United States, 1889–1918* (New York: Arno, 1969); James E. Cutler, *Lynch-Law: An Investigation into the History of Lynching in the United States* (New York: Longmans, Green, & Co., 1905); Joel Williamson, *The Crucible of Race: Black-White Relations in the American South Since Emancipation* (New York: Oxford, 1984); Jacquelyn Dowd Hall, *Revolt Against Chivalry: Jessie Daniel Ames and the Women's Campaign Against Lynching* (New York: Columbia University Press, 1979). Because of the unwillingness of law enforcement officials at the time to document incidents of mob violence against African Americans, the statistics assembled tend to begin their count in the 1880s. As George Wright has established in studying newspaper records in the state of Kentucky, however, more than one-third of the reported lynchings in that state that

took place between the Civil War and the Civil Rights Movement were executed between 1865 and 1874, so there is good reason to suspect that reports that focus on the period immediately following Reconstruction offer, at best, only a partial accounting. See George C. Wright, *Racial Violence in Kentucky, 1865–1940: Lynching, Mob Rule, and "Legal Lynchings"* (Baton Rouge: Louisiana State University Press, 1990), esp. 40–44.

45. Robyn Wiegman, to whom much of my analysis is indebted, is the exception here; Trudier Harris, too, offers extensive analysis and accounts of ritual castrations far more detailed than I have provided but on which I have drawn in my discussion below. See Robyn Wiegman, *American Anatomies: Theorizing Race and Gender*, esp. Chapter Three; Trudier Harris, *Exorcising Blackness: Historical and Literary Lynching and Burning Rituals* (Bloomington: Indiana University Press, 1984).

46. Trudier Harris, *Exorcising Blackness: Historical and Literary Lynching and Burning Rituals*, 22. Another account of the public display of such relics is offered by W.E.B. Du Bois, who once told of walking through the streets of Atlanta shortly after the well known lynching of a black man by the name of Sam Hose. On his way to entreat the editor of the *Atlanta Constitution* to "try to put before the South what happened in cases of this sort," Du Bois passed by a meat market, and discovered that its owners "were exhibiting the fingers of Sam Hose" in their display. See W.E.B. Du Bois, "The Reminiscences of W.E.B. Du Bois," New York: Columbia University Oral History Research Office, 1960. Also recounted in Martha Hodes, *White Women, Black Men: Illicit Sex in the Nineteenth-Century South*, 207–8.

47. Robyn Wiegman, "The Anatomy of Lynching," *Journal of the History of Sexuality* 3:3 (1993), 446.

48. For a number of detailed accounts of specific instances of castration ritual, see Trudier Harris, *Exorcising Blackness: Historical and Literary Lynching and Burning Rituals*.

49. Robyn Wiegman, *American Anatomies: Theorizing Race and Gender*, 99.

50. Robyn Wiegman, *American Anatomies: Theorizing Race and Gender*, 99.

51. Benedict Anderson, *The Spectre of Comparisons: Nationalism, Southeast Asia and the World* (New York: Verso, 1998), 367.

52. See Eric Foner, *Reconstruction: America's Unfinished Revolution, 1863–1877*, 160–170.

53. On the Black Codes, see Eric Foner, *Reconstruction: America's Unfinished Revolution, 1863–1877*, 199–201.

54. Mary Gabriel, *Notorious Victoria: The Life of Victoria Woodhull, Uncensored* (Chapel Hill: Algonquin Books, 1998), 240.

55. Mary Gabriel, *Notorious Victoria: The Life of Victoria Woodhull, Uncensored*, 240–55; see also Barbara Goldsmith, *Other Powers: The Age of Suffrage, Spiritualism,*

and the Scandalous Victoria Woodhull (New York: Alfred A. Knopf, 1998), Chapter Thirty-four.

56. The analysis that follows is based on the essay version of Woodhull's speech, published considerably later in a collection of her speeches and essays. See Victoria Claflin Woodhull, "The Garden of Eden; or, Paradise Lost and Found," *The Human Body, The Temple of God; or, The Philosophy of Sociology* (London, 1890), 3–58.

57. Recall that for Locke, writing in the Second Treatise, the individual's ownership of his body in the state of nature becomes the means by which the concepts of wage labor and private property are naturalized as political rights guaranteed by the liberal social contract, as well as the means by which slavery is denaturalized in modern political society. See John Locke, *Two Treatises of Government*, ed. Peter Laslett (Cambridge: Cambridge University Press, 1965), II, §27.

58. Victoria Claflin Woodhull, "The Garden of Eden; or, Paradise Lost and Found," 11. Emphasis in original.

59. Genesis 3:3.

60. Victoria Claflin Woodhull, "The Garden of Eden; or, Paradise Lost and Found," 38.

61. Victoria Claflin Woodhull, "The XIVth and XVth Amendments to the Constitution of the United States: A Speech Before the National Woman's Suffrage Convention," *The Human Body, The Temple of God*, 181–82. Emphasis in original.

62. Quoted in Woodhull, "The Garden of Eden; or, Paradise Lost and Found," 8.

63. Genesis 3:20. Quoted in Victoria Claflin Woodhull, "The Garden of Eden; or, Paradise Lost and Found," 8.

64. Victoria Claflin Woodhull, "The Garden of Eden; or, Paradise Lost and Found," 13.

65. Victoria Claflin Woodhull, "The Garden of Eden; or, Paradise Lost and Found," 24.

66. Victoria Claflin Woodhull, "The Garden of Eden; or, Paradise Lost and Found," 25.

67. Victoria Claflin Woodhull, "The Garden of Eden; or, Paradise Lost and Found," 33.

68. Victoria Claflin Woodhull, "The Garden of Eden; or, Paradise Lost and Found," 30.

69. For details, see Mary Gabriel, *Notorious Victoria: The Life of Victoria Woodhull, Uncensored*, 240–42.

POSTSCRIPT

RESTATING NEW POSSIBILITIES

[C]onsider the possibility that the primary threat to citizenship might be found in the very forces that protect citizenship.

Thomas L. Dumm[1]

IS THERE A SPECTER HAUNTING THE LIBERAL TRADITION IN AMERICA? Surely the guarantee of women's suffrage secured by the Nineteenth Amendment, as well as the prohibition of racial and gender discrimination mandated by the Civil Rights Act of 1964 and its successors, have effectively transformed the ground of American citizenship, ensuring that the conditions that once made the body politically meaningful no longer hold. Recent history, it seems, suggests otherwise. Rather than having been rendered inessential within politics, or banished altogether from it, the citizen's body has come to figure more visibly and more powerfully than ever in the American political imagination over recent decades. Since at least the mid-1980s, a series of increasingly rancorous political disputes about how Americans understand their past, and how that understanding might shape our vision of who we are as a people, have dominated public discussions about citizenship. Foregrounding questions of race, gender, and sexuality, the so-called culture wars have placed the citizen's body, yet again, at the very center of the nation's political agenda. What I want to suggest, by way of concluding, is that these debates represent a late twentieth-century replay of the tensions and anxieties I have traced throughout the preceding chapters, and that they are at least partially a function of American discourses of citizenship themselves. This is to say that citizenship in America remains, problematically, a spectral politics of the body that ties us conceptually to the past, and resists our best attempts at meaningful politics in the present.

The demise of the common?

It has been just over a decade since Allan Bloom's surprise bestseller, *The Closing of the American Mind*, linked an array of political problems that Bloom identified as characteristic of the post-Vietnam era—a decline in moral standards, the devaluation of norms, the demise of faith in the great works of western culture, and the dissolution of a common language and a common culture in America—directly to changes in the curricular focus of higher education. The move to liberalize liberal education that followed in the wake of the student protests of the 1960s, Bloom argued, produced consequences that reverberated far beyond lecture halls and seminar rooms and tragically altered our understanding of what it means to be American and what it means to be democratic citizens. Specifically, he charged the "recent education of openness," associated with the development of academic programs in Women's Studies and Ethnic Studies, with obscuring shared goals and notions of the public good. Gone is the day, Bloom suggests, when "by recognizing and accepting man's natural rights, men found a fundamental basis of unity and sameness. Class, race, religion, national origin or culture all disappear or become dim when bathed in the light of natural rights, which give men common interests and make them truly brothers."[2] Installed, now, in the place once held by respect for natural rights is something akin to the state of nature described "by the founding fathers of modern thought."[3] This late modern state of nature is notably different from its early modern counterpart in that it no longer functions as a rhetorical device designed to help us imagine the terms and conditions under which a common public order becomes necessary and beneficial. Instead, Bloom contends, a once fictive state of nature has become reality in a world fraught with rampant tribalism, open hostility to doctrines of moral universalism, and the celebration of closed minds and petty distinctions.

The Closing of the American Mind struck a sensitive nerve and was followed in short order by a variety of likeminded works that sought to expose the purported political excesses committed by "tenured radicals," sparking a series of culture wars that quickly spilled outside the academy and into the domain of American popular culture.[4] But the lament for a lost or alienated common life, and the identification of feminism and multiculturalism as bearing responsibility for the demise of commonality, is by no means the exclusive province of American conservatives. In recent years it has been taken up by some of the same "tenured radicals" charged by Bloom and others with politicizing higher education. In the hands of thinkers like Todd Gitlin and Richard Rorty,

Bloom's criticisms have been transformed into a kind of Left self-critique that asks how a politics rooted in the idea of the beloved communities of the Civil Rights movement could end in what Gitlin calls *The Twilight of Common Dreams*.

While Gitlin and Rorty by no means adopt Bloom's political or educational agendas (indeed, in some very important senses their conclusions challenge Bloom's own) they nonetheless take aim at many of the same targets, and in this sense (if only in this sense) might be said to occupy the same axis of the culture wars. Gitlin's work is framed by an account of the 1992 disputes in Oakland over the adoption of a new textbook series for the California public schools' history-social science curriculum, a series that in Gitlin's analysis "offer[ed] little comfort to . . . anyone inclined to see American history as the unbroken progress of benign Europeans across a savage and underutilized continent."[5] As Gitlin tells the story, despite the fact that the series offered substantial and sympathetic treatment of women and ethnic minorities, the new curriculum was most vociferously attacked not by conservatives, but by groups representing "the cultural Left," self-described spokespersons for precisely those ethnic, religious, and sexual minorities whose history was, for perhaps the first time, being highlighted with generally respectful treatment in state authorized textbooks.[6] While Gitlin acknowledges that some of this criticism "pointed to . . . genuine instances of establishment bias," he treats the majority of it as "trivial and hypersensitive."[7] This "identity politics," he concludes, "is a set of false solutions proclaimed for real problems," and the Left "which once stood for universal values, seems to speak today for select identities, while the Right, long associated with privileged interests, claims to defend the common good."[8]

Gitlin's book is an impassioned address directed at an American Left that, by his account, has become both politically and intellectually paralyzed by the centrifugal tendencies of identity politics, a Left rendered unable to "reduce the sickening inequality between rich and poor" that reigns in post-Reagan America insofar as it has lost all desire or ability to envision a common public life.[9] In *Achieving Our Country*, Richard Rorty, too, attributes the enfeeblement of the Left to its loss of political vision, its inability, in his words, to "replac[e] shared knowledge of what is already real with social hope for what might become real."[10] It has become a "spectatorial, disgusted, mocking Left rather than a Left which dreams of achieving our country,"[11] assigning to "cultural politics preference over real politics," and ridiculing "the very idea that democratic institutions might once again be made to serve social justice."[12] Together, Gitlin and Rorty counsel that an effective Left that might again serve as a counterweight to economic, environmental, and social depredation must abandon its romantic attachment to the "cultivation of separate identities" and to "cultures of resistance" that simply reinforce political marginalization. For Rorty in particular, this means declaring a "moratorium on theory. . . . [the Left] should try to kick its philosophy habit . . . [and] try to mobilize what remains of our pride in being Americans."[13] Both propose the forging of a new majoritarianism that would entail a return, in Gitlin's case, to the principles of the Enlightenment if not its acknowledged failures, or in Rorty's, to a hardheaded reformist politics of engaged pragmatism.[14]

It is tempting to read Bloom, Gitlin, and Rorty as little more than nostalgic mourners for a past that is long past, or more likely never was. To be sure, there is certainly a measure of nostalgia in all three. With Bloom, it is a nostalgia for the academy as city on the hill, and with Rorty, for the engaged politics of the Old Left. Of the three, Gitlin is perhaps the least inclined toward the backward glance, for as he acknowledges, "the golden years were mighty white."[15] Yet even Gitlin's vision is animated by the past, by the early years of the New Left, before the triumph of what he views as the "separatist urge."[16] Nonetheless, I would suggest that a number of more complicated forces are at work here, and that we view these early and late writings from the culture wars in slightly different terms. In each case, a vision for the future is not animated by the desire to return to the past so much as it is structured by a retrospective logic that treats the past as a moment prior to, and therefore immune from, the difficulties of the present. In their writings, the past is not so much a place to retreat to, or strategically reinstate, as it is a a decisive turning point in public life in which Americans abjured their almost providential purpose in the world. If each of these thinkers seeks to recapture that moment, they do so not to suggest that we return to it in order to live there permanently, but reinhabit it only long enough to begin again.

All three articulate their claims through the classic conventions of the jeremiad, enjoining their fellow Americans to remember our national mission, to forget our petty social distinctions, to reclaim once and for all the longstanding promise of the liberal tradition in America. I am not suggesting that there is any unanimity among them about what constitutes a petty social distinction, nor that they necessarily share a common vision of what America's promise entails. Rather, what I mean to draw attention to is the way that each assumes a kind of linear (if not strictly progressive) account of American liberalism that filters out its paradoxes and the counterprinciples at work within it. Insofar as each apprehends competing languages of citizenship at work in contemporary America, they treat these as ideologies that we may either embrace or reject at will. What they fail to recognize is that these are not simply ideologies (though they are that), but also constitutional discourses, practices and techniques of power that produce different kinds of citizens. Both the universal citizen that all three seem to endorse, and the queer citizen, the ethnic citizen, and the female citizen that each views as indicative of decline, are identities born of constitutional practices developed during Reconstruction. In living those practices, we both become those identities and produce them anew, as persistent conflicts within the American polity.[17] If Bloom, Gitlin, and Rorty are right to sense profound conflict over both ideals and techniques of citizenship in contemporary American public life, they are naive to counsel a return to some distinctively American liberal ideal, for it is precisely American liberalism that is at work in shaping both these debates and the citizens who engage them. There is no place or moment or liberal ideal to which we can return, for we are—all of us—already there.

This is not to deny, however, the problem represented by the culture wars themselves. The triumph of a "minoritarian thinking"[18] that premises political identification in separate and incompatible local identities does seem to raise the specter (both memory and prospect) of civil war, of the collapse of public life and the consequent suffocation of democratic engagement. This seems on the face of it to be the lesson of Bosnia. I am skeptical, however, of any call for an abandonment of "cultural politics" in the name of reclaiming American democratic liberalism. As I have suggested here, the conceptual, rhetorical, and political practices that come under the rubric of identity politics comprise neither a deviation from, nor an alternative to, the liberal tradition in America, but a historically-specific strand within it, a tendency (like abstract universalism) born of post-Civil War Reconstruction.[19] If the emergence of identity politics or cultural pluralism poses problems for American public life, these are better understood as problems *of* rather than as challenges *to* liberal thought. For it may well be that what Bloom views as a betrayal of liberal thought in America, or what Gitlin and Rorty see as a failure of political imagination on the American Left, is symptomatic of a longstanding problem within the liberal tradition itself.

My point in turning to this relatively recent episode in American public life is not to suggest that we settle the question of whether identity politics or abstract universalism better underwrites an expansive, democratic order, but instead to suggest that the persistent opposition of these two languages obscures the existence of other potentially more creative possibilities. Perhaps both languages promise (impossible) delivery and (improbable) resolution all too readily. Rather than perceiving ourselves as forever caught between these two rather too stark alternatives, perhaps we might consider the possibility that the appearance of being caught is itself a function of American languages of citizenship. How we understand American history, how the story of the American past is told, who gets to tell it and why, and whether we understand competing accounts of the past as commensurable or incommensurable—all of these questions suggest the degree to which the recent culture wars are also efforts to *remember* a nation genealogically. This is as true of those who would displace the body from citizenship as it is of those who stake their political claims on it, if only as a rhetorical foil. In both cases, something historic and political comes to be treated as essential, and perhaps even more problematically, as ontological.

Nations, citizenship, and the future

Americans are fabled as creatures of both the present and the future who have somehow evaded the determinism of the past. Romanticizing this absent past, however, does not so much secure our escape from history as it effects the reincorporation of the past in new form, creating new and ever more obstinate forms of determinism. The past is neither banished nor overcome but is produced as an archaism within the present, a relic that is both origin and outcome. In the United States, all three constitutional languages of citizenship examined here—the aggregate universalism of 1787, and the embodied citizenship and abstract universalism that emerge from Reconstruction—position the citizen's body as an immutable origin of public life. Each in its own way seeks to establish closure around the citizen's local body, a body made meaningful by, and suffused with, history. In each case, the circumscribed, time-bound body comes to dominate both present and future possibilities.

Lest we be tempted to dismiss this as past history, it is important to grasp just how central citizenship is to the day-to-day experiences of thinking and living as nationals and as moderns. Obviously, citizenship per se neither enables nor really even affects the mundane activities of everyday life: living, working, raising families, and so on. These activities might be performed as well by noncitizens resident in a given national territory. However, national citizenship provides us with a fundamental sense of power and protection as we negotiate the various activities of everyday life. Let me pause here, for a moment, to consider the example of a 1958 Supreme Court decision, *Trop v. Dulles*, as cited by Lauren Berlant in *The Anatomy of National Fantasy*. While serving in the U.S. Army in French Morocco in 1944, Private Trop was convicted of desertion, sentenced to three years of hard labor, and given a dishonorable discharge. He was later denied a passport to reenter the United States, and informed that his citizenship had been revoked following his conviction for wartime desertion. Writing for the Court's majority in overturning Trop's involuntary expatriation, Earl Warren argued that stripping a citizen of his status in the national and international political community constitutes "a form of punishment more primitive than torture, for it destroys for the individual the political existence that was centuries in development."[20] As Berlant suggests, "the modern state's assurance of national citizenship [is here seen as] more fundamental to the person than any of his other historical affiliations," and denaturalization "violates the citizen through a virtual ontological torture."[21] National citizenship permeates even the most banal activities of daily life and tranforms them into the more or less discernible practices of living the nation. The injunction that we should "Buy American" (whether it refers to automobiles or anything available from Wal-Mart), the increasingly familiar refrain that appears on highway motel signs announcing that they are "American Owned and Operated," or the ads for an Indian restaurant in the town where I live that proclaim "We also serve American food cooked by American chefs," are all examples of the variety of ways that we live the nation through mundane activities. In these cases, buying, sleeping, cooking, and eating figure not simply as daily activities but as practices through which we express and confirm (or betray) our identities as Americans.[22]

"If nation-states are widely conceded to be 'new' and 'historical,'" Benedict Anderson writes, "the nations to which they give political expression always loom out of an immemorial past, and, still more important, glide into a limitless future. It is the magic of nationalism to turn chance into destiny."[23] In America our ability to think the citizen is also caught up in the arts of memory and projection, of thinking both backward and forward without rift or rupture, from the position of the present. In both of the constitutional moments I have discussed here, the American nation and the American citizen (in their various guises and permutations) have come to bear within them the mark of a past that both establishes their position in the present and commits them to a particular vision of the future. While it seems clear from this analysis that the backward glance is fundamental to foundings and that contemporary citizens can no more escape their history than could their predecessors, still we might ask if that history must turn to destiny. Can we break the spell of citizenship? Can we, as Nietzsche put it, conceive of a "past from which we may spring rather than that from which we seem to have derived?"[24] The transformation of chance into destiny and of citizenship into ontology succeeds only to the degree that politics manages to obscure the forces of contingency that point to other possibilities, that indicate that history might have turned out otherwise and that political pasts might be refigured and recombined to different effect and with different consequence. If citizenship is understood as inhering in the very conditions of our historical being—of our being national, of our being modern, of our being American—then we might begin to break the hold of historical determinism by asking what it would mean to think about citizenship in terms of action rather than essence, in short, by directing our attention toward what it means to act as citizens rather than what it means to be citizens.[25]

What could it mean to imagine an active citizenry formed of and through history? Addressing that question, if only in a preliminary way, involves viewing our own past with new eyes: Jefferson's genealogical nationalism formed of a fabulous kinship with Native Americans; *The Federalist*'s technique of aggregating unlike things; the early identity politics (if I may be allowed the anachronism) of Reconstruction's direct embrace of the citizen's local body; the abstract universalism of the same era. What makes each of these strategies work is its ability to put old elements to new use, to tap into history and deploy history as politics. They succeed precisely to the degree that they are able to appropriate past political languages for the purposes of the present. The problem we confront at the start of the twenty-first century is how to exploit the creative possibilities of foundings without reifying or reiterating the past. Doing this requires rethinking the past in ways that do not so much confirm the present as unsettle it, breaking up the identity of past and future by treating the political present as a moment that is born of, and shaped by, contingent forces. If American languages of national citizenship rely on a figure of the body as the origin of politics, they also dramatize the fact that both origins and bodies are formed through perpetual reinterpretation, reconfiguration, and resignification. It is precisely this process by which the body is positioned retrospectively as (past) origin that confirms that it is neither originary nor static, but rather the (present) site upon which and through which we imagine worldly relations.

Enhancing the creative possibilities contained within the liberal tradition in America, then, entails more than simply reappropriating and rearranging the elements central to American conventions, though reappropriation and resignification are certainly important aspects of such a project. In drawing on tradition, we might also think about resyncopating traditions, locating within them what is treated as archaic, not so that we can overcome, transcend, or dissolve America's modern archaisms, but so that we can put them to work and set them into motion differently by (to paraphrase Sheldon Wolin) restating new possibilities.[26] Working with the confines of what is already given in order to produce something that is new and different is, after all, one of the classic tasks of political life; drawing upon past conceptual and political languages in ways that do not confirm the givenness and familiarity of the present but alert us to its strangeness, moreover, is a classic enterprise of political theory; and remaking the past as a means of innovating in the present describes a classic practice of thinking (as) American(s). This means, contra Rorty, that America does not need less theory, but more. To that end, and by way of concluding, I'd like to return to the vision of citizenship that closed the last chapter: Victoria Woodhull's account of the Garden of Eden, and through Woodhull, another axis of the recent culture wars, and another set of political possibilities.

Feminism, politics, and tragedy

It is difficult to know precisely what to do with Woodhull, and this is only partially because of the strange combinations of political realism and prophetic vision that coalesce in her writings. In some ways, Woodhull's treatment of the Garden of Eden, with its effort to map the Garden onto the human body, recalls Thomas Jefferson's earlier project of mapping a nation onto the land, projecting a particular future by virtue of *re*presenting the past anew. In Woodhull's hands, Jefferson's romance of national freedom incarnate is replayed as elegy for (women's) freedom vanquished. The tale of the rape of Eve is used by Woodhull as a metaphor for the way Reconstruction is mapped onto the citizen's body and to suggest how Reconstruction's denial of political subjectivity to women might be transformed into a new ground for feminism. While Woodhull's text itself has faded into obscurity, her narrative of violation and the origins of political power most assuredly has not. To the contrary, that narrative gives shape to a variety of post-Reconstruction identitarian movements that seek to secure a place within American public life for questions of race, gender, and sexuality. The idea of the violated body as both the alienated origin of politics and the source of an oppositional imaginary is common, for example, to a number of strands of contemporary feminist thought. While I would argue that this tradition all too often gives way to a countertendency that is ultimately self-defeating, I would also suggest that it nonetheless contains creative potential.

In "The Violence of Rhetoric," Teresa de Lauretis offers an account of the emergence of sexual difference as socially meaningful that in many ways recalls Woodhull's. De Lauretis argues that a broad range of literatures in the human sciences treat the question of violence in ways that assume but do not challenge (or even necessarily acknowledge consciousness of) its inextricability from gender, and in fact "en-gender" violence such that "the representation of violence is inseparable from the notion of gender."[27] For example, social scientists who treat domestic violence as a social fact without inquiring into the patriarchal conditions that structure it, she contends, end up replicating rhetorically the very acts of violence that they claim only to document. Similarly, structuralist accounts of myth that posit an opposition between characters who are active, mobile, and vigorous, and those upon whom violence is enacted, construct action and mobility as masculine even as they "construct the object [of action] as female and the female as object."[28] Much of this scholarship on violence, as well as empirical-historical acts of violence themselves, she concludes, represents distinct moments in a larger struggle by which both a particular social order and a specifically gendered organization of power are produced and maintained. Scholarly rhetoric thus produces and reproduces the object of violence, and reproduces it, moreover, as always symbolically feminine, even when not literally female.[29]

For de Lauretis, violence names an activity—indeed, the primary activity—that bestows gender on individual subjects, on individual bodies that, though they are always already present to social life, are as yet unmarked by it.[30] In her formulation violence is at once the environment of, and a tool in, the technology of gender. It names the actions through which gender is produced and it is the means by which the actor is distinguished from the object of his action, a pairing that in de Lauretis' reading, like Woodhull's, is always figured respectively as masculine and feminine.[31] Insofar as violence produces gender as an ontological condition, it produces subject-citizens as sexually differentiated. Like Woodhull, de Lauretis offers a narrative that powerfully situates the emergence of public order and of socially meaningful forms of sexual difference in an identical set of acts that places men and women in a world that is common to both but experienced differently by each, a world that frees men by miring women in the very terms of their originary subjection.

I do not think that de Lauretis means to offer us a narrative of the origins of either social life or gender in "The Violence of Rhetoric," at least, not to the degree that Woodhull does in "The Garden of Eden." In fact, it could be said that de Lauretis' project represents more an effort to expose the unacknowledged narrative terms that structure gender within a broad range of critical traditions in the human sciences, than to construct an alternative account of gender. Moreover, it is certainly the case that her meditation about gender is unconcerned with making any claims that might be read as distinctive to American life, or in defining a distinctive product of the American political imagination. There is nonetheless a sense in which de Lauretis' effort to re-referentialize the relation between gender and violence, and thus to expose the place of Woman in modern thought as vacant and altogether uninhabitable by women,[32] like Woodhull's collapses all forms of political action as necessarily implicated in the sweep of an "en-gender[ing]" violence. In this respect, I think it can be said that de Lauretis's formulation responds to the continuing power of patriarchal thought in late twentieth-century America in much the same way as Woodhull responded a century earlier to Reconstruction's reformulation of patriarchal citizenship.

It is also in this sense that de Lauretis' narrative, again like Woodhull's, becomes as politically problematic as it is insightful, on at least two counts. First, in her terms, sexual difference entails the (structurally necessary) opposition of masculine and feminine with respect to the wielding of power: the opposition of one who acts and another upon whom violence is enacted, of one who wields power and another against whom power is exercised, in short, the opposition of the political subject and the politically subjugated. De Lauretis' account is organized by what Sharon Marcus has called a "gendered grammar of violence, where grammar means the rules and structure which assign people to positions within a script." The problem lies in the degree to which this grammar tends to structure our imagination so comprehensively that we are unable to think our way out of it, even when it offers us a means for doing so in and of its own terms.[33] Dependent upon both a vocabulary and a syntax that is already overdetermined by engendered violence at the moment we begin to employ it, we become unable to ask how asymmetries of power figured through the violence of rape (and thus, by analogy, the exercise of political power in ways that produce and enforce sexual or racial difference) might be refigured through a set of feminist counterpractices that redirects and reorganizes power itself.[34] Gendered asymmetries might actually be reproduced by narratives like those of Woodhull and de Lauretis insofar as they articulate powerful scripts that do not simply describe the grounds of women's subjugation in subjection, but ultimately (mis)represent those grounds as totalizing and unbroken, untouchable in political terms and through political action.

This suggests a further problem. Insofar as this "gendered grammar of violence" identifies political power with patriarchal power, it tends to conflate the establishment of the political world with the violent subjugation of women, particularly if we read it in light of Woodhull's earlier formulation. In this light we need to ask what are the implications for feminism, or for any other identitarian movement, if politics itself comes to be seen as the (or even *a*) source of originary trauma and permanent disempowerment? In her recent work, Wendy Brown has suggested that identitarian movements founded in the apprehension of political injury form "wounded attachments" with the terms of the injury itself, and consequently conflate the tending of that injury with emancipation from it. Such movements tend to turn the fact of social injury into a moral righteousness born of rage against it, and envision change only in the blindered and self-limiting terms of retribution and revenge, rather than in systematic critical engagement and transformation.[35] "Revenge as a 'reaction,' a substitute for the capacity to act," Brown writes, "produces identity as both bound to the history that produced it and as a reproach to the present which embodies that history." Politicized identity, in this sense, finds its origins in a past that cannot be redeemed without relinquishing political action itself: "it installs its pain over its unredeemed history in the very foundation of its political claim, in its demand for recognition" and "thus becomes attached to its own exclusion for its very existence as identity." Politicizing the terms of injury as protest against subordination or marginalization takes the problematic and (self-)destructive form of rancor rather than alternative vision, of the perpetual revivification of a painful past, rather than incitement to transform and innovate in the present.[36]

If Brown is right (and I am inclined to think she is) the question becomes, how might contemporary feminists, and others, engage the critical content of Woodhull's (or de Lauretis') fable about the gendered character of public life without embracing the injury it recounts? It is in this light that we might pause to reconsider the genealogy of the languages of citizenship that I have developed thus far. As I have argued in Parts I and II of this book, the body has always been present on the scene of American politics, and yet American political practices and political institutions have never quite accommodated themselves to this fact, even as they have sought, repeatedly, to fix and contain the body's political meaning. For both Jeffersonian democracy and for the aggregate universalism of the 1787 Constitution, the body represented an important foundation of politics, but the incorporation of different bodies (with different histories and different interests) within the political was possible only at the cost of difference itself. For the Founders of 1787, supplying for the citizen a prosthetic body to replace his local body meant that citizenship was not so much disembodied as departicularized. In spite of the obvious allure of a disincorporated body unconstrained by the sociological facts of private life, this technique of citizenship was bound to falter, brought down by its own internal heresies. The Reconstruction era's attempt to find a place for different bodies within a constitutional language of citizenship has fared no better, however, bequeathing to us a political landscape caught between an identity politics better poised to reject power than to reimagine it, and an abstract universalism (a pale deformation of the aggregate universalism of the Founders) that too easily reconfirms dominant structures of power.

Contra the verdict of thinkers like Allan Bloom, Todd Gitlin, and Richard

Rorty, we might say that the problem of identitarian movements is not their rejection of the commons, nor their apprehension of the violent origins of that commons, but rather their rejection of politics itself. This is the tragedy that lies at the very heart of Victoria Woodhull's response to Reconstruction. But there is another possible reading of Woodhull's narrative that, while it may not be generalizable to the full universe of contemporary identitarian movements, can nonetheless help us to see a degree of critical promise in it. This reading entails viewing Woodhull's account not narrowly as an interpretation of the events of Reconstruction per se, but instead as a commentary on the problems of political foundings more generally. For if Woodhull's text is structured by an undeniable sense of women's victimization in and through the acts that establish political order, there is also a counternarrative suggested by her reading of the book of Genesis, one that understands the Fall as an important moment, symbolic of a world at odds with itself. Woodhull recounts the tale of an event that marks an irreversible change in worldly life, a moment around which our awareness of common life and of mortality itself is concentrated, and in light of which all life in common will henceforth be lived.[37] It is a moment that, like the events recounted in ancient tragedy, dramatizes to us the genesis of politics, and the apprehension of power that is always already at work within it—a world that does not yield, or does not yield simply, to human design. If violent acts attend or even initiate political foundings, the subject positions that differentiate those who wield violence from those forced to yield to it are neither natural nor permanent, but contingent and therefore alterable. Political life and, at least in Woodhull's account, sexual difference are brought into being in the same moment and by virtue of the same set of acts that also marks the demise of innocence. We need not understand this moment as locking us into subject positions where the fixed moral referents of origins overwhelm the contingent possibilities of politics. For our own positions with respect to those founding acts are themselves contingent, and though Woodhull does not develop this line of reasoning herself, what she offers to feminist and democratically-minded political theorists are the resources for imagining a language of politics that no longer romanticizes the moral superiority of a lost or abandoned past, but instead acknowledges conflict, contest, and dissonance as the necessary ground of politics itself.

In this reading, Woodhull does not require us to choose between political life and feminist life, but offers the means for recognizing how one entails and radicalizes the other. Both represent different aspects of a public life distinct from the utopian fantasy of a world without division, supplanting that ideal with a postutopian, postlapsarian vision of life in common. There are, of course, tensions, but they are constitutive tensions, and the point is neither to resolve them in some transcendent ideal of universal harmony, nor to dissolve them by resigning ourselves to a permanently and irreparably fractured public, embracing a part as if it were a whole. For whatever the attractions of simplifying or harmonizing a complex world, or of trying to absent ourselves from the difficulties that come of being forced to make political judgments in it, reading Woodhull's account as tragedy serves to remind us of the impoverished and impoverishing effects of grasping at too easy resolutions to dilemmas that, though they may not be resolved or even resolvable, may nonetheless offer us a structure by which we might reformulate them in creative ways and to productive effect.[38]

Thus, at the turn of a century—which is also, as it happens, the start of a new millenium—Americans find themselves embroiled in a conflict between two languages of citizenship constitutive of American liberalism. In this late modern world, fraught with anxieties about the dissolution of a common culture and a common language, numerous commentators bemoan the loss of a common vision about how to achieve "our" country, insisting that we choose one language of citizenship over the other. In the very demand that we choose, there is a kind of impoverishment of the rich, if not unproblematic, tradition that shapes the American political imagination, and what is more, a kind of political myopia that obscures alternative angles of vision. What I have in mind as alternatives, however, are alternatives only in the sense that they present themselves not as substitutes or exemplars of some "third way," but as variations and innovations on the very traditions from which they emerge. Developing them requires that we view the body not as the origin, but rather as an important site, of conflicts over the meaning of difference and identity in discussions about how we act as citizens of a multiethnic America.

Endnotes

1. Thomas L. Dumm, *united states* (Ithaca: Cornell University Press, 1994), 22.

2. Allan Bloom, *The Closing of the American Mind* (New York: Simon & Schuster, 1987), 27.

3. Allan Bloom, *The Closing of the American Mind*, 109.

4. Works in the genre established by Bloom are far too numerous to cite comprehensively here, but include Roger Kimball, *Tenured Radicals: How Politics Has Corrupted Our Higher Education* (New York: Harper & Row, 1990); Dinesh D'Souza,

Illiberal Education: The Politics of Race and Sex on Campus (New York: Free Press, 1991); William J. Bennett, *The De-Valuing of America: The Fight for Our Culture and Our Children* (New York: Summit, 1992); Russell Jacoby, *Dogmatic Wisdom: How the Culture Wars Divert Education and Distract America* (New York: Doubleday, 1994). To my mind, the most intellectually- and politically-incisive criticism of this literature can be found in J. Peter Euben, *Corrupting Youth: Political Education, Democratic Culture, and Political Theory* (Princeton: Princeton University Press, 1997), esp. Chapter One.

5. Todd Gitlin, *The Twilight of Common Dreams: Why America is Wracked by Culture Wars* (New York: Metropolitan Books, 1995), 7.

6. Todd Gitlin, *The Twilight of Common Dreams: Why America is Wracked by Culture Wars*, 9.

7. Todd Gitlin, *The Twilight of Common Dreams: Why America is Wracked by Culture Wars*, 9–10 *passim*.

8. Todd Gitlin, *The Twilight of Common Dreams: Why America is Wracked by Culture Wars*, 36.

9. I have not touched upon what I find most troubling in Gitlin's book. As I read it, the story of the textbook wars in Oakland is suffused with a distressing moralism, for Gitlin seems to take a perverse satisfaction, if not pleasure, in the consequences of the "tribalism" he decries. As Americans commemorated the quincentennial of Christopher Columbus' discovery of the continent, Gitlin points out, the Oakland public schools were still locked into a dispute about textbooks and as a consequence the very series that included more—and more sympathetic—coverage of Native American life was unavailable to them. "Columbus Day of 1992 should have been the perfect occasion for teaching schoolchildren about American Indians or, as the city of Oakland, California, officially calls them, Native Americans," he begins. But in consequence of what Gitlin depicts as political gridlock born of identity politics, "when Columbus Day rolled around in 1992, Oakland's fourth-, fifth-, and seventh-grade teachers had no textbooks at all to help them teach about California's Indians or, indeed, about anyone else." What troubles me, here, is the deliberate thoughtlessness with which Gitlin relates the tale—a thoughtlessness that retreats into moral righteousness and the complacency of the given. I would certainly agree that this is a tragic story. However, Gitlin narrates it not as tragedy but as morality play where, to his mind, the critics of the textbooks, and by extension proponents of "identity politics," get exactly what they deserve from an America that even to Gitlin's mind has treated them as (at best) second-class citizens: less than nothing. If Gitlin's text is an adequate exemplar of a genre of late twentieth-century political writing in America, then I think we might extend the critique of identity politics movements that Wendy Brown develops in *States of Injury*—namely, that they are shaped by a certain moral *ressentiment* that attaches them to the

very social injuries for which they seek vindication—to some of the most vocal critics of identity politics as well. Todd Gitlin, *The Twilight of Common Dreams: Why America is Wracked by Culture Wars*, 236, 7, 13.

10. Richard Rorty, *Achieving Our Country: Leftist Thought in Twentieth-Century America* (Cambridge: Harvard University Press, 1998), 18.

11. Richard Rorty, *Achieving Our Country: Leftist Thought in Twentieth-Century America*, 35.

12. Richard Rorty, *Achieving Our Country: Leftist Thought in Twentieth-Century America*, 36.

13. Richard Rorty, *Achieving Our Country: Leftist Thought in Twentieth-Century America*, 91–92.

14. See Todd Gitlin, *The Twilight of Common Dreams: Why America is Wracked by Culture Wars*, esp. Chapters Seven and Eight; Richard Rorty, *Achieving Our Country: Leftist Thought in Twentieth-Century America*, esp. 41–71.

15. Todd Gitlin, *The Twilight of Common Dreams: Why America is Wracked by Culture Wars*, 236.

16. Todd Gitlin, *The Twilight of Common Dreams: Why America is Wracked by Culture Wars*, 100.

17. For a more detailed discussion of the ways in which ideologies work as productive discourses, see Elizabeth Wingrove, "Interpellating Sex," *Signs* 24:4 (Summer 1999), 869–93.

18. The phrase is Gitlin's. See Todd Gitlin, *The Twilight of Common Dreams: Why America is Wracked by Culture Wars*, 231.

19. Judith Butler offers a different, and very useful, challenge to the opposition between "cultural" and "real" politics. As she argues, using the case of stuggles to combat homophobia as an example, this counterposition between a "politics of difference" and "political economy" dissolves under scrutiny: "Why would a movement concerned to criticize and transform the ways in which sexuality is socially regulated not be understood as central to the functioning of political economy? Briefly, of course, we know that the family, . . . which involves the reproduction of sexuality and the reproduction of gender was clearly established by both Marx and Engels as properly part of the materialist conception of social life. And it seems to me that in that Marxist paradigm that socialist-feminism so profited from, the reproduction of gendered persons . . . depended on the social regulation of the family and indeed on the reproduction of [the] heterosexual family as a site for the reproduction of heterosexual persons. Sexuality was, indeed, part of the analysis of material life and linked clearly with the mode of production. . . . How is it that suddenly sexuality goes from being part of material life to being merely cultural when the focus of critical analysis turns from the question, how is normative sexuality reproduced . . . to the queer question, how is it that that very nor-

mativity is confounded by the non-normative sexualities it harbors within its own terms, as well as the sexualities that thrive and suffer outside those terms? . . . Is one's material livelihood not at issue in those instances in which lesbians and gays are rigorously excluded from state sanctioned notions of the family, . . . deemed inadmissable to citizenship, selectively denied the status of freedom of speech, and freedom of assembly, denied the [questionable] benefit of being a member of the military who might speak his or her desire, deauthorized by the law to make emergency medical decisions about one's dying lover, to receive the property of one's dead lover, to have received from the hospital the body of one's dead lover?" See Judith Butler, "Left Conservatism, II" *Theory & Event*, 2:2, ¶11. Available at http://www.press.jhu.edu/journals/theory_&_event/v002/2.2butler.html. See also Judith Butler, "Merely Cultural," *Social Text* 52/53, vol. 15:3–4 (Fall/Winter 1997), 265–77; and Nancy Fraser, "Heterosexism, Misrecognition, and Capitalism: A Response to Judith Butler," *Social Text* 52/53, vol. 15:3–4 (Fall/Winter 1997).

20. Quoted in Lauren Berlant, *The Anatomy of National Fantasy: Hawthorne, Utopia, and Everyday Life* (Chicago: The University of Chicago Press, 1991), 13.

21. Lauren Berlant, *The Anatomy of National Fantasy: Hawthorne, Utopia, and Everyday Life*, 13.

22. For an analysis of liberal nationalism at work in everyday life in the United States, see Anne Norton, *Republic of Signs: Liberal Theory and American Popular Culture* (Chicago: The University of Chicago Press, 1993).

23. Benedict Anderson, *Imagined Communities: Reflections on the Origin and Spread of Nationalism*, (New York: Verso, 1993), 11–12.

24. Friedrich Nietzsche, *The Use and Abuse of History*, trans. Adrian Collins (Indianapolis: Bobbs-Merrill, 1949), 24.

25. Wendy Brown treats this problem of understanding politics as an expression of ontological circumstances in its more specific expression as feminist standpoint epistemology. Brown ventures the suggestion that in our public conversations, we might begin to redirect public speech from the ontological to the political by reshaping the question "who am I, and what, therefore do I think?" as "what do I want for us?" See Wendy Brown, *States of Injury: Power and Freedom in Late Modernity* (Princeton: Princeton University Press, 1995), esp. 51.

26. Sheldon S. Wolin, "Political Theory as a Vocation," *American Political Science Review* 63:4 (December, 1969), 1082.

27. Here is de Lauretis, glossing an argument made by Wini Breines and Linda Gordon: "[Insofar as] the great majority of scholarly studies still come short of a coherent understanding of family violence as a social problem, the reason is that, with the exception of feminist writers, clinicians, and a few male empirical researchers, the work in this area fails to analyze the terms of its own inquiry, especially terms such as *family,*

power, and *gender*. For . . . violence between intimates must be seen in the wider context of social power relations; and gender is absolutely central to the family . . . [Hence Breines and Gordon] counter the dominant representation of violence as a 'breakdown in social order' by proposing instead that violence is the sign of 'a power struggle for the *maintenance* of a certain kind of social order.'" Teresa de Lauretis, "The Violence of Rhetoric: Considerations on Representation and Gender," *Technologies of Gender: Essays on Theory, Film, and Fiction* (Bloomington: Indiana University Press, 1987), 33–34 *passim*. See also Wini Breines and Linda Gordon, "The New Scholarship on Family Violence," *Signs: A Journal of Women in Culture and Society* 8, no. 3: 490–531.

28. Teresa de Lauretis, "The Violence of Rhetoric: Considerations on Representation and Gender," 45. See also Jurij Lotman, "The Origin of Plot in the Light of Typology," trans. Julian Graffy, *Poetics Today* 1:1–2, 161–84.

29. Teresa de Lauretis, "The Violence of Rhetoric: Considerations on Representation and Gender," 43.

30. Significantly, this is the point where Woodhull and de Lauretis differ, I think, and where Woodhull's account may give way to a more classically tragic reading (as discussed below), and de Lauretis' does not. For unlike de Lauretis, Woodhull does not posit the body as preexisting acts of violence that bring social order, and a social order of sexual difference, into being—at least not in any way that would be recognizable to those of us who live in the aftermath, and with the consequences, of that violence. If the Garden of Eden in Woodhull's reading symbolizes the (violated) human body, it is recognizable as such only after the fact of the violation; the body, in other words, is not a stable entity that simply "holds" meaning, but one that can be apprehended only in light of the activities that make it meaningful.

31. Teresa de Lauretis, "The Violence of Rhetoric: Considerations on Representation and Gender," 31–50.

32. Teresa de Lauretis, "The Violence of Rhetoric," 32.

33. For example, what Marcus calls the "rape script" tends to cast women as weak victims, yet posits (and eroticizes) considerable amounts of force and violence as necessary to overcome women who resist. See Sharon Marcus, "Fighting Bodies, Fighting Words: A Theory and Politics of Rape Prevention," *Feminists Theorize the Political*, eds. Judith Butler and Joan W. Scott (New York: Routledge, 1992), 392, 402 n14.

34. I am uncertain that Marcus' proposed means of intervening in and altering the discursive construction of rape by promoting both physical and rhetorical forms of women's self-defense is as effective a counterforce to the tyranny of this gendered grammar of violence as her critical engagement with the means by which this grammar is predicated is valuable. For, while Marcus is very right to insist that women under attack merely accede to a gendered script of feminine politeness when they follow advice not to fight back but to instead attempt to dissuade their attackers, I think she idealizes

physical self-defense as a transformation of a (gendered) script that requires us to think of rape as "subject-object violence" to one of "subject-subject violence." "By talking back and fighting back we place ourselves as subjects who can engage in dialogic violence and respond to aggression in kind," she suggests (397). I cannot help but wonder about the ways in which Marcus' own formulation leaves untouched the formation of subjectivity in and through the exercise of violence. Is not a more productive task for a critical feminism not to secure a space for feminine subjectivity in and through the wielding of violence, but instead to promote alternative visions of the means by which subjects may be produced, that is, to envision forms of subjection that do not rely on—and may in fact challenge—violent acts?

35. Wendy Brown, *States of Injury: Power and Freedom in Late Modernity*.

36. Wendy Brown, *States of Injury: Power and Freedom in Late Modernity*, 73–74.

37. I am drawing here on the language of Helen Bacon, "Aeschylus," *Ancient Writers: Volume I*, ed. T. James Luce (New York: Charles Scribner and Sons, 1982), 108.

38. In their readings of very different tragic texts, both George Shulman and Peter Euben suggest similar possibilities. See George Shulman, "American Political Culture, Prophetic Narration, and Toni Morrison's *Beloved*," *Political Theory* 24 (1996), 295–314; J. Peter Euben, *The Tragedy of Political Theory: The Road Not Taken* (Princeton: Princeton University Press, 1990), esp. 34–38.

Index

Abolition movement, 109, 112
Abstract universalism, xxviii
Achieving Our Country (Rorty), 171
Adams, John, xxviii, 2, 4, 31, 33, 67–69, 74, 80, 121–122
Adultery, 109; see also Beecher-Tilton scandal
African Americans, 21, 139; *see also* Reconstruction; Reconstruction Amendments
    in Jefferson's *Notes*, 35–40
    political process, 95
    suffrage rights, 95–96
African colonization, 36
Aggregate universalism, 59, 84–85, 97, 173–174, 180
America
    in European political imagination, xxi
    as expression of Natural Law, xxi
    feudal tradition of, xxii, 59–61
    genealogical nationalism, xxvi, xxviii
    historical and conceptual bases of, xxii
American citizenship, 59; *see also* Aggregate universalism
American culture, Native past and, 34
American democracy, 43
American feudalism, 59–61
American founding
    Arendt on democracy, 6–11
    concept of nature and, 2
    pastlessness of, 3–6, 12n
American liberalism, vs. European liberalism, xxiii

American Revolution, 7
    feudal tendencies of, 59–61
The Anatomy of National Fantasy (Berlant), 174
Anderson, Benedict, 20, 33–34, 41, 139, 156, 175
Anthony, Susan B., 110
Antifederalists, 75
Antislavery movement, 109, 112
Appleby, Joyce, 57, 65
Arendt, Hannah, 3, 6–11, 44, 58, 81, 118, 121–122
Aristotle, 115–117, 128, 132n, 138n
Articles of Confederation, xxii, xxvii, 60, 65, 77
"Ascriptive Americanism" of Smith, xv–xvi, xviii, xxviii

Baker, Paula, 81–82
Bauman, Zygmunt, 101
Beard, Charles, 93
Beard, Mary, 93
Beecher, Henry Ward, xxviii, 109–114, 116–117, 120, 122–123
Beecher, Lyman, 109–111, 117, 125–127, 130n
Beecher-Tilton scandal, 109–111, 125–127, 130n
    crisis of homosocial desire, 156
    friendship of men, 113–114
    as public property, 111
    public vs. private lives, 112
Belated Feudalism (Orren), xxii

Benjamin, Walter, 19–20
Bennett, Jane, 58
Bensel, Richard, 94
Bentham, Jeremy, 44
Berlant, Lauren, 25, 43, 66, 68, 84, 112, 174–175
Between Men (Sedgwick), 126
Bhabha, Homi K., 139, 146
Bill of Rights, 78, 80
Birth of a Nation (Griffith), 140–141
Black Codes, 145, 157
Bloom, Allan, 170–173, 180
Body politic
  African Americans and, 96
  as archaic figure, xx
  demise of the common, 170–174
  early conception of, xvii
  Reconstruction Amendments, 97
Bosnia, 173
Brandon, Mark, 98–99
Brown, Wendy, xviii–xix, 179–180
Buffon, Comte de, 22–23, 28–29
Burgett, Bruce, 9, 42, 118

Castration, 154–155
  homoeroticism of, 156
Centralized government, 77
Christian moralism, 161–162
Citizen
  natural man and, xx
  as "prosthetic person," 95
Citizenship
  action vs. essence of, 176
  Adams *Defense* and boudoir metaphor, 68–71
  Constitution of 1787, 66
  current political agenda and, 169
  in *The Federalist*, 65
  of Founders, xv, xxvii, xxiv–xxvii, 94

from homosocial to heterosexual, 123, 126–127
the future and, 174–177
Jay's *Federalist* Number Two and, 78
liberal tradition and, xiv
loyalists vs. American citizenship, 62–64
nature of, 62
ontology of, 62
"passion for distinction" and, 121–122
post-Civil War Reconstruction and, xv, xxiv
property ownership and, 66
public life participation and, 121–122
race and gender and, 100
white male privilege, 66–67
women's claim to, 84
"Civic Ideals" (Smith), xv–xvi
Civil rights, 97, 171
Civil Rights Act of 1964, 169
Civil War, 93
  as fratricide, 148
Claflin, Tennessee, 110
Clarke, Charity, 62
The Closet Companion, 64
The Closing of the American Mind (Bloom), 170
Columbus, Christopher, 147
Committee of Five, 8, 15n
Compromise of 1877, 93
Confederate Memorial monument, 144–145
Connolly, William E., 57, 86
Constitution of 1787, 43, 58–60, 99, 102, 117, 122, 148
  aggregate universalism of, 85, 151, 180
  Amendments of, 93–94; *see also* Reconstruction Amendments
  citizenship and, 66, 78–80

republican motherhood, xxii, xxvi, 82–86
   supremacist groups and, 147
   women's citizenship and, 81–86
Constitutional Convention of 1787, 74, 94
Constitutional moment, term defined, xxiv–xxv
Continental Congress, 8, 21, 44
Cruden's Concordance, 160
Culture wars, xiv

De Lauretis, Teresa, 177–182
Decentralization, 60, 75
Declaration of Independence, 6, 8–9, 19, 35
   American "We" collective, 9
   Arendt on, 6–11
   monarchy as violation of nature, 23
Declaratory Acts, 158–159
Defense of the Constitutions of Government of the United States (Adams), 68–71
Democracy
   Jefferson's vision of, 2
   lineage of concept, 4
Democracy in America (Tocqueville), xvi
Derrida, Jacques, 8, 10, 15n
Discourses on Davila (Adams), 121
Disempowerment, 71
Douglas, Ann, 117
Douglass, Frederick, 95, 104n
Dred Scott v. Sandford, 96–97, 104n
DuBois, Paige, 3
Dumm, Thomas L., 73, 169

Edwards, Jonathan, 117
Emancipation, 35–36
Equality, 94
   lineage of concept, 4

Ethnic identitarian movements, xx
Ethnic Studies, 170
Ethnicity, 99
Euben, Peter, 102
European liberalism, vs. American liberalism, xxiii
Evans, C.A., 144

Fathers and Children (Rogin), 33
Federal vs. state authority, 93
Federalism, 2
The Federalist Papers, xxvi–xxvii, 60, 65, 74–82, 85–85, 93, 103, 176
   counterexamples of, 75
   factious spirit as danger, 76–77
   Federalist No. Two, 78
   Federalist No. Four, 96
   Federalist No. Ten, 76
   Federalist No. Fifteen, 77
   Federalist No. Twenty, 78
   Federalist No. Seventy-four, 80
   human nature in, 76
   national citizenship in, 65
Feminism, 170
Feudal-republicanism, xxvi
Feudalism, 142
Fifteenth Amendment, 97, 100, 107n, 129, 153
Fliegelman, Jay, 27, 31
Foner, Eric, 139
Forrest, Nathan, 153
Foucault, Michel, xxvi, 58, 71–74, 109, 151
Founding of nation
   Reconstruction as second founding, xxv, 94, 103
Fourteenth Amendment, 99–100, 107n, 129, 155
Fox, Richard Wightman, 117

Frank, Jill, 118
Franklin, Benjamin, 46
Fraternal citizenship, 140, 142
Fraternity/fraternal love, 118–119
Free love doctrines, 110, 161
Freedman, lynching and castration of, 154–155
Freedman's Bureau, 139, 142
Freedman's Bureau Act of 1865, 139
Freedom, lineage of concept, 4
French Revolution, 7
Freud, Sigmund, 152
Friendship (*philia*), 115–116
  public life and, 118
Fry, Joshua, 40–41

Gallatin, Albert, 44
"The Garden of Eden; or, Paradise Lost and Found" (Woodhull), 157, 177–178, 181–182
Gender, 99
  public life, 180
  violence and, 177–178
Genealogical nationalism, xxvi, xxviii, 20–21, 39–42, 148, 150–151, 176
Genealogy of Mortals (Nietzsche), 151
General rules, 122
  suffrage rights and, 94–98
Georgia Supreme Court, 153
Gitlin, Todd, xx, 170–173, 180, 183n
The Gleaner, republican motherhood and, 82–86
Goodell, William, 95
Government, effective institutions and, 81
Governmental rationality, 72–73
Governmentality, 58, 71
  political operation of, 58
The Great Sensation (Oliver), 111
Griffith, D. W., 140–141, 143

Hamilton, Alexander, 74, 76–78, 80, 85, 118–120
Hamilton, Alexander, 4
Harris, Trudier, 154–155
Hartz, Louis, xiii–xvi, xxii–xxiii, 3, 12n, 59, 141–142
Hegel, G. W. F., xiii, xxi
Hellman, Lillian, 102
Histoire Naturelle (Buffon), 22
Hobbes, Thomas, xix
Hodes, Martha, 152
Holmes, Lorenda, 63
Homonoia, 118
Homosocial desire, 119–120, 122
Honig, Bonnie, 6, 10
The Human Body, The Temple of God (Woodhull), 161

Identitarian movements, 179, 181
Identity politics, 99, 171, 173, 180
Independence Hall, 44
Intellectual freedom, xiii
Interracial marriage, 152–153, 156, 165n
Interracial rape, 154, 166n

Jackson administration, 33
Jacksonian era, 95
Jay, John, 20, 78–79, 96
Jefferson, Peter, 31, 40–41
Jefferson, Thomas, xxvi, 2–4, 8–9, 21–25, 31–32, 57–58, 78, 103, 122, 176
  on African Americans, 35–40
  natural history of nation, 43–45
  on nature and nationalism, 19–20
Jehlen, Myra, xxi, 22, 29
Jones, Joseph, 21

Katz, Jonathan Ned, 118, 123–126

King George III, 8
Knights of the White Camelia, 147–148, 154
Ku Klux Klan, 97, 140–141, 147

Lafayette, Marquis de, 45
Laurens, John, 118–120
Lefort, Claude, xvi–xx, xxv
Leslie, Margaret, 5
Liberal constitutionalism, xiv
Liberal egalitarianism, 142
Liberal tradition
 citizenship and, xiv, 173
 modern thought and, xvi, 12n
 rethinking of, xiii, 170–174
The Liberal Tradition in America (Hartz), xiii–xiv
Liberal universalism, xiv
Localism, 60, 62
Locke, John, xiii, xxi–xxii, 158
Louisiana Purchase, 31–32
Love, public action and, 116–117
Lowndes, Joseph, 34
Loyalists, 63–64
Ludlow, William, 23, 28
Lynchings, 154–155, 166n
 castration rituals and, 154–155

Madison, James, 4, 27, 76, 78
Majoritarianism, 172
Male homosocial desire, 119–120, 122
Male public homosociabity, 154, 156
Manning, Susan, 27
Marbois, François, 21–22, 35
Marcus, Sharon, 179
Mayflower Compact, 147
Media, 61–62
Mill, John Stuart, 157
Miller, Charles A., 19

Minor v. Happersett, 100, 125
Minoritarian thinking, 173
Mob violence, 154
Modernity and modern government, 101
 the Constitution and, 75
 danger and, 73
 emergence of, xvii–xviii
 temporal modes of understanding and, 20
Monarchy
 princely power, xvii
 as violation of nature, 23
Morrison, Toni, xxiii
Mr. Vigillius; *see* Murray, Judith Sargent
Multiculturalism, 170
"Multiple traditions" thesis, xv
Murray, Judith Sargent ("Mr. Vigillius"), 83–86
Mylne, James, 43

Nation
 as family, 140
 gendered metaphors for, 140
 memory and forgetting, 146
National citizenship, 43, 80, 97–98
 African-American men and, 143
 Trop v. Dulles, 174–175
National consciousness, 41
National debt, 27
National genealogy, 148, 150–151
 of white supremacists, 141, 150–151
National identity, white male privilege and, 67
National memory, 146
National reconciliation, 152
National unity, 78
 people as one, 79
National Woman's Suffrage Convention, 159

Nationalism, 24
Native Americans, 21, 176
  in Jefferson's *Notes*, 28–35
Natural Law
  America as expression of, xxi
  commonality and, 170
Natural man, transition to citizen, xx
Nature, state of, xx, 7
  concept of, 2
  Jefferson's nationalism and, 19–20
  monarchy as violation of, 23
  social/political conservatism and, 46
  state of nature, xx
New-Harmony (utopian socialist community), 45–46
Nietzsche, 5, 151, 175
Nineteenth Amendment, 100, 169
Norms, 127
Norton, Anne, xxi, 94
Norwood; or Village Life in New England (Beecher), 109
Notes on the State of Virginia (Jefferson), 19–20, 58, 103
  African Americans in, 35–40
  correspondence with publisher, 25, 27
  creole nationalism of, 31–34
  genealogical nationalism of, 20–21, 39–40
  historical perspective of, 21–25
  Jefferson's map, 40–43
  Jehlen's critique of, 22
  Native Americans
    ancient past, 28–35, 176
    conversion of, 34
  Natural Bridge as metaphor for new political order, 25–28
  nature and politics of, 22–23
  Outassete and kinship, xxvi, 31

Oliver, Leon, 111–112
On Revolution (Arendt), 7
Ordinance (of 1784), 41
Origins myth (Genesis), 157
  the Fall and sin of rape, 159–160, 162, 177
  Woodhull on, 158–165
Orren, Karen, xxii
Outassete, 31, 33
Owen, Robert Dale, 45

Paine, Thomas, 1–2, 4
"Passion for distinction," 121–122
Past, as still-living foundation, 102
Pastlessness, America's myth of, 3–6
Pastoral model, care of populations, 73
Peale, Charles Willson, 44
People-as-One, xvii
Perfect friendship, 115
Personal life vs. political, 120
Pilgrim Fathers, 147
Pleasure friendship, 115
Pluris, 96
Polis, 116–117
Political citizenship, 101
Political fragmentation, 70
Political friendship, 112–114, 129
  defined, 115
Political identity, 101
  emancipated slaves, 99
Political rights, 101
Politics
  domestication of, 82
  gendered division of political labor, 81–82
Polity, 98, 128
Postslavery society, 93
Princely power, xvii

Print media, 61–62
Private lives, 112
Progressive Era, 140–141
Prohibition, 82
Public action, love and, 116–117
Public vs. private lives, 61, 112

Race, public discourse of, 96, 99
Racial equality, 98
Racial separation, 153
Racism, 143, 149
Radical Reconstruction, 114, 139, 148
Radical Republicans, 98
Raleigh, Sir Walter, 147
Rawls, John, 3
Reactionary Enlightenment, 141
Reason of State, xviii
Reconstruction, 93–103
    black political participation, 154
    Constitutional amendments, 93
    ex-Confederates' lost cause, 145
    gender and nation, 144
    political/economic reforms, 142
    Radical Republicans and, 98
    Southern proslavery and, xxvii, 142, 144
Reconstruction Amendments, 96
    accomplishments of, 97
    political identity for emancipated slaves, 99
    political imagination and, 98–101
    political significance of, 97
    race and gender, 99, 152, 180
    as second founding, 94, 103
    transformations of, xxviii, 129
Refashioning Futures (Scott), 101
Regional conflict, 140
Renan, Ernest, 145–146, 151, 157, 161

Republican motherhood, 82–86
Richards, Elizabeth, 109–110, 114, 123–126
Rogin, Michael, 33, 141
Rorty, Richard, 170–173, 177, 181

Said, Edward, 2
Salecl, Renata, 38
Scandals, 127–129
Scott, David, 101
"Second American Revolution," 93
Sedgwick, Eve Kosofsky, xxviii, 119–120, 126
Self-confession, public practices of, 86
Self-governance, 62, 65
Self-identity, 62–64
'76 Association, 147
Sexual reconstruction, 109–129
Sharecropping, 98, 157
Sheehan, Bernard, 33
Shklar, Judith, 2–3, 12n, 20, 42–43
Shuffelton, Frank, 21
Silber, Nina, 140
Slavery, 35–36, 41–42, 97, 148
    antebellum defenses of, 141
    end of, 93
Slotkin, Richard, 27
Smith, Rogers, xv–xvi, xviii, xix, xxviii, 142–143
Social conventions, 110
Social equality, 152
Social status, 153–154
Sollors, Werner, 34
Southern feudal thought, 141
Southern Homestead Act, 139
State
    founded in violence, 157
    male power and, xix

sovereign state, xix
State of nature; *see* Nature, state of
Suffrage movement, xxvii, 99, 110–111
Suffrage rights, 82, 93, 129, 139
  African Americans, 95–96
  general rules and, 94–98
  property and tax-paying qualifications, 95
  women and, 95, 100, 169
Sullivan, James, 67

Thirteenth Amendment, 97
3/5ths Compromise of Article I (Fourteenth Amendment), 97
Tilton, Theodore, 109–116, 120, 123
Tocqueville, Alexis de, xiv, xvi, 1, 59
Tories, 63–64
Totems, 152
Trelease, Allen, 147
Trop v. Dulles, 174–175
Tucker, St. George, 36
The Twilight of Common Dreams (Gitlin), 171

United States Supreme Court
  Dred Scott v. Sandford, 96
  Minor v. Happersett, 100
Unum, 96
Utility friendship, 115, 117
Utopian communities, 45–47

Violence
  gender and, 177–178
  gendered grammar of, 179
"Violence of Rhetoric" (de Lauretis), 177–182
Voting rights, women and, 100

Waite, Morrison, 100, 129
Waller, Altina, 117
War of 1812, 33
Warner, Michael, 61–62, 66, 84
Warren, Earl, 175
Washington, George, 118
Welfare-State Reason (*Wohlfahrtsstaatr'son*), xviii
Wells-Barnett, Ida B., 154
"What Is a Nation?" (Renan), 145
White League, 147, 149–151
White supremacist organizations, 99, 103, 141, 143, 147
Whites, LeeAnn, 144–145
Wiegman, Robyn, 143, 155–156
Wilde, Oscar, 114
Williams, Patricia, 140
Winichakul, Thongchai, 41
Wolin, Sheldon, xvii–xix, 3, 10, 59–61, 65, 75, 84, 176
Women
  citizenship and, 81–86
  moral reform movements and, 82
  republican motherhood, 82–86
  voting rights, 95, 100, 169
Women's equality, 161
Women's rights, 109
Women's Studies, 170
Wood, Gordon, 5
Woodhull, Victoria, xxviii–xxix, 100, 110, 123–126, 157–165, 177–179, 181–182
Wright, Frances, 43, 45–46

Yacavone, Donald, 119
Yack, Bernard, 116

2077